The Ethics of Management

LaRue Tone Hosmer
Durr-Fillauer Chair in Business Ethics
Culverhouse College of Commerce
University of Alabama

Fourth Edition

McGraw-Hill Irwin

Boston Burr Ridge, IL Dubuque, IA Madison, WI New York
San Francisco St. Louis Bangkok Bogotá Caracas Kuala Lumpur
Lisbon London Madrid Mexico City Milan Montreal New Delhi
Santiago Seoul Singapore Sydney Taipei Toronto

McGraw-Hill Higher Education

A Division of The **McGraw-Hill** *Companies*

THE ETHICS OF MANAGEMENT
Published by McGraw-Hill/Irwin, a business unit of The McGraw-Hill Companies, Inc. 1221
Avenue of the Americas, New York, NY, 10020. Copyright © 2003, 1996, 1990, 1987, by The
McGraw-Hill Companies, Inc. All rights reserved. No part of this publication may be reproduced or
distributed in any form or by any means, or stored in a database or retrieval system, without the prior
written consent of The McGraw-Hill Companies, Inc., including, but not limited to, in any network
or other electronic storage or transmission, or broadcast for distance learning.
Some ancillaries, including electronic and print components, may not be available to customers
outside the United States.

This book is printed on acid-free paper.

1   2   3   4   5   6   7   8   9   0   DOC/DOC   0   9   8   7   6   5   4   3   2

ISBN 0-256-26459-7

Publisher: *John E. Biernat*
Senior sponsoring editor: *Andy Winston*
Editorial coordinator: *Sara E. Ramos*
Marketing manager: *Lisa Nicks*
Project manager: *Karen J. Nelson*
Production supervisor: *Debra R. Sylvester*
Senior designer: *Jenny El-Shamy*
Associate supplement producer: *Joyce J. Chappetto*
Cover design: *Jenny El-Shamy*
Compositor: *GAC Indianapolis*
Typeface: *10.5/12 Times Roman*
Printer: *R. R. Donnelley & Sons Company*

Library of Congress Control Number: 2001099458

www.mhhe.com

Preface

I believe that a course on the ethics of business should be both rigorous and fun. Rigorous because there is a lot of material to cover, and a need to cover it well. Fun because these are controversial issues in which each student should learn to make up his or her mind as to what solution is "most right," "most just," and "most fair" through class discussions and group projects. I also believe that it is not enough just for students to be able to make up their own minds; they have to be able to convince others because that conviction, if widespread, can pull a company together in a way that creates cooperation and innovation and builds unified efforts.

This book is going to make five basic arguments on that path between controversial issues and unified efforts. The first is that moral problems in business are complex and difficult to resolve because some individuals and/or groups associated with the firm are going to be hurt or harmed in ways outside their own control, while others will be benefited or helped. Further, some of those individuals and/or groups associated with the firm will have their rights ignored or denied, while others will have their rights recognized and expanded. There is a mixture of benefits and harms, of right exercised and rights denied, and this mixture makes it very difficult for business managers to

The Complex Nature of Moral Problems in Business Management

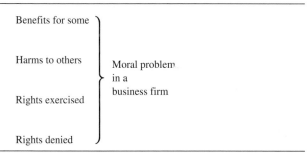

decide upon a course of action that they can confidently say is " right" and "just" and "fair" when faced with a moral problem.

The second basic argument is that business managers cannot rely upon their moral standards of behavior, or the intuitive ways they automatically feel about what actions are "right" and "just" and "fair," to make their decisions when faced with a moral problem. Moral standards of behavior differ between people, depending upon their personal goals, norms, beliefs and values, which in turn are dependent upon their religious and cultural traditions and their economic and social situations. The individuals and groups in a global economy come from very different traditions and live in very different situations, and consequently their moral standards of behavior, being subjective, are bound to differ greatly.

The third basic argument is that business managers have to recognize that the individuals and groups associated with their firms will have different moral standards as to what they believe to be "right" and "just" and "fair." It is not enough for a manager to simply reach a decision on what he or she

The Derivation of Subjective Standards of Moral Behavior in Management

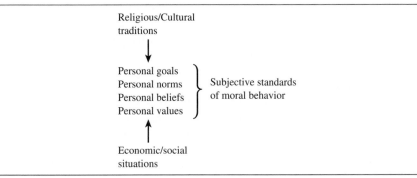

The Application of Objective Models of Moral Analysis in Management

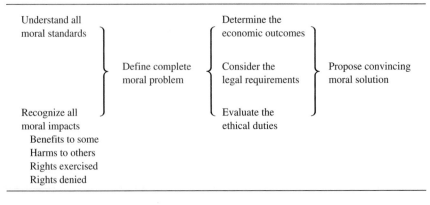

believes to be a proper balance of benefits and harms, of rights recognized and denied, in any given situation. Managers have to go further, and *be able to explain convincingly why that balance should be viewed as "right" and "just" and "fair."* A convincing explanation requires objective methods of analysis rather than subjective standards of behavior. These objective methods of analysis include: (1) economic outcomes based upon impersonal market forces, (2) legal requirements based upon impartial social and political processes, and (3) ethical duties based upon universal human goals.

Building Trust, Commitment and Effort within an Organization

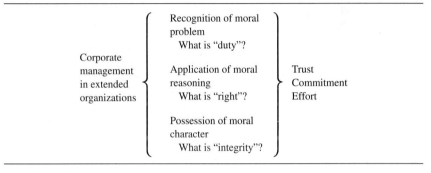

Extending Cooperation, Innovation, and Unification throughout the Organization

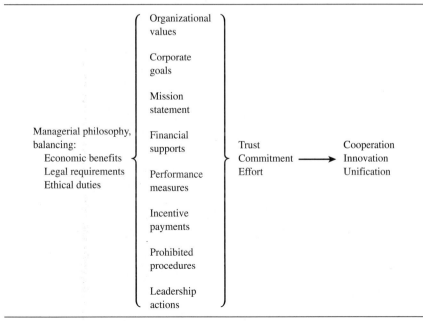

The fourth basic argument is that if this analytical procedure is followed on a consistent basis, with moral solutions that are logically convincing to the individuals and groups associated with the firm, the result will be an increase in trust, commitment and effort among those individuals and groups. Business firms have not only grown in size recently. They have also become extended in form. That is, they are now dependent upon a much larger number of individuals and groups, with a much wider range of capabilities and skills, that extend beyond the company, throughout the industry and the society. The committed efforts of all of those individuals and groups, many of them far outside the formal structure and the hierarchical control of the company, are essential if the firm is to act as an integral whole.

The fifth, and last, basic argument is that it is not enough for the senior executives in a firm to consistently recognize moral problems, present moral solutions, and exhibit moral integrity, in order to bring all of the individuals and groups associated with the firm into an integral whole. Instead, this sense of integrity has to be spread throughout the firm, and that requires a mission statement based upon organizational values and corporate goals and sustained by financial supports, performance measures, incentive payments, prohibited procedures, and leadership actions. Given the increasing intensity of global competition, companies cannot continue to operate successfully without the resulting cooperation, innovation, and unification.

I believe that we have to cover all five arguments to have a course in business ethics that is, once again, rigorous and fun. Good luck in your efforts. If I can help you in any way, please don't hesitate to call or use e-mail. My telephone number is (205) 348-8931 and my e-mail address is LHosmer@cba.ua.edu.

LaRue Hosmer

Contents

4   Moral Analysis and Ethical Duties   85

Definition of Normative Philosophy. The Concept of Ethical Relativism. The Principle of Eternal Law. The Principle of Personal Virtue. The Principle of Utilitarian Benefits. The Principle of Universal Duties. The Principle of Distributive Justice. The Principle of Contributive Liberty. Conclusions on the Principles of Normative Philosophy.

5   Why Should a Business Manager Be Moral?   121

Trust, Commitment, and Cooperative Effort. Extended Organizations. Cooperation, Innovation and Unification. Unify and Guide. A New Method of Management.

6   How Can a Business Organization Be Made Moral?   143

Example of a Major Moral Disaster. Management of a Moral Company. *Philosophy of Management. Corporate Values. Organizational Goals. Mission Statement. Financial Supports. Performance Measures. Incentive Payments. Prohibited Procedures. Leadership Actions.*

CHAPTER 1

Moral Problems in Business Management

Moral problems occur frequently in business management. They extend far beyond the commonly discussed issues of bribery, collusion, and theft, reaching into such areas as corporate acquisitions, marketing policies, and capital investments. A large corporation has taken over a smaller one through the common practice of negotiating for the purchase of stock. Then, in merging the two firms, it is found that some of the positions in one are duplicated in the other. Is it "right" to fire or demote executives holding those duplicate positions, many of whom have served their respective firms for years? A manufacturer that has grown rapidly in an expanding market was helped greatly during that growth by wholesale distributors that introduced its products to retail stores. Now the market has become large enough to make direct distribution from the factory to the store in truckload lots much less expensive, and the market has become competitive enough to make the cost savings from direct distribution much more meaningful. Is it "just" to change distribution channels? A paper company in northern Maine can generate power and reduce its energy costs by building a large dam on land that it owns, but the dam will block a river that canoeists and vacationers have used for years. Is it "fair" to ruin recreational opportunities for others?

"Right" and "just" and "fair" are moral terms. They express a judgment about our behavior towards other people that is felt to be morally correct. We believe that there are "right" and "wrong" ways to behave toward others, "just" and "unjust" actions, "fair" and "unfair" decisions. These beliefs help to form our moral standards of behavior. They reflect our sense of obligation to other people, our feeling that it is better to help rather than to harm other persons. The problem, however, is that frequently it is difficult to avoid harming other people, and this is particularly true in business management. Why? Various groups are involved in business—managers at different levels and functions, workers of different skills and backgrounds, suppliers of different materials, distributors of different products, creditors of different types, stockholders of different holdings, and citizens of different communities, states, and countries—and benefits for one group frequently result in harms for others.

We can illustrate this problem of mixed benefits and harms with examples from the introductory paragraph. It would seem "wrong" at first glance to fire executives who happened, through no fault of their own, to hold duplicate positions in the merged firms. Yet, let us assume that the two companies are in a very competitive industry and that the basic reason for the merger was to become more efficient and better able to withstand foreign competitors. What will happen if the staff reductions are not made? Who will be hurt, then, among other managers, workers, suppliers, distributors, creditors, stockholders, and members of the local communities? Who will benefit if the company is unable to survive? Even if survival is not an issue, who will benefit if the company is unable to grow or if it lacks the resources necessary for product research and market development? The basic questions are the same in the other two examples. Who will benefit, and how much? Who will be penalized, and how greatly? These are easy questions to ask, but difficult ones to answer. In many instances, fortunately, alternatives can be considered. Duplicate managers, instead of being fired, might be retrained and reassigned. Inefficient distributors are a more difficult problem, though a place might be made for them by introducing new products or developing new markets or allowing them to participate in the new distribution processes. The dam across the waterway poses the most difficult problem: It either exists or it doesn't, and making it smaller or putting it in a different location does not really resolve the dilemma.

Moral problems truly are managerial dilemmas. They represent a conflict between an organization's financial performance (measured by revenues, costs, and profits) and its social performance (stated in terms of obligations to persons both within and without the organization). The nature of these obligations is, of course, open to interpretation, but most of us would agree that they include protecting loyal employees, maintaining competitive markets, producing safe products, and preserving environmental features.

Unfortunately, the dilemma of management is that these obligations are costly, both for organizations evaluated by financial standards and for managers subject to financial controls. The manufacturer that distributes direct from the factory to stores will be more profitable and better able to withstand competition than the manufacturer that ships to wholesale warehouses for additional handling and transport. The salesperson, to use a new and more troublesome illustration, who gives small bribes to purchasing agents will have a better record and receive higher commissions than the salesperson who refuses to countenance unethical payments. The design engineer who finds questionable ways to sharply reduce material costs is more likely to be promoted than the design engineer who places product quality and consumer safety above cost considerations. The plant manager who dumps toxic chemicals out in back of the plant will show greater profits than the one who pays for proper disposal.

Some of these problems doubtless appear very clear to you. Others may seem much more debatable. Frequently there is a balance between the financial outcome and the social impact of an organizational decision or action, and the dilemma of management comes in attempting to find the point upon that balance that is "right" and "just" and "fair." The purpose of this book is to examine the factors that enter into that balance and to consider a very specific analytical structure that should help *you* reach a point *you* consider to be "right" and "just" and "fair." Those factors, and that analytical structure, is shown in Figure 1–1.

Before going on to describe each of these steps in greater detail, let us consider an example of a large and complex moral problem. It is one that for many people truly does constitute a managerial dilemma in that it generates substantial benefits for some individuals and great harms for others, and it both recognizes and denies the rights of different groups. It is, in short, an issue in which one side cannot be said to be absolutely "right," or the other side clearly "wrong." We will use it later in the chapter to illustrate the seven steps in the analytical process.

EXAMPLE OF A LARGE-SCALE MORAL PROBLEM

Hydro-Quebec, a large public utility owned by the province of Quebec, has proposed building a huge hydroelectric generating station in the remote wilderness of northern Canada. The company plans to construct a dam 17 miles long across the valley of the Great Whale River, close to the mouth of the river where it empties into James Bay. The dam will create a lake covering 9,100 square miles, leaving only isolated peaks and upland areas as islands in a partially forested but primarily open tundra region. That region stretches 300 miles to the east, almost to the border with Newfoundland, and 200 miles to the north, nearly to the Arctic Circle. It is an area with heavy snowfall in the winter and plenty of rainfall in the summer. The soil is rocky, and the water does not penetrate the ground; instead it collects in rivulets and streams. The

FIGURE 1–1 _____

Analytical Process for the Resolution of Moral Problems

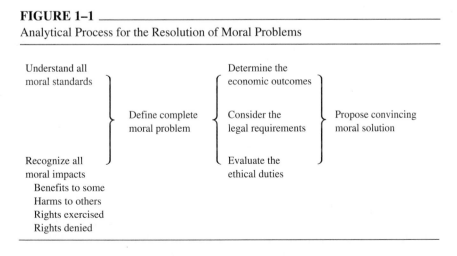

land has a constant slope towards the west, and the rivulets and streams are channeled into larger rivers which coalesce into the Great Whale River near the coast. One dam will store massive amounts of water covering this extensive area for hydroelectric power generation.

The dam would serve a hydroelectric generating station that could produce 14,000 megawatts of electric power, equivalent to the total output of 14 modern coal-fired or nuclear-based generating plants, but of course without the acid emissions or radioactive residues that are associated with those energy sources. Approximately half of the power would be used in southern Quebec, where it would aid in the industrialization of that region. The balance of the power would be sold to the six New England states and New York City, where it would eliminate any need for the utilities in that area to build additional generating capacity for the next 10 years. Because Hydro-Quebec is owned by the province of Quebec, profits from the sale of the power would be used to fund improvements in education and health care throughout the province, in both the south and the north.

The electric power the dam would generate is needed in a region of the United States that for years has been dependent upon the importation of foreign oil for both home heating and industrial expansion. The profits are needed in an area of Canada that for years has suffered from insufficient funding for primary and secondary education, and for health care. Improved health care in the north will bring lower infant mortality and longer life spans. Improved education in the south will bring greater graduation rates and higher personal incomes. The only possible problem with the project is the opposition of a majority of the Cree and Inuit Indians who live in the area to be flooded, a total of 2,000 families. The chief of the Cree has refused to sell the land (which had never been formally deeded to his people by treaty) saying, "It is hard to explain to white people what we mean when we say our land is part of our life. We are like rocks and tree, beaver and caribou. We belong here. We will not leave." A minority of both tribes, about 800 families, however, are perfectly willing to sell the land, and want to adopt what they consider to be more modern and more comfortable ways of living in a cold, harsh, and unforgiving climate.

How do you decide when faced with this issue? Millions of people will benefit. Only 2,000 families, about 8,000 individuals, will be harmed. Certainly you could pay all of the Indian families, majority and minority alike, a fair price for their land. But how do you establish a "fair" price for scrub forests and frozen tundra that has no commercial value but evidently a high emotional worth to most of the families? There is no equivalent land in Canada that is not currently occupied either by native peoples or recent immigrants, so that you cannot simply ask the objecting majority of the Cree and Inuit to move either further east into Newfoundland or further west into Ontario. Both moves would disrupt the lives of other people already there. The majority of the Cree and the Inuit say that they do not want your money. They want to stay right where they are, living their lives exactly as they have for hundreds if not thousands of years, on land they consider to belong solely if not legally to them, without interference from the provincial government that wants to build hydroelectric dams and generating plants in what they consider to be their wilderness.

How do you decide, and particularly how do you reach a decision that all can accept as being "right" and "just" and "fair"? It is suggested that you work through the decision process in Figure 1–1, step by step. Understand the moral standards, or the intuitive judgments on "right and "wrong," and the reasons they differ between different peoples. Look at the benefits and the harms, the rights exercised and the wrongs imposed, for all of those peoples. Then, propose the moral question—is it "right" and "just" and "fair" that we generate these benefits and exercise these rights for ourselves, given that others will be harmed and have their rights ignored—as clearly as possible. Finally, answer that moral question by considering the economic outcomes, the legal requirements, and the ethical duties. See if you can reach a solution that you not only believe personally to be "right" and "just" and "fair," but also that you believe you could explain convincingly to others. The theme of this book is that it is not enough to make up your own mind. You have to be able to justify your decision to others.

Understand the Moral Standards

Most people, when they first encounter a situation in which the well-being of some individuals or groups is going to be hurt or harmed in some way, or in which the rights of those individuals or groups are going to be ignored or compromised in some other way, turn first to their moral standards of behavior. Moral standards of behavior are our gauges of individual and organizational actions. They are the means we all use to decide whether our actions, and those of the other people and other groups with whom we live and work, are "right" or "wrong," "fair" or "unfair," "just" or "unjust."

The problem is that our moral standards of behavior are subjective. They are personal. They are the way each of us intuitively feels about our actions and those of our neighbors, friends, and associates, but we can't really justify those feelings. You may feel that lying is wrong under any and all circumstances. I may feel that lying to avoid causing embarrassment or anguish to a close friend is perfectly all right. We can't or at least we generally don't resolve those differences, and so we usually just agree to disagree on the question. Such an understanding is perfectly acceptable when we are dealing with a minor moral problem such as lying to avoid causing discomfort to a friend. Such an understanding—to agree to disagree—is not acceptable when we are concerned with a substantial moral problem such as building a huge hydroelectric dam that will benefit millions of people who live far away, yet harm the thousands of individuals who live right there.

We have to decide the issue, not ignore the conflict, and the first step is to understand that moral standards are not an adequate framework for decision because they are variable as well as personal. They vary by individual, by group, by region, by country, by culture, and by time. We all have evidence of that variation. Business managers in South and Central America and large parts of Africa and Asia think that it is perfectly acceptable to make small payments to government officials to facilitate needed documents and permits. That is termed *bribery* in the United States. Government officials in the United States feel that it is perfectly acceptable to work for foreign firms that have business relationships with the government after they retire. That is termed *treason* in South and Central America and large parts of Africa and Asia.

Moral standards of behavior differ between peoples because the goals, norms, beliefs, and values upon which they depend also differ, and those goals, norms, beliefs, and values in turn differ because of variations in the religious and cultural traditions and the economic and social situations in which the individuals are immersed. These relationships are shown in Figure 1–2.

We will take up each of these elements in sequence, starting with the personal goals, norms, beliefs, and values, and showing their derivation from the religious and cultural traditions and the economic and social situations of each individual:

- *Personal goals.* Goals are our expectations of outcomes. They are the things we want out of life and the things we expect others probably want out of life as well. They include material possessions (cars, homes, boats, and vacations), lifestyle preferences (money, position, workload, and power), personal goods (family, friends, health, and respect) and social aims (justice, equality, a clean environment, and a world at peace). If I want more money and power and you want greater justice and equality, then probably we are going to differ on what we think is "right" and "wrong."

- *Personal norms.* Norms are our expectations of behavior. They are the ways we expect to act and the ways in which we expect others to act in given situations. Norms differ from moral standards in that they have no close association with judgments about "right" or "wrong." Norms are expectations of behavior; morals

FIGURE 1–2 _____

Individual Determinants of Moral Standards

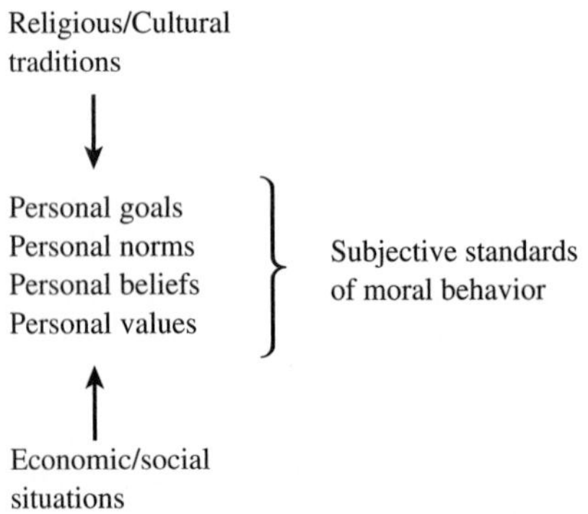

Religious/Cultural traditions

Personal goals
Personal norms   } Subjective standards
Personal beliefs   of moral behavior
Personal values

Economic/social situations

are gauges of behavior. I expect you to drive on the right-hand side of the road; that is a norm. If you persist on driving on the left-hand side (in the United States), I will say that you are "wrong;" that is a moral standard.

- *Personal beliefs.* Beliefs are our expectations of thought. They are the ways we expect to think, and the ways in which we expect others to think, about given situations. Our beliefs generally support our norms, and our norms usually lead towards our goals. For example, I believe that cigarette smoke causes cancer, and consequently I expect you not to smoke in my presence because one of my goals is good health. If you persist in smoking, despite my repeated (and heated) objections, I am going to say that you are "wrong" for you have acted against my moral standard derived from those goals, norms, and beliefs.

- *Personal values.* Values are our priorities between goals, norms, and beliefs. They are the ways we judge the relative importance of what we want to have, how we want to act, and why we believe as we do. Most people do not consider that all of their goals, norms, and beliefs are of equal importance. Generally there are some that seem more important, more "valued" than others. Let us say that you and I value democracy (a belief) very highly; if someone offers both of us money (a goal) to vote a given way (a norm), we are going to say that they are "wrong."

The goals, norms, beliefs, and values of a person will vary depending upon the cultural and religious tradition of that person, and those variations will in turn affect the moral standards. Clearly the cultural and religious traditions of the Cree and Inuit who have long been established in northern Quebec are going to differ markedly from the cultural and religious traditions of the European immigrants who have been comparatively recent (within the past 300 years) settlers in southern Quebec. Assume that both sides hold their religious beliefs and cultural norms in equally high esteem; their differing goals, norms, beliefs, and values are going to affect the ways in which each group views the proposed hydroelectric generating project.

The goals, norms, beliefs, and values of a person will also vary depending upon the economic and social situation of that person. The economic situation includes the relative income and financial security of the individual. The social situation does not mean the social status of the person; instead it refers to his or her membership in different organizations whose members can influence his or her goals, norms, beliefs, values, and—ultimately—his or her moral standards. Clearly once again, the relative incomes and the organizational memberships of the Cree and Inuit in northern Quebec are going to differ markedly from the relative incomes and organizational memberships of the European immigrants in southern Quebec. Once again, their differing goals, norms, beliefs, and values are also going to affect the ways in which each group views the desirability of the big hydroelectric generating project.

How should you attempt to bridge those different moral standards and project views to arrive at an ethical solution that you believe to be "right" and "just" and "fair," *and* that you think you could logically explain to all of the other groups involved in the project in order to reach a morally acceptable compromise? The argument of this book is that you work through each of the next six stages in the moral analysis, starting with an explicit recognition of the moral impacts.

Recognize the Moral Impacts

Moral problems were described earlier as being complex because they result in benefits for some and harms for others, and because they exercise the rights of some and deny the rights of others. Those benefits and harms, that exercise and denial of rights, together compose the "impacts" of the problem. Those impacts—the benefits and harms, the rights and wrongs—are what people think about when they consider a morally controversial project such as the construction of the large hydroelectric project in northern Quebec. Consequently it is suggested that you start your analysis of the problem, and your determination of the solution, by first identifying exactly who is going to be benefited and who is going to be harmed. Then identify exactly who is going to be able to freely exercise their rights and who is going to be prevented from an equally free exercise of their rights. People feel strongly about being harmed. People feel even more strongly about being denied their rights. Your first step is to make certain that everyone involved in the moral problem understands what is happening to everyone else.

- *Benefits.* Whose well-being will be substantially improved by the present or proposed action (what is being done, or what is planned to be done) either by yourself or by the organization to which you belong? Focus on material or financial or personal benefits to identifiable groups of people, not to inanimate companies or communities or countries. Moral problems involve a mixture of outcomes. List the positive outcomes of that mixture. Specifically, identify the major groups of people whose well-being you believe will be improved, and give a short description of the nature of that improvement for each group.

- *Harms.* Whose well-being will be substantially harmed by the present or proposed action (what is being done, or what is planned to be done) either by yourself or by the organization to which you belong? Focus on material or financial or personal harms to identifiable groups of people, not to inanimate companies or communities or countries. Moral problems, once again, constitute a mixture of outcomes. List the negative outcomes of that mixture. Identify the major groups of people whose well-being you believe will be damaged, and give a short description of the nature of that damage for each group.

- *Rights.* Whose rights will be exercised and made more certain by the present or proposed action either by yourself or by the organization to which you belong? Focus on the rights of identifiable groups of people, not of inanimate companies or communities or countries. Be selective. Make certain that there is a clear right or claim of a privilege to do something important that is being exercised, not just a general desire to do something beneficial. Identify the major groups of people whose rights you believe will be sustained or expanded in some way, and give some indication of the nature of those rights.

- *Wrongs.* Whose rights will be denied and made less certain by the present or proposed action either by yourself or by the organization to which you belong? Focus on the wrongs of identifiable groups of people, not of inanimate companies or communities or countries. Again, be selective. Make certain that there is a clear right or claim of someone to do something important that is being denied, not just a general desire to do something beneficial. Identify the major groups of these people whose rights you believe will be denied or reduced in some way, and give an indication of the nature of those rights.

The benefits and the harms, the rights and the wrongs, for the different groups involved in the proposed construction of the Great Whale hydroelectric generating project are summarized in Figure 1–3.

A major harm and an important wrong are both shown in Figure 1–3 that were not included in the earlier description of the project. This is the technical issue of the possibility of methyl mercury poisoning. Mercury, which is a highly toxic heavy metal, occurs naturally in the soil and consequently in the low scrub vegetation of the tundra area of northern Quebec. When that tundra vegetation is submerged under water, the plant matter decays and the mercury combines with the organic hydrocarbons to form methyl mercury, a water-soluble form of the toxic metal. Being water soluble it will quickly enter into the aquatic life of the massive lake. It will probably affect the fish and, if humans eat the fish, will probably affect the humans as well. No one knows the extent of that affect upon either the fish or the people because there has never

FIGURE 1–3

Comparison of the Benefits and Harms of the Hydro-Quebec Great Whale Generating Project

People Affected	Benefits Received	Harms Allocated
Residents of northern Quebec	Improved housing Improved health care Lower infant mortality Longer life spans Better education	Loss of flooded land Loss of native culture Poisoning of local fish Harm to human health
Residents of southern Quebec	Lower-priced power Greater industrial growth More jobs Higher income Better education	None
Residents of northeastern U.S.	Available electric power No new generating plants No acid rain No global warming	None

been a reservoir of this size (9,100 square miles) built this far north (in the tundra area) before. The only proposed solution has been a legal prohibition on eating the fish. Methyl mercury poisoning thus is a probable harm (loss of the local fish as a food product) and possible wrong (denial of the right to health) for the Cree and Inuit peoples that must be included though, as stated earlier, the exact impact is not known with certainty.

The rights exercised and rights denied perhaps need greater explanation than can be compressed into the short descriptions in Figure 1–3. The residents of southern Quebec would doubtless feel that, if an election were held on building the hydroelectric project, the percentage voting "yes" would easily win because the benefits of lower-priced power, greater industrial growth, more jobs, and higher incomes would go to a vast majority of the population. Those residents of southern Quebec would probably also feel that, if a trial were held on the issue, the verdict would be "go ahead" because the right of eminent domain (right of the government to expropriate private land for a public use, such as a highway or airport) is solidly established in the law. Further, the legal ownership of the land by the Cree and Inuit has never been formally established; their concept of ownership does not extend to land. Land in their culture is owned communally by the tribe, not individually by the person. It is possible in their culture for a person to own a house; it is not possible for that person to own the land upon which that house rests. This is another example of the way in which misunderstandings between Native American and Western cultures are so easily possible. The next step, then, in the analytical process is to clearly state the moral problem so that everyone fully comprehends the issues, regardless of their religious and cultural traditions and of their economic and social situations.

State the Moral Problem

If your listed balance of benefits received and harm imposed, and your described contrast of rights exercised and rights denied, conflict with your personal moral standards, then clearly you have what you believe to be a moral problem. But, remember that not everyone will agree with you due to the differences in moral standards that come from variations in goals, norms, beliefs, and values, and from the contrasts in religious and cultural traditions and economic and social situations.

To reach a solution you want to get everyone to fully comprehend your side of the issue. Doubtless other groups will want to get everyone— including you—to fully comprehend their sides of the issue as well. If all groups fully comprehend all sides, clearly and accurately, then a compromise that meets the tests of economic benefits, legal requirements, and ethical duties is at least possible. That is why you want to first define and then state the moral problem as clearly as you can. Get agreement here, and the rest of the decision process will be much easier.

It is strongly suggested that you state the moral problem in the form of an extended question. A question is much less threatening and far more considerate than a statement. And the question format explicitly recognizes the concerns of others and makes it possible to include those concerns in the subsequent analysis, discussion, and conclusion:

> Is it "right" that Hydro-Quebec build a large hydroelectric generating plant in northern Quebec, on land that has been inhabited by the Cree and Inuit Indians for centuries? The project will result in substantial benefits (lower-priced power, greater industrialization, more jobs, higher incomes, reduced pollution, improved education, and better health care) for large groups of people in southern Quebec. It will even further result in substantial benefits (better housing, education, and health care; longer life spans; and reduced infant mortality) for the native peoples of northern Quebec. But, it will also result in a loss of their land and culture, and possible harms to their health. A strong majority of the Indian peoples in the north do not want the project built. A strong majority of the European immigrants in the south do want the project built. The residents of southern Quebec have a right to democratic rule and legal process regarding that project, but the inhabitants of northern Quebec have an equal right to decide their own future and a critical right to ensure their own health.

Determine the Economic Outcomes

"Economic outcomes" in moral analysis refer to the net balance of benefits over costs for the full society, given that the values of those benefits and costs are determined by all of the people within that full society, acting through open and free markets. This is the concept known as Pareto Optimality. The underlying belief is that people express their preferences for the goods and services they most want through output product markets, and their preferences for the capital (money), labor (time), and land (raw materials) they least desire through input factor markets. Capital, labor, and land are the resources owned by members of society. Producing firms purchase or rent that capital, labor, and material at the lowest possible costs, convert those factors into products with the greatest possible efficiencies, and then sell the output goods and services at the highest possible prices. Competition in the output product markets keeps the prices from becoming improperly high, and competition in the input factor markets keeps the costs from becoming unfairly low. The full society, then, gets as many as possible of the products they most want while having to give up as little as possible of the factors they least want.

The analytical method of "economic outcomes" can also be expressed as three easily understood dictums: (1) More is better than less. (2) Specifically, more is better than less when that "more" consists of what people really want, as expressed through their preferences in the product markets. (3) And even more specifically, that more of what people really want is better than less when that "more" is produced as efficiently as possible by using as little as possible of what people least want, as expressed by their preferences in the factor markets.

In the example of the huge hydroelectric generating plant proposed by Hydro-Quebec, the analytical method of "economic outcomes" would first conclude—following the first two dictums—that more electricity, as long as it was wanted in the output product markets and would not be surplus, would be better than less. The problem would come in the third dictum. People would have to give up what they least wanted in the input factor markets. But, there are no input factor markets for tundra land and native culture, and consequently the members of the full society are unable to express their preferences in an economically understandable way. Also, there is the troubling issue of the methyl mercury poisoning. This is termed an "external cost" in economic theory; it is outside the production process, but the potential consequences will be imposed upon the native peoples without their consent.

The concept of the greatest possible economic benefits at least possible economic costs, which is the "more is better than less" doctrine or the Pareto Optimality theory, is considered to be a valid means of morally evaluating the benefits and harms of a moral problem as long as three conditions are met:

- All markets must be free. Open and competitive product markets must exist for all goods and services, and open and competitive factor markets must exist for all input capital, labor, and material, to generate a true net benefit for society. Without open and free markets the preferences of the members of that society cannot be expressed.

- All laws must be obeyed. The analytical method of economic benefits does not consider the balance of rights exercised and rights denied. It focuses on the outcomes, not on the rights. It is assumed that all legitimate rights are expressed by democratically enacted laws, and therefore the spirit as well as the letter of those laws must be followed.

- All costs must be included. External costs are those outside the productive process; they are frequently ignored because no one in the producing firm has to write out a check as they must to purchase capital, labor, and material. It is assumed that they will be recognized, computed, and then included in the purchase price of the output goods and services.

Consider the Legal Requirements

Legal requirements in moral analysis refer to the laws adopted by members of society to regulate the behavior of members of that society. Clearly some regulation is needed. If everyone pursued their own self-interests, without regard to the self-interests of others, there would be disruption and chaos, and no economic benefits would be possible for anyone. The problem is that every regulation limits, to some extent, the rights of some individuals and groups within society, even though it protects the rights of other individuals and groups within that same society. Legal requirements, in one sense, are very similar to economic outcomes. Economic outcomes in moral analysis focus upon a balance between benefits and harms. Legal requirements in moral analysis also focus upon a balance, though in this instance it is a balance between rights and wrongs, or between rights exercised and rights denied.

The balance between rights exercised and rights denied clearly has to be "fair," which would mean equitable to the full society. The economic outcomes method attempts to determine what would be beneficial to the full society. The legal requirements method attempts to determine what would be equitable, or evenhanded, to that society. I own a considerable amount of land in a pleasant residential community. You are my next-door neighbor. I own the land outright and consequently I think that I have a right to do what I please with that land and make as large a profit as possible. A real estate developer offers me a very high price to build a very large shopping center. My right to sell what I own without interference will be exercised. Your right to live quietly, in your own home, will be denied.

How do we determine what would be equitable under those circumstances? We could take a vote, and because there will be many more residents who don't want a new shopping center in our community than there will be those that do, you will win. But, would that be "right"? A majority can override the rights of a minority. The method proposed in the legal requirements method of moral analysis to determine fairness is to consider what would be the balance of rights versus wrongs if everyone within society considered what regulations should be adopted *while ignorant of his or her own self-interest.* This is the concept known as the Social Contract. It is usually expressed as a question: What regulations would people agree should be the basic laws of our society *if they did not know the position they held within society?*

This is obviously an impossible condition. People do know the positions they hold within society. I know that I own the land and want to build the shopping center. You know that you are my next-door neighbor and don't want the shopping center built. You particularly don't want it built because I plan to keep it open until 12:30 every night to maximize revenues, with bright lights in the parking lots that will shine directly into your bedroom windows and loud music on the speaker systems that will prevent you from sleeping. But let us say that we move back in time, before there are shopping centers and residential communities. What agreement would we make then as to regulations that would limit the rights of ownership of land? I would be as worried as you about the possibility that my neighbors might use their land in ways that would detract from my use of my land. If we could reach an agreement and pass a law under those conditions, termed the "Veil of Ignorance," then it would be possible to say that that agreement and that law would be "right" and "fair" and "just." It would reflect the social interests of all of us rather than the self-interests of a portion of us.

In the example of the huge hydroelectric generating plant proposed by Hydro-Quebec, the analytical method of legal requirements, following the concept of the Veil of Ignorance, would help each side understand the rationale of the other side. The native peoples of northern Quebec would be forced to recognize the many benefits and rights of the residents of the south. The residents of southern Quebec would be forced to recognize the many harms and wrongs to the peoples of the north. The concept of a law that focuses on the social interests of all of society rather than on the self-interests of a portion of society can be considered to be a valid means of evaluating the balance of rights and wrongs of a moral problem as long as one condition exists:

> All parties must be willing to evaluate the balance of benefits and harms, and of rights and wrongs, as if they were ignorant of their positions within society. Everyone must be willing to adopt the method of the Veil of Ignorance to examine the issue, and look at social interest rather than self-interest.

This is a difficult condition, but it is not an impossible one.

Evaluate the Ethical Duties

"Ethical duties" in moral analysis refer to the obligations owed by members of society to other members of that society. Clearly, some obligations do exist. We ought not to lie to each other, or agreements will not be possible. We ought not to cheat each other, or contracts will not be possible. And we ought not to steal from each other, or communities will not be possible. A society without agreements, without contracts, and without communities would be impossible to sustain. The problem is that if I could lie just a little bit, cheat just a little bit, and steal just a little bit the society could still be maintained, although weakened, and I would be advantaged though you would be harmed. Once again, the focus in moral analysis is between self-interest and social interest.

Ethical duties is a method of moral analysis that attempts to provide a set of rules as to what would be in the interest of society under all conditions and in all situations. There is no moral balance between social interest and self-interest as there is in the analytical methods of economic outcomes and legal requirements. The doctrine of economic outcomes attempts to find a balance between benefits for some people within society and harms for others that will result in an overall improvement for the full society. The doctrine of legal requirements attempts to find a similar balance between rights for some people and wrongs for others that also will result in an overall improvement for our society. The doctrine of ethical duties does not look for a balance between duties. It does not say that a little more lying, cheating, or stealing by one group can be balanced by a little less lying, cheating, and stealing by another, and society will be better off. Instead, it attempts to set the rules or conditions under which some very specific instances of lying, cheating, and stealing would be permissible.

I feel, as I explained in an example given earlier in this chapter in the section on moral standards of behavior, that lying to avoid causing discomfort to a friend is permissible. You may disagree. But how about stealing to save the life of a child, particularly if the theft is from persons or groups who have more than enough for their own sustenance? Is that morally correct in your judgment? Ethical duties get down to the absolute essence of what is "right" and "just" and "fair" for everyone. Remember this "for everyone" condition; an ethical principle is meaningless unless it can be applied to all. There are six of these universal rules or conditions that are summarized below, in the historical sequence of their initial formulation:

- *Personal virtues* (Aristotle, 384–322 B.C.). The argument here is that we can do as we like, and follow our own self-interests, as long as we adopt a set of standards for our "right," "just," and "fair" treatment of one another. We have to be honest, open, and truthful, for example, to eliminate distrust, and we should live temperately so as not to incite envy. In short, we have to be proud of our actions and of our lives, for it is hard to be proud of actions that exploit or oppress others. The principle, then, can be expressed as "never take any action that is not honest, open, and truthful, and that you would not be proud to see reported widely in national newspapers and on network television programs."

- *Religious injunctions* (St. Augustine, 354–403 A.D. and St. Thomas Aquinas, 1225–1274). Honesty, truthfulness, and temperance are not enough; we also have to have some degree of compassion and kindness towards each other to form a truly "good" society. Compassion and kindness are best expressed in the Golden Rule, which is not limited to the Judeo-Christian tradition, but is part of almost all of the world's religions. Reciprocity and compassion together build a sense of community. The principle, then, can be expressed as "never take any action that is not kind, and that does not build a sense of community, a sense of all of us working together for a commonly accepted goal."

- *Utilitarian benefits* (Bentham, 1747–1832, and Mill, 1806–1873). Compassion, kindness, and a sense of community would be ideal if everyone was compassionate and kind and worked for the community rather than for themselves, but everyone won't and so we need a means of evaluating self-centered acts rather than eliminating them. An act, then, is "right" if it leads to greater net social benefits than social harms. This is the rule that is often summarized as "greatest good for the greatest number," though in reality the society itself has to benefit. The principle can be summarized as "never take any action that does not result in greater good than harm for the society of which you are a part."

- *Universal rules* (Kant, 1724–1804). Net social benefit is elegant in theory, but the theory does not say anything about how we should measure either the benefits or the harms—what is your life or health or well-being worth?—or how we should distribute those benefits and allocate those harms. What we need is a rule to eliminate the self-interest of the person who decides in any given situation, and we can do that by universalizing the decision process. The principle, then, can be expressed as "never take any action that you would not be willing to see others, faced with the same or a closely similar situation, also be free and even encouraged to take."

- *Distributive justice* (Rawls). The problem with the "willingness to see others be free and even encouraged to take" rule for actions that allegedly come from a good intent to promote social interest rather than a selfish desire to advance self-interest is that people differ in their social and economic situations. People have different social and economic wants. We need a rule to protect the poor and the un-educated who lack the power and position to achieve those wants. If we did not know who among us would be poor and uneducated—the Social Contract—every-one would be in favor of such a rule. The principle, then, can be expressed as "never take any action in which the least among us will be harmed in any way."

- *Contributive liberty* (Nozick). Perhaps liberty, the freedom to follow one's own self-interest within the constraints of the law and markets, is more important than justice, the right to be protected from extremes of that law and those markets. If so, then the only agreement that could be made under the conditions of the Social Contract—in which people do not know who would be rich or poor, who powerful or weak—would be that no one should interfere with the rights of any-one else to improve their legal abilities and marketable skills. The principle, then, can be expressed as "never take any action that will interfere with the rights of others for self-development and self-improvement."

The method of moral analysis recommended in this text is that you look first at *your* moral standards of behavior—what do you intuitively believe to be "right" and "wrong," "fair" and "unfair," "just" and "unjust," based upon *your* goals, norms, beliefs, and values. Then, look at the situation that you have en-countered. Who will be benefited and who will be harmed? Who will be able to exercise their rights and who will be denied an equally free exercise of their rights? If those conditions in that situation conflict with your moral standards, then you have a moral problem. Express that moral problem as clearly as you can, so that everyone else will understand your concerns. Then, analyze that moral problem through the perspectives of economic outcomes, legal require-ments, and ethical duties to arrive at your moral solution. This process was ear-lier expressed in graphic form, which is repeated in Figure 1–4 for emphasis.

Chapter 2 will discuss in greater detail the analytical procedure of eco-nomic outcomes. Chapter 3 will deal with legal requirements. Chapter 4 will describe the ethical duties. Chapter 5 will focus on the reasons to be moral: the

FIGURE 1–4 _____

Analytical Process for the Resolution of Moral Problems

Understand all moral standards		Determine the economic outcomes	
	Define complete moral problem	Consider the legal requirements	Propose convincing moral solution
Recognize all moral impacts Benefits to some Harms to others Rights exercised Rights denied		Evaluate the ethical duties	

trust, commitment, and effort that can develop among all of the participants within an extended organization in response to decisions and actions they perceive to be "right" and "just" and "fair." Chapter 6 will consider the managerial and organizational changes needed to achieve exactly those results, and the resultant cooperation, innovation, and unification that are needed for success in a competitive global environment.

CASE 1–1

Cruise Ships and the Disposal of Waste at Sea

Vacation cruises have become very popular. Approximately 85 cruise ships, primarily based in Miami, Florida, offer three-, five-, or seven-day trips to Bermuda, the Bahamas, the Caribbean, and the Yucatan Peninsula in Mexico. Some of these cruise ships are very large, carrying 2,000 to 3,000 passengers and 500 to 700 staff, the equivalent of a medium-sized town. The large size is a major cause of the pollution problem.

The large cruise ships are essentially floating hotels, but unlike land-based hotels they are not connected to municipal water and sewer systems. They carry the fresh water needed for drinking, washing, laundry, and kitchen use in huge tanks. Human wastes from toilets are stored in large tanks that are pumped out when the ship returns to the home port. Nonhuman wastes are stored in much smaller tanks that are discharged each night, at sea.

The nonhuman wastes are called "gray water," a euphemism that brings to mind the soapy water from baths and showers. That is certainly included, but also included is wastewater from the clothes washers for sheets and towels in the ship's laundry, from the dishwashers for plates, utensils, and pans in the ship's kitchen, and from the many garbage disposals. It is an unsavory, smelly mess that is discharged at night in order not to concern or disturb the guests.

Officials in the companies that own the cruise ships, such as Royal Caribbean Cruises, say that they cannot afford to carry tanks large enough to store all of the nonhuman wastes until they return to their home port. The ships add fresh water to their tanks when they stop at islands in the Caribbean or at ports in the Bahamas or Bermuda. But, those ports do not have waste treatment plants large enough to accept either the human or nonhuman wastes for processing.

The space needed for much larger tanks to store nonhuman wastes would, company officials claim, substantially take away from the space available for the accommodation of paying passengers. No one is hurt, they add, by disposal at sea because these are chemical (soap) and biological materials that quickly disperse in the wave actions of the sea. It is true that marine life has declined severely in this area, but company officials say this is due to poor waste treatment practices on the islands themselves and to overfishing by ships from many foreign countries.

The island nations don't like gray water dumping just off their coasts, but they are dependent upon the dollars brought by tourists shopping for souvenirs, gifts, and clothing at the ports-of-call during the cruise. Island nations that objected too strongly in the past have been told that the cruise ships would simply find a different port-of-call. International maritime law provides no assistance to those nations; it is not illegal for ships to dump wastes "at sea," which is usually defined as three miles from the nearest point of land.

Some of the smaller Caribbean nations appealed to the World Health Organization. They claimed in their appeal that nutrients from the garbage and chemicals from the detergents had greatly increased the growth of viral and bacterial agents throughout the Caribbean. Now, they added, dense clouds of these tiny organisms can be found in the seawater, and many sea creatures, such as fish, turtles, and dolphins, are showing signs of external rashes and internal tumors. The World Health Organization said in reply that it had no authority to act as long as it could not be proven that human health was affected.

Senior executives at the major cruise lines were concerned, but they believed that there was little they could do. Ship designers had estimated that it would decrease passenger accommodations by 15 percent to 20 percent to add the much larger tanks needed to store the "gray water" wastes. Those tanks, due to their weight when full, would have to be built below the waterline in space currently used for the crew's quarters. The crew, now housed in very crowded conditions that cannot be further compressed, would have to be moved into new facilities built where passenger cabins now exist.

Those same executives believed that, if those changes in the physical layout of the ships were made, ticket prices would have to be increased by an equivalent 15 percent to 20 percent to make up for the lost revenue. This, it was feared, would decrease customer demand. Now, because of their huge economies of scale and the scenic attractiveness of the region they visit, cruise ships offer highly desired and relatively inexpensive vacations. On the other hand, the executives admitted that apparently the quality of the seawater had deteriorated to some extent, and that at least part of the responsibility for that deterioration might be due to the waste dumping practices of the cruise lines.

Class Assignment.   What should be done? What recommendations should you, as a leading member of the Board of Directors, make to the other members of the board, and how should you convince them to adopt those recommendations? The first chapter of this text suggested that you use the following pattern of analysis:

1. What groups will be benefited from continuing the present "dump at sea" policy?

2. What groups will be harmed from continuing the present "dump at sea" policy?

3. What groups will be able to fully exercise their rights if the present policy is continued?

4. What groups will be denied many of their rights if the present policy is continued?

5. How would you express the moral problem (if you believe this to be a moral problem) so that everyone involved will believe that you fully recognize and truly understand their particular problems and concerns?

6. What are the economic benefits? The rule is that you should always take the action that will generate the greatest profits for the company because this will also generate the greatest benefits for the society, provided it can be shown that all markets are fully competitive, all customers are fully informed, and all external and internal costs are fully included.

7. What are the legal requirements? The rule here is that you should always take the action that most fully complies with the law because the law in a democratic society represents the combined moral standards of all of the people within that society, provided it can be shown that the goals, norms, beliefs, and values of all of the various individuals, groups, and organizations have been equitably combined in the formulation process.

8. What are the ethical duties? The rule here is that you should always take the action that you (1) would be proud to see widely reported in national newspapers; (2) that you believe will build a sense of community among everyone associated with the action; (3) that you expect will generate the greatest net social good; (4) that you would be willing to see others take in similar situations in which you might be the victim; (5) that you believe does not harm the "least among us"; and (6) that you think does not interfere with the right of everyone to develop their skills to the fullest.

9. What is your recommendation, and how would you explain your recommendation to the other individuals, groups, and organizations that are going to be affected by that decision or action if it is adopted?

CASE 1–2

Napster and the Free Exchange of Recorded Music

Napster is an Internet-based music-sharing service. Any person with a home computer and access to the Internet can reach the Napster home page and then enter the name of the musician and the title of the song that he or she wishes to obtain. That song is not then made available directly from the hard drives on its server; instead the Napster program connects the user who wants a specific title to the hard drive of another user who happens to have that specific title. The music is shared, not purchased, and that sharing, legally, makes all the difference.

The Audio Home Recording Act of 1992 exempts consumers from lawsuits for copyright violations when they record or exchange music for private, noncommercial use. It is perfectly legal for people to copy a song from a radio or television program and keep it in their own collection. It is also perfectly legal for people to copy a song from their collection and give it to a neighbor or friend. And lastly, it is perfectly legal for a company to sell the equipment necessary for all this recording, as long as there is no commercial (that is, no paid) usage of the song or of the record.

The Audio Home Recording Act of 1992 was passed when almost all music was analogue (sequential variations in pitch) rather than digital (numerical representations of pitch). Analogue recordings made on home equipment were universally acknowledged to be far lower in quality than those made on commercial equipment; consequently the executives at recording companies, the composers who wrote the music, and the artists who performed it were not overly concerned about the protection of their property against unpaid analogue exchange.

Now music is represented digitally by literally billions of bits of binary data. Compact disks can store this immense amount of information in binary form fairly cheaply, but it would be impossible to transmit the data in that form over the Internet without taking far too much time, or to store it in that form on a hard drive without taking far too much space, were it not for the development of MP3 technology. This is a compression technology that essentially transmits and stores statistically probable patterns in the data rather than the data itself. It is possible, using compression technology, to download a song from the Internet in minutes rather than hours, and to store those songs on the hard drive of a personal computer in thousands rather than tens of thousands of megabits.

The digitalization of sound and the compression of data made possible the sharing of music over the Internet though the Napster service. The Recording Industry Association of American, the trade group representing companies that are active in recording, distributing, and selling music on records and compact disks, believes that this service is absolutely wrong, the moral equivalent of theft. Spokespeople for that trade group allege that persons who are using Napster are simply stealing the music of established artists, taking their intellectual property without paying for it, and making it much more difficult for beginning musicians and all others associated with the recording industry to earn a living:

> Napster is enabling and encouraging the illegal copying and distribution of copyrighted music. Just because Napster itself may not house the infringing recordings does not mean Napster is not guilty of copyright infringement. (Statement of RIAA spokesperson, quoted in "Napster Lawsuit Q&A" under RIAA/Current Issues on the RIAA website, riaa.com, October 24, 2000)

> When you post digital music files on the Internet for anyone to take and keep, it's not promotion but distribution. It should be up to the artist and copyright owner to decide how their music will be heard, distributed and promoted. Though

most people do not realize it, only about 15% of all releases sell enough copies to make a profit and those record sales support the other 85%, including those from new and emerging artists. When someone decides to take distribution into his or her own hands, that decision can impact not only the artist whose music is being taken, but the artists that may have been supported by those sales. It's also important to remember that sales of recordings don't just support the musical artist. Piracy cheats producers, composers, sound engineers, studio musicians, publishers, and vocalists out of their share of royalties on which they generally depend for their livelihoods. (RIAA spokesperson, quoted in "Napster Lawsuit Q&A" posted under RIAA/Current Issues on riaa.com, October 24, 2000)

I think the fact is that Napster is stealing recorded music, something that we have to stop. It's taking food out of my kid's mouth. That's the way I look at it. It's wrong. It's inherently wrong. It's stealing. (Art Alexakis of the rock group Everclear, quoted in "What Do Artists Think of Napster's System," posted under RIAA/Current Issues on riaa.com, October 24, 2000)

Why is it all of a sudden okay to get music for free? Why should music be free, when it costs artists money to record and produce it? No other occupation provides its services for free that we know of. Do mechanics, contractors, plumbers, machinists, doctors, etc. provide their services in exchange for no compensation. We certainly know that lawyers don't. (Lars Ulrich of the rock band Metallica, quoted in "A Note from the Band," posted under Metallica/Napster Forum on metallica.com, June 13, 2000)

Many users of the Napster service disagree totally. Their belief is that it is not stealing to exchange property between friends. They argue that they can let a friend borrow any other item they own, without any concern by the original manufacturer of that item, so why should it be different with recorded music? The attitude is often expressed as an analogy to sharing printed materials. I can let a friend take a book or magazine that I bought, and there is no problem. I can even xerox copies of an article that I like, and as long as I don't sell those copies, there is again no problem. Why can't I let a friend copy a song that I like, as long as I don't sell that copy for cash?" This proposal for noncommercial and nonprofit use was fully supported by executives at Napster and one of the recording industry's largest firms:

Napster is innocent and simply facilitates communications between people interested in music by giving them the ability to sample and preview music before buying it. Napster does not copy files and does not make or transfer MP3 files. It provides access among users logged onto its site at a given time and lets them reach into each other's hard drives and share files under legally acceptable fair use terms, which precludes making a profit. (Hank Barry, CEO of Napster, in "Senate Committee Questions Napster," *Infoworld*, July 17, 2000)

Thomas Middlehoff, CEO of Bertelsmann [a very large European recording and distribution company that was attempting to enter the American market] said, "Napster has pointed the way for a new direction for music distribution, and we believe it will form the basis of important and exciting new business models for the future." Middelhoff declared that Bertelsmann intended to challenge the industry's objections to file sharing, pointing out that "Napster's 38 million users can't all be criminals." (Thomas Middelhoff, CEO of Bertelsman, in "Bookster? Napster Gets Down with Bertelsmann," *Publisher's Weekly,* November 6, 2000)

Many users of the Napster service also believed that the free exchange of recorded music benefited beginning bands and emerging artists, who found it difficult to establish a market for their recordings through the normal trade distribution channels that so heavily emphasized price. This was a belief that was shared by some of those beginning bands and emerging artists:

> Regardless of Napster's ultimate fate, Limp Bizkit [a metal rap group] stands to be a winner for years to come. Its advocacy of Napster has moved the band into national debates about e-commerce, the political and legal ramifications of online music, and the future of music distribution. And the band's free shows have made loyalists of a nation of kids unable to afford the high cost of concert tickets. (Michael Clark, "Limp Bizkit Stirs Fans to a Frenzy," *Houston Chronicle*, August 2, 2000)

> Napster and defenders such as Public Enemy, Courtney Love and Byrds founder Roger McGuinn say the industry association has never done much for the huge majority of artists, and is only protecting its massive profits. They also argue that online music delivery is the way of the future, and will spur sales by giving people the chance to listen to new genres and styles of music, giving the artist back control that they've lost to the big recording labels. (Karin Lillington, "Nabbing Napster Won't Stop the Music," *Irish Times*, July 21, 2000)

Many users of the Napster service also believe that the recording companies have brought this problem of the free exchange of recorded music upon themselves by overcharging their customers for years. Those customers frequently complain that they can buy a blank disk for 50 cents at a computer store, yet to buy a recording on that same disk costs $18 at a music store. If the recording companies would sell their albums for a reasonable price and accept a reasonable profit, these customers continue, then nobody would bother with the free exchange. Some of the artists agree:

> It's like this. There's a fat guy on a street corner selling M&Ms to all the people waiting in line. He's making all that money, and the people, they're not very happy about it. Then the bottom of the bag rips, and the candy goes all over the sidewalk. What are the people going to do? They start grabbing it up, and he's standing there saying, "No, wait, that's my candy!" That fat kid. He's the recording industry. (Chuck D, member of the rap group Public Enemy, in "What Will Be the Net Effect?" *Los Angeles Times*, July 4, 1999)

The actual impact of Napster upon payments to the performing artists, and upon profits of the recording companies, is not clear. Sales of commercially produced recordings have increased since the start of Napster, and some Napster supporters say that this is the result of popularizing the music by making it better known. Many Napster opponents, however, say that this is the result of the extended prosperity of the country and the relative newness of Napster, and that sales at record stores will go down as soon as the Napster service becomes more widely understood. It has to be admitted that sales of commercial recordings at music stores near college campuses—students are the primary users of the Napster service—have already started to go down.

Class Assignment.   There has been a proposal that Napster collect a fee, perhaps one or two dollars, to pay the artists for each exchange. The problem is that collecting money implies a sale, and that would in all likelihood end Napster's existing exemption from the law. The Recording Industry Association of America is currently pushing Congress to enact a new law making the home recording and Internet exchange of digitally compressed music illegal. What do you think should be done? How would you balance the benefits and harms, the rights and wrongs, of this particular situation? Chapter 1 of this text suggested that you use the following pattern of analysis:

1. What groups benefited from the "free exchange" policy?

2. What groups were harmed from the "free exchange" policy?

3. What groups were able to exercise all of their rights under the "free exchange" policy?

4. What groups were denied some of their rights under the "free exchange" policy?

5. How would you express the moral problem (if you believe this to be a moral problem) so that each individual and group involved will believe that you fully recognize and completely understand their particular problems and concerns?

6. What are the economic benefits? The rule is that you should always take the action that will generate the greatest profits for the company because this will also generate the greatest benefits for the society, provided it can be shown that all markets are fully competitive, all customers are fully informed, and all external and internal costs are fully included.

7. What are the legal requirements? The rule here is that you should always take the action that most fully complies with the law because the law in a democratic society represents the combined moral standards of all of the people within that society, provided it can be shown that the goals, norms, beliefs, and values of all of the various individuals, groups, and organizations have been equitably combined in the formulation process.

8. What are the ethical duties? The rule here is that you should always take the action that (1) you would be proud to see widely reported in national newspapers; (2) you believe will build a sense of community among everyone associated with the action; (3) you expect will generate the greatest net social good; (4) you would be willing to see others take in similar situations in which you might be the victim; (5) you believe does not harm the "least among us"; and (6) you think does not interfere with the right of everyone to develop their skills to the fullest.

9. What would you recommend, and how would you explain your recommendation to the other individuals, groups, and organizations that are going to be affected by that decision or action if it is adopted?

CASE 1–3

Whirlpool Corporation and the Sale of Dish Antennas

The Whirlpool Corporation is the world's largest manufacturer of major home appliances such as washers, dryers, ovens, stoves, refrigerators, dishwashers, freezers, trash compactors and air conditioners. It is a global firm. Manufacturing plants and marketing divisions are located in North America, Central and South America, Southeastern Asia, the Near East, Europe, Africa, and Japan. Company headquarters are in Benton Harbor, Michigan. Sales in 1998 totaled $10.3 billion; profits were $325 million; and 62,000 persons were employed.

Whirlpool, as do many other manufacturers of "long life" consumer products such as appliances, has a customer finance division that was started to provide financing to the retailers who stocked the company's products and to the customers who purchased those products. Whirlpool had a good credit rating; it was able to borrow money at low market rates and then lend that money at higher commercial rates to their distributors for inventory support and to their customers for installment purchases.

Over the years the customer finance division expanded beyond its original mission of supporting company sales through inventory financing for dealers and installment loans for customers, and began offering leases on heavy equipment for highway contractors, mortgages on real estate for mall developers, and contracts on "open-end" notes for sales agents. Sales agents are companies or even individuals who may or may not have a store location but do most of their business by seeking out and direct selling customers. Frequently they rely on telemarketing to get leads and then visit those potential customers to get orders.

All of these new forms of financing developed by Whirlpool carried higher interest rates, and consequently generated larger profits, then did their regular inventory support loans and installment purchase contracts. The open-end notes were particularly profitable. They were a form of credit card debt and carried the high interest rates—18% to 22%—associated with credit cards, and yet were used to finance single item purchases of the type sold by the direct sales agents, such as roofing repairs, aluminum siding and complete furniture suites.

An open-end note is essentially a credit card that is issued for a single sale. Little or no down payment is required, and the customer agrees only to make a minimal payment each month. The interest rates are high, and there are penalties for missing the minimal payment each month, but money is made available for people with low income and poor credit to purchase products that they otherwise probably could not afford. The problem is that these loans are on the edge of legality.

Under traditional or closed-end financing the seller is required by the Federal Truth-in-Lending Act to disclose in a simple, clear written contract the amount of the total loan, the size of the monthly payment, and the number of months before the loan will be fully repaid. Under credit card or open-end financing there are far fewer disclosure requirements. The interest rate has to be stated on the contract (though this can be in small type at the bottom of the page), and the full amount of the loan has to be included. The monthly payment, however, is only a minimal amount, generally just large enough to cover the interest. Consequently the number of months for full repayment cannot be computed and that figure is never disclosed. The lack of full disclosure has led in many instances to customer confusion and legal action. It did in this instance.

The Whirlpool Financial National Bank was one of two defendants, along with a Mr. Don Gantt, D/B/A Gulf Coast Electronics, named in a lawsuit filed by Barbara Carlisle and George and Velma Merriweather alleging that they had been misled by the defendants concerning the terms for the open-ended or credit card financing of the dish antennas they had purchased to improve television reception at their homes in rural Alabama. D/B/A/ means "doing business as"; it refers to an individual who operates under a company name that in reality is a proprietorship, not a corporation. Mr. Gantt, the individual in this case, was the sales agent whose proprietorship had sold the dish antennas. By the time of the trial Mr. Gantt was bankrupt, and he could not be located to appear either as a defendant or as a witness. (Trial transcript, p. 163, lines 4 to 6)

Television reception tends to be poor in much of rural Alabama. The broadcasting stations are in the major cities—Birmingham, Huntsville, Montgomery, and Mobile—and operate with low to medium power. Their signals do not carry throughout the state, and the rural regions lack the alternative of cable transmission. During the 1970s and 1980s persons living in those areas relied upon tall antennas, often attached to the roof or chimney of a home, with a directional control so that the receptor could be positioned to "catch" the signals from a specific station. It was not a totally satisfactory solution; the number of channels that could be received was very limited.

In the 1990s satellite dish antennas become available. They could receive an almost limitless number of channels, rebroadcast from satellites circling the earth in space. The problem was that the early models of the satellite dish antennas were expensive, and many of the persons living in the rural regions were poor and unable to afford the full purchase price, or even to make a substantial down payment upon that purchase price. Consumer financing was needed, and Gulf Coast Electronics—together with approximately 10 other sales agents within the state—used the open-end consumer financing provided by Whirlpool Financial National Bank to sell satellite dish antennas to poor customers in the rural regions of Alabama.

These sales agents generally had an office, not a store. They would use telephone calls to establish customer contacts, and then make home visits to get customer orders. Gulf Coast Electronics employed 10 persons who performed both functions. They were paid substantial commissions depending upon their number of completed sales, and they tended to be very aggressive. They were trained to demonstrate the advantages of the new antenna system, quote a total price of $1,124 that included delivery and installation, and then offer "nothing down" financing from Whirlpool Financial National Bank with minimal payments of $34 per month.

The primary issue at trial was the verbal description of the terms of that "nothing down" financing agreement given to the potential customers within their homes by sales agents working for Gulf Coast Electronics. The plaintiffs claimed that those sales agents had promised that payments of $34 per month for 36 months would totally pay for the antenna, delivery, and installation. In reality that would occur only if no interest were charged. According to the sales contract that was signed prior to installation, interest at the rate of 22 percent per year was to be added to the unpaid balance at the end of each month, which meant that total repayment—given that no late charges or other penalties were added to the total—would take five years.

Underlying the primary legal issue of whether the terms of the sales contract had been accurately revealed was a secondary concern over the equitable nature of the full sales transaction. The total sales price, with tax and installation, for the 19-inch RCA satellite dish antenna, termed a DSS system, sold by Gulf Coast Electronics was $1,124.24. Apparently the same system, prior to the sales tax and without the system installation, could have been purchased at a major electronics retailer such as Radio Shack or Circuit City for about $400. Thomas Methvin, attorney for the plaintiffs, questioned David Carroll, a witness for the plaintiffs, early in the trial:

Q. Today, how much can you go to a store and buy a DSS satellite dish for?

A. $199, and in some places.

Q. Back in 1995 when these victims bought theirs, how much did the same DSS satellite dishes by themselves cost in the store, not the package [tax and installation], but just the DSS [digital satellite system].

A. In '95, to the best of my recollection, as far as I remember, they were $199 I know. I don't know what date. But at one time you could buy them for close to $400. So no more than $400. (Trial transcript, p. 48, line 17 to p. 49, line 1)

The $1,124 charged by Gulf Coast Electronics also included sales tax and installation. The sales tax would have been $32 (8 percent of $400), and installation was described as very simple. The complete DSS system came with a stand, the antenna, a length of coaxial cable, and a control box. It was necessary only to position the stand close to the house, set the antenna on the stand, drill a hole through the wall of the home, connect the antenna to the control box, and then the box to the television set. Witnesses testified that this installation took no more than 30 minutes.

Mr. Carroll, the witness who testified to the much lower cost of the DSS system when purchased at a retail store rather than through a sales agent, had been in charge of training for Centevision. Centevision was a sales agent similar to Gulf Coast Electronics; it also sold TV antennas and financed them through Whirlpool Financial National Bank. Mr. Carroll testified that he had trained between 10 and 20 new salespeople each week for Centevision, during a period of peak demand, and then the following exchange took place between Mr. Carroll and Mr. Methvin, attorney for the plaintiffs:

Q. And between the several, I believe you said two hundred or so sales people that you trained yourself, was there a target market when you were selling these satellite dishes and home theater packages?

A. Yes, sir. We were trained to basically target the blacks, you know, any type of people living in trailers. People like that.

Tripp Haston [for the defendants]: Judge, could we have an objection for relevancy. This man worked for a company named Centevision and not Gulf Coast Electronics. He didn't train anyone from Gulf Coast Electronics, who was the merchant in this case.

Mr. Methvin [for the plaintiffs]: Judge, we think it's evidence to show not only was Gulf Coast Electronics one dealer that was doing it, but it came from the very top, that Whirlpool had lots of bad dealers. And we're going to have testimony from other witnesses that dealt with other dealers. And so that's why it's relevant. (Trial transcript, p. 28, line 21 to p. 30, line 19)

Two of the plaintiffs then testified that they had been told that payments of $34 per month would pay off the entire debt in three years. The first plaintiff, Mrs. Barbara Carlisle, explained that she had not only gotten an antenna for herself, but also arranged for her parents, Mr. and Mrs. Merriweather, the second plaintiffs, to have one installed at their home. After paying on the debt for two years she grew concerned that the balance on her monthly statements was not going down as rapidly as she had expected and, after talking with others at her church, found that she had been misled:

Q. Mrs. Carlisle, how did it make you feel when you found out you had been flim-flammed by these people?

A. It made me angry. It made me worry. I mean upset, very hurt. I got my parents involved in it, and I knew they were hurting from it. I've had headaches, sleepless nights, worrying, because I knew they were worried. And we're not rich people. We work hard for the little that we have. And we just don't deserve to be treated like that. And I think they should be punished for what they did.

Q. Mrs. Carlisle, as you sit here today, are you certain that February, 1995, when you were on the phone with those individuals from Gulf Coast, that you were told your payments would be $34.00 a month for three years and it would be paid for?

A. I'm positive.

Q. And when you called back for your parents, are you certain that you were told that their payments would be $34.00 a month for three years?

A. Yes. (Trial transcript, p. 127, line 21 to p. 128, line 12)

Mrs. Merriweather, the second plaintiff and Mrs. Carlisle's mother, also testified that she felt that she had been cheated by the company:

Q. When they told you that these people came in your house, and you trusted them because you couldn't read the papers yourselves, your husband couldn't read the papers, that you trusted to be telling you the truth. And when that lawyer told you they lied to you, were you upset?

A. I was sick, and I couldn't sleep [Mrs. Merriweather continued with a graphic description of her various illnesses]

Q. You think it was right for those people—ma'am, do you know how much the satellite costs today? Did you know you can buy a satellite for less then $300 to-day?

A. No. I didn't know it.

Q. When those people sold you that satellite—well let me ask you this way, how do you feel paying over a thousand and something dollars for a satellite you can buy for $300.00?

A. Huh, I don't feel right.

Q. You feel mad about that?

A. Sure is.

Q. You ever talk to you husband about this?

A. Yeah, I talk to him. He was just walking saying, "I'm tired of these folks doing us like this." (Trial transcript p. 184, line 13 to p. 185, line 20)

The final witness was a senior executive in the Whirlpool National Financial Bank, Brian Chambliss. The following exchange took place between Mr. Methvin, attorney for the plaintiffs, and Mr. Chambliss:

Q. Let me just ask a question that's very simple. If what the jury has heard from this witness stand from Mr. David Carroll and several of these witnesses, from Mrs. Carlisle and the Merriweathers, if what they heard is the truth, Whirlpool is a pretty sorry company, aren't they.

Mr. Haston (attorney for the defendants): Judge, I'd object to that question as argumentative.

Mr. Methvin (attorney for the plaintiffs): Well, let me just strike and ask it this way [Mr. Methvin then continued the examination]

Q. Will you stand behind what Whirlpool is selling, back them up one hundred percent? You're proud to be a part of this company?

A. Yes, I am.

Q. You're proud of what they did?

A. I'm proud to be a part of that company.

Q. Are you proud of what they did in this case?

A. I don't think we've done anything wrong.

Q. Nothing wrong. So if somebody goes into people's homes, sometimes unsophisticated people, armed with your documents, get them signed up, and they make payments to y'all and you find out they've been lied to, you say there's nothing wrong with that?

A. At this point I don't think we've done anything wrong. I think that there probably could have been a misunderstanding.

Q. Misunderstanding?

A. In what was presented to them.

Q. How about those roughly two hundred people that Mr. Carroll talked to? You reckon all two hundred of them had a misunderstanding?

Mr. Haston [attorney for the defendants]: Objection to the question as argumentative, Judge.

Class Assignment.   Clearly Mr. Chanbliss, the executive from Whirlpool Financial National Bank, believes that his company has done nothing wrong. Another executive at Whirlpool, Christopher Wyse, reiterated that position in the following e-mail received by the case writer:

> As we have recently reached a confidential, out-of-court, settlement in this litigation, we will not be able to speak to your class on January 19. While we were looking forward to providing our views on these matters, the unreasonable risk associated with litigating in front of improperly impassioned juries and the potential cost in time and money in litigating such meritless claims made settlement an option the Bank had to consider. I'm sure you understand our position. (E-mail message from Whirlpool dated Dec 7, 1999)

Do you agree that the case is a matter of "misunderstanding" and that the claims are "meritless"? Assume that the facts are reasonably as stated in the case; they were not disputed by the attorneys for the company at the trial except one stated that a competitive price for the DSS system at the time of the original transactions was $499 rather than $400. One of the concepts of this course is that, if you disagree with someone about the social and moral implications of their actions, you have to be able to logically convince them by arguing from some basic principles as to what is best for society. You can't just say, "This is my opinion." You have to be able to say, "This is my opinion, and these are the reasons why I think that it is right. If you disagree, tell me the reasons why you think it is wrong." Chapter 1 of this text suggested that you use the following method of analysis to fully explain your decisions:

1. What groups were benefited from the "antenna sales and financing" program?

2. What groups were harmed from the "antenna sales and financing" program?

3. What groups were able to fully exercise all of their rights with the use of that program?

4. What groups were denied some of their rights by the use of that program?

5. How would you express the moral problem so that each of the individuals and groups will believe that you fully recognize and completely understand their particular situation?

6. What are the economic benefits? The rule is that you should always take the action that will generate the greatest profits for the company because this will also generate the greatest benefits for the society, provided it can be shown that all markets are fully competitive, all customers are fully informed, and all external and internal costs are fully included.

7. What are the legal requirements? The rule here is that you should always take the action that most fully complies with the law because the law in a democratic society represents the combined moral standards of all of the people within that society, provided it can be shown that the goals, norms, beliefs, and values of all of the various individuals, groups, and organizations have been equitably considered in the formulation process.

8. What are the ethical duties? The rule here is that you should always take the action that you (1) you would be proud to see widely reported in national newspapers; (2) that you believe will build a sense of community among everyone associated with the action; (3) that you expect will generate the greatest net social good; (4) that you would be willing to see others take in similar situations in which you might be the victim; (5) that you believe does not harm the "least among us"; and (6) that you think does not interfere with the right of everyone to develop their skills to the fullest.

9. What is your recommendation, and how would you explain your recommendation to the other individuals, groups, and organizations that are going to be affected by that decision or action if it is adopted?

Moral Analysis and Economic Outcomes

We are concerned in this book with ethical dilemmas: decisions and actions faced by managers in which the financial performance (measured by revenues, costs, and profits) and the social performance (stated in terms of obligations to individuals and groups) of the organization are in conflict. These are the moral problems in which some individuals and groups to whom the organization has some form of obligation—employees, customers, suppliers, distributors, creditors, stockholders, local residents, national citizens, and global inhabitants—are going to be hurt or harmed in some way outside their own control while others are going to be benefited and helped. These are also the moral problems in which some of those individuals or groups are going to see their rights ignored or even diminished while others will see their rights acknowledged and even expanded. The question is how to decide: how to find a balance between economic performance and social performance when faced by an ethical dilemma, and how to decide what is "right" and "just" and "fair" as the solution to the underlying moral problem.

In the previous chapter it was suggested that you first recognize the moral impacts—the mixture of benefits and harms, the contrast between rights and wrongs—and compare those impacts to the moral standards of the various individuals and groups who will be affected by the managerial decision or action. People's moral standards are bound to differ due to differences in their religious and cultural traditions and their economic and social situations. Everyone will not agree with your intuitive viewpoint. To get widespread understanding, you will have to address their moral concerns. It was suggested that you do this by first clearly stating the moral problem in a way that recognizes the concerns of all, and then examining those concerns through the analytical methods of economic outcomes, legal requirements and ethical duties. The intent is to reach a decision, or strike a balance, that can be understood and—hopefully—accepted by all. The process of reaching this decision, or striking this balance, is shown in Figure 2–1:

"Economic outcomes" in moral analysis do not refer just to the net balance of revenues over costs for the company that has proposed a given decision or action. *Economic outcomes in economic theory refer to the net balance*

FIGURE 2–1 _____

Analytical Process for the Resolution of Moral Problems

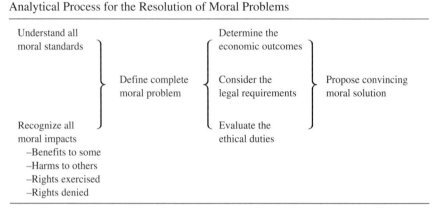

---

of benefits over harms for the full society as a result of that decision or action. This, as was described very briefly in the prior chapter, is the concept known as Pareto Optimality. It forms the moral basis of economic theory.

THE MORAL BASIS OF ECONOMIC THEORY

For many persons, the concept of a moral basis for economic theory is a contradiction in terms. They learned economic theory as a logical and mathematical approach to markets, prices, and production, devoid of moral substance. As a result of this education, most noneconomists, and perhaps a few economists as well, appear to focus almost entirely on profit maximization. They view the theory of the firm as descriptive, designed to rationalize the behavior of business managers, and believe that such single-minded pursuit of profit automatically excludes any consideration of environmental health, worker safety, consumer interests, or other "side issues."

Overconcentration on profits doubtless has resulted in these and other problems within our society, but that is neither a consequence nor a corollary of economic theory. Economic theory, in its more complete form, addresses these issues and includes ethical as well as economic precepts. Economic theory in its complete form is more a normative theory of society than a descriptive theory of the firm. Profit maximization is a part of the theory but only a part, certainly not the central focus, though it must be admitted, and this adds to the lack of understanding, that techniques for profit maximization occupy a central portion of the curriculum at most schools of business administration.

The central focus of the larger theory of society is the efficient utilization of resources to satisfy consumer wants and needs. At economic equilibrium—and an essential element in reaching equilibrium throughout the entire economic system is the effort by business managers to balance marginal increases in revenues against marginal increases in costs, which automatically results in maximum profits for the firm within market and resource constraints. At this economic equilibrium, it is theoretically possible to achieve Pareto Optimality.

Pareto Optimality refers to a condition in which the scarce resources of society are being used so efficiently by the producing firms, and the goods and services are being distributed so effectively by the competitive markets, that it would be impossible to make any single person better off without harming some other person. Remember this phrase: "It would be impossible to make any single person better off without making some other person worse off." This is the ethical substance of economic theory encapsulated in Pareto Optimality: Produce the maximum economic benefits for society, recognizing the full personal and social costs of that production, and then broaden the receipt of those benefits if necessary by political, not economic, actions.

Pareto Optimality provides the ethical content of economic theory. Without this concept of maximum social benefit at minimal social cost, the theory deteriorates into a simple prescription for individual gain and corporate profit. With this concept, the theory becomes a means of achieving a social goal: maximum benefits of most wanted goods and services produced at minimum costs of least wanted resources.

The theory requires that every business manager attempt to optimize profits. Consequently the decision rule that an economist would propose for finding the proper balance between the economic and social performance of a business firm would be to always be truthful (don't mislead), honorable (observe contracts), and competitive (set prices and costs at marginal levels), and always decide for the greater financial return. The question of this chapter is: Can we use this decision rule when faced with an ethical dilemma?

For many economists, the concept of Pareto Optimality excludes any need to consider ethical dilemmas in management. This view is very direct and can be summarized very simply. "Ethics are not relevant in business, beyond the normal standards not to lie, cheat, or steal. All that is necessary is to maintain price-competitive markets and recognize the full costs of production in those prices, and then the market system will ensure that scarce resources are used to optimally satisfy consumer needs. A firm that is optimally satisfying consumer needs, to the limit of the available resources, is operating most efficiently and most profitably. Consequently, business managers should act to maximize profits, while following legal requirements of noncollusion and equal opportunity and adhering to personal standards of truthfulness and honesty. Profit maximization, according to economic theory, leads automatically from the satisfaction of individual consumer wants to the generation of maximum social benefits. Profit maximization, again according to management, is the only moral standard needed for management."

Is this summary an overstatement of the microeconomic view of ethics and management? Probably not. The belief that profit maximization leads inexorably to the well-being of society is a central tenet of economic theory and has been stated very succinctly and very clearly by both James McKie of the Brookings Institution and Milton Friedman of the University of Chicago:

The primary goal and motivating force for business organizations is profit. The firm attempts to make as large a profit as it can, thereby maintaining its efficiency and taking advantage of available opportunities to innovate and contribute to growth. Profits are kept to reasonable or appropriate levels by market competition, which leads the firm pursuing its own self-interest to an end that is not part of its conscious intention: enhancement of the public welfare. (James McKie, "Changing Views" in *Social Responsibility and the Business Predicament,* Washington: Brookings Institute, 1974, p. 19)

    The view has been gaining widespread acceptance that corporate officials. . . . have a "social responsibility" that goes beyond serving the interest of their stockholders or their members. This view shows a fundamental misconception of the character and nature of a free economy. In such an economy, there is one and only one social responsibility of business—to use its resources and engage in activities designed to increase its profits, so long as it stays within the rules of the game, which is to say, engages in open and free competition, without deception or fraud. . . . Few trends could so thoroughly undermine the very foundations of our free society as the acceptance by corporate officials of a social responsibility other than to make as much money for their stockholders as possible. (Milton Friedman, *Capitalism and Freedom*, Chicago: University of Chicago Press, 1962, p. 133)

The statement by Milton Friedman was expanded in an article, "The Social Responsibility of Business Is to Increase Its Profits" that was published in the *New York Times Magazine* a number of years ago (Sept. 13, 1970, p. 32f). This article is often assigned for students at business schools in classes on business ethics or business and society. It is a frustrating article to read and then to discuss in class because it never makes clear the theoretical basis of Pareto Optimality; Professor Friedman assumed that readers would recognize and understand that basis of his contention.

THE MORAL OBJECTIONS TO ECONOMIC THEORY

What is your opinion? Can we accept the microeconomic premise that maximum profits for a firm lead directly to maximum benefits for society? The response of people trained in other disciplines is often much more pragmatic than theoretical, and it too can be summarized very simply. "Yes, we know the theory, but look at where the blind pursuit of profit has led us: foreign bribes, environmental problems, unsafe products, closed plants, and injured workers. We need something more than profit to measure our obligations to society." This view, I think, has been most sensibly expressed by Manuel Velasquez of the University of Santa Clara:

Some have argued that in perfectly competitive free markets the pursuit of profit will by itself ensure that the members of society are served in the most socially beneficial ways. For, in order to be profitable each firm has to produce only what the members of society want and has to do this by the most efficient means available. The members of society will benefit most, then, if managers do not impose their own values on a business but instead devote themselves to the singleminded pursuit of profit, and thereby devote themselves to producing efficiently what the members of society themselves value.

Arguments of this sort conceal a number of assumptions. . . . First, most industrial markets are not "perfectly competitive" as the argument assumes, and to the extent that firms do not have to compete they can maximize profits in spite of inefficient production. Second, the argument assumes that any steps taken to increase profits will necessarily be socially beneficial, when in fact several ways of increasing profits actually injure society: allowing harmful pollution to go uncontrolled, deceptive advertising, concealing product hazards, fraud, bribery, tax evasion, price-fixing, and so on. Third, the argument assumes that by producing whatever the buying public wants (or values) firms are producing what all the members of society want, when in fact the wants of large segments of society (the poor and the disadvantaged) are not necessarily met because they cannot participate fully in the marketplace. (Manuel Velasquez, *Business Ethics: Concepts and Cases*, New York: Prentice-Hall, 1982, pp. 17–18)

This pragmatic response, which can obviously be supported by many examples within our society, is not compelling to most economists. They believe that the issues cited—the lack of competitive markets, the presence of injurious practices, and the exclusion of some segments of society—are part of economic theory and would be prevented by its strict application. How would they be prevented? Here, it is necessary to provide an explanation of the extensive structure of economic theory and of the logical interrelationships that exist among the components in that structure: the individual consumers, product markets, producing firms, factor markets, factor owners, and public institutions. The "factors" in that listing above are the scarce resources of labor, capital, and material used in the production of goods and services.

Doubtless an explanation of this structure and these interrelationships will be dull for those with a good grasp of economic theory, and trying for all others, but this explanation is necessary to deal with the ethical problems in the theory on a meaningful basis. If you truly are bored with economic theory, and willing to accept the rationality of the structure, skip ahead a few pages and dive directly into the section, "The Moral Claims of Economic Theory."

THE LOGICAL STRUCTURE OF ECONOMIC THEORY

Economic theory is complex. Perhaps, to make this brief explanation more comprehensible, we should start with an overall summary. The focus of the theory, as stated previously, is the efficient utilization of scarce resources to maximize the production of wanted goods and services. The mechanism of the theory is the market structure: Each firm is located between a "factor" market for the input factors of production (labor, material, and capital) and a "product" market for the output goods and services. The demand for each good or service is aggregated from the preference functions of individual consumers, who act to maximize their satisfactions from a limited mix of products. The supply of each good or service is aggregated from the production schedules of individual firms, which act to balance their marginal revenues and marginal costs at a limited level of capacity.

The production of goods and services creates derived demands for the input factors of labor, material, and capital. These factors are substitutable—they can be interchanged—so the derived demands vary with the costs. These costs, of course, reflect the constrained supplies in the different factor markets. A firm attempting to minimize costs and maximize revenues will therefore use the most available resources to produce the most needed products, generating not only the greatest profits for itself but the greatest benefits for society. The components of the theory and the relationships among these components, which together produce corporate profits and social benefits, may be more understandable in graphic form, as shown in Figure 2–2.

Now it is necessary to work through each of the six sections in Figure 2–2 in greater detail so that the relationships between revenues, costs, and social benefits will be clear. Those relationships, and their consequent outcomes, constitute the ethical content of economic theory.

FIGURE 2–2

Graphic Summary of Microeconomic Theory

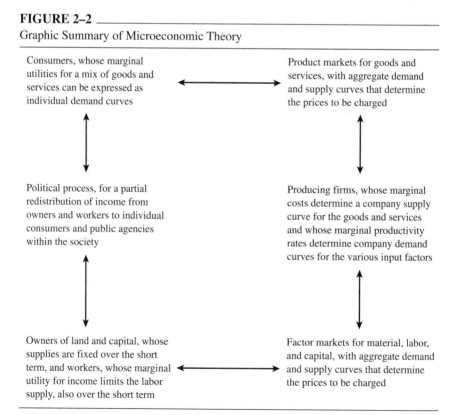

Individual Consumers

Each consumer has a slightly different set of preferences for the various goods and services that are available, and these preferences can be expressed as "utilities," or quantitative measures of the usefulness of a given product or service to a specific customer. The "marginal utility," or extra usefulness, of one additional unit of that product or service to that customer tends to decline, for eventually the person will have a surfeit of the good. The price that the person is willing to pay for the good also declines along with the marginal utility or degree of surfeit. Price relative to the number of units that will be purchased by a given person at a given time forms the individual demand curve, as shown in Figure 2–3.

Price can also be used to compare the relative usefulness of different goods and services to an individual. It can be expected that a person selecting a mix of products will choose an assortment of goods and services such that marginal utility per monetary unit would be equal for all the items at a given level of spending for this individual. Each good would be demanded up to the point where the marginal utility per dollar would be exactly the same as the marginal utility per dollar for any other good. If a customer had a higher marginal utility relative to price for any particular good, he or she would doubtless substitute more of that good for some of the others to achieve a better balance among his or her preferences. The final balance or mix, where the marginal utilities per monetary unit are equal for all products and services, can be termed the point of equilibrium for that customer.

FIGURE 2–3
Personal Demand Curve

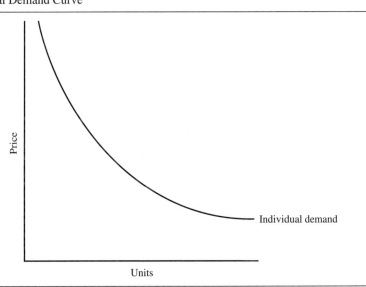

The concept of consumer equilibrium is an important element in the structure of the economic condition termed Pareto Optimality. A customer with balanced marginal utilities per monetary unit for all available goods and services cannot be made better off at his or her level of spending, according to his or her standards of preference. The customer may buy hamburgers, French fries, and beer, and we may think that he or she should be buying fish, fresh vegetables, and fruit, but that person is satisfying his or her standards, not our own, and they are being satisfied up to the limits of his or her ceiling on expenditures. Consequently, that person cannot be made better off without an increase in disposable income. Now, let us look at the determination of the level of disposable income in microeconomic theory. This is more complex than the determination of the mix of desired purchases, but the logical structure can be followed through the product markets, the producing firms, the factor markets, the private owners of those factors, and the public processes for redistribution of factor income.

Product Markets

A product market consists of all the individual customers for a given good or service, together with all the producing firms that supply that good or service. The demand curves of all those customers can be aggregated to form a market demand curve. This market demand curve reflects the total demand for a good or service, relative to price. If price is the vertical axis and demand the horizontal axis, the market demand curve will generally slope downward and towards the right, indicating increased potential purchases at the lower price levels.

Crossing this market demand curve is a market supply curve that portrays the total available supply, again relative to price. The market supply curve generally slopes upward and towards the right, for the higher the price, the more units in total most companies can be expected to produce, until they reach a short-term limit of capacity. The market price, of course, is set at the intersection of the curves representing aggregate demand and aggregate supply, as shown in Figure 2–4 on the following page.

Producing Firms

The aggregate supply curve, the "other half" of each product market relationship, is formed by adding together the individual supply curves of all the producing firms. These individual supply curves are generated by the cost structures of those firms at different levels of production, while the actual level of production for each firm is determined by a comparison of "marginal revenues" and "marginal costs."

The marginal revenue of a producing firm is the extra revenue that the firm would receive by selling one additional unit of the good or service. To sell that additional unit in a fully price-competitive market, it is necessary to

FIGURE 2–4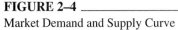

Market Demand and Supply Curve

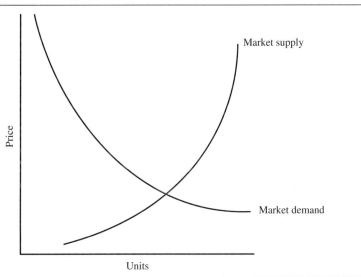

move down the aggregate demand curve to a slightly lower price level. To sell that additional unit in a non–price-competitive market, it is necessary to spend greater amounts on advertising and promotion to differentiate the product from those manufactured by other firms. Under either alternative, the marginal revenue from selling the last unit will be less than the average revenue from selling all other units. Marginal revenues inevitably decrease with volume.

The marginal cost of the producing firm is the obverse of the marginal revenue. Marginal cost is the extra expense that the firm would incur by producing one additional unit of the product or service. Marginal costs initially decline with volume due to economies of scale and learning curve effects, but they eventually rise due to diminishing returns as the physical capacity of the plant is approached. The rising portion of the marginal cost curve forms the supply curve of the firm; it represents the number of units that the firm should produce and supply to the market at each price level, as shown in Figure 2–5 on the following page.

The producing firm achieves equilibrium when marginal costs are equal to marginal revenues. At the intersection of the marginal cost and marginal revenue curves, the profits of the firm are maximized. The firm can increase profits only by improving its technology; this would change the marginal costs and consequently the supply curve. However, over the long term, all firms would adopt the new technology and achieve the same cost structure. Production equilibrium would be reestablished at the new intersections of the marginal cost and marginal revenue curves for all firms within the industry.

FIGURE 2–5

Marginal Cost Curve

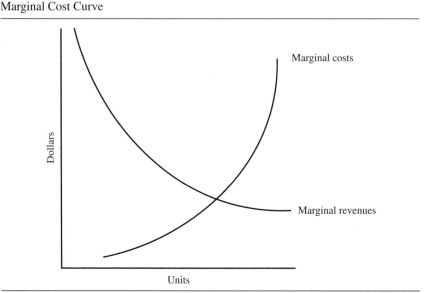

All the costs of production have to be included in computing the marginal cost curve for a firm. This is the second of the ethical constructs in microeconomic theory, along with the individual selection of goods and services according to private preference standards, or "utilities." The internal personal costs (e.g., hazardous working conditions) and the external social costs (e.g., harmful environmental discharges) have to be computed, so that customers pay the full costs of production. The technology, of course, can be changed to improve working conditions and reduce environmental discharges, and this should be done to bring marginal costs down to marginal revenues at a new, nonhazardous and nonpolluting equilibrium, but it is an essential element in economic theory that product-market prices reflect the full costs of production.

Factor Markets

The technology of the producing firm determines the maximum output of goods and services that can be achieved for a given mix of input factors. The input factors of production are land (an apparently obsolete term that instead refers to all of the basic raw materials), labor, and capital. Charges for the input factors are rents for the land and other basic resources, wages for the labor, and interest for the capital. These charges are interdependent because the factors are interrelated; that is, one factor may be substituted for others in the production function.

The relationships among these input factors, and the amount of one that would have to be used to substitute for another, are determined by the technology of the production function and by the "marginal productivity" of each factor for a given technology. The marginal productivity of a factor of production is the additional output generated by adding one more unit of that factor while keeping all others constant. For example, it would be possible to add one additional worker to a production line without changing the capital investments in the line or the material components of the product. There should then be an increase in the physical output of that production line, and that increase, measured in units or portions of units, would be the marginal productivity of that worker. To maximize profits, a company should increase the use of each factor of production until the value of its marginal product (the increase in unit output, or productivity, times the price of those units) equals the cost of the input factor.

Factor Owners

The aggregate demand for each factor of production is equal to the proportion of that factor used in the production function of each firm times the output of those functions supplied to meet the product market demand. The demand for each factor of production is therefore "derived" from the primary markets for goods and services.

The aggregate supply of each factor of production, however, is limited. Over the long term, stocks of the basic materials may be expanded by bringing into production marginal agricultural lands, oil fields, and ore mines, while the reserves of investment capital may be increased by raising the rate of capital formation. Over the short term, however, the supply amounts are fixed. Aggregate supplies of labor are also limited, though for a different cause: Each worker has a marginal utility for income that decreases and becomes negative as his or her desire for greater leisure exceeds his or her preference for further work. This negative utility function creates a "backward sloping" supply curve for labor and sharply limits the amounts available at the higher wage rates, as shown in Figure 2–6 on the following page.

The price system in the different factor markets, therefore, ensures that the limited factors of production will be used in the most economically effective manner to produce the goods and services to be sold in the product markets, and that the rents, wages, and interest paid for these factors will reflect both the productivity of the factor and the derived demand of the goods.

Political Processes

The owners of the factors of production, within a capitalistic society, are also the customers for the products and services generated by the production functions at the various firms. The owners receive the rents, the wages, and the

FIGURE 2–6

Factor Supply Curves

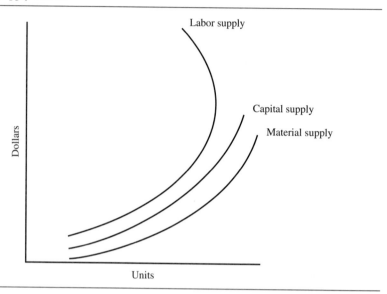

interest payments for the use of the resources they want to sell and then purchase the goods and services they want to buy, following their personal preferences or utilities.

A political process for the redistribution of the rents, wages, and interest payments works through both tax provisions and welfare allocations, so that all individuals and groups within a given society have a minimal ability to participate in the product markets for the various goods and services to the extent determined by the members of that society. This political process is the third ethical construct in microeconomic theory. It ensures that the distribution of the revenues for material, capital, and labor will be "equitable," following a democratically determined definition of equity.

THE MORAL CLAIMS OF ECONOMIC THEORY

Now that there is a common understanding of the basic structure of economic theory, or the logical system of relationships among individual customers, product markets, producing firms, factor markets, resource owners, and political processes, it is possible to look at the claims of that theory relative to the social welfare. There are five explicit assertions:

- *Effective use of resources.* The price mechanisms of the factor markets allocate the scarce resources of society to their most effective uses. The marginal productivity of each factor together with the cost (reflecting supply versus demand) determines the relative usage of the factors by the producing firms. At factor equilibrium, it would be impossible to expand total production without an increase in resource supply.

- *Efficient conversion of resources into products.* The production functions of the producing firms convert the limited input factors into the wanted output goods and services by the most effective methods (process technologies) and at the most efficient rates (output amounts). A firm's technology and capacity are long-term decisions, while the operating rate is a short-term choice, but all are based upon the balance between marginal revenues and marginal costs. Internal personal harms and external social damages are included in the marginal costs. At process equilibrium, it would be impossible to convert resources into products more efficiently and with less personal harm or social damage without an advance in technology.

- *Effective distribution of products.* The price mechanisms of the product markets distribute the wanted goods and services of society to their most effective uses. The marginal utilities of each customer together with the prices (again reflecting supply versus demand) for the various products determine the relative consumption of the goods and services. At market equilibrium, it would be impossible to improve consumer satisfaction without an increase in personal income.

- *Political adjustment of inequalities.* The political processes of the national society determine the personal income of each consumer through democratic means. The income may be distributed according to ownership of the factors of production or according to an individual's need, effort, contribution, or competence. Distribution of the overall benefits of the economic system is a political, not an economic, process.

- *Managerial responsibility for profits.* Provided the managers of the producing firms act to maximize profits, the customers for the goods and services act to maximize satisfactions, and the owners of the resources act to maximize revenues, the economic system will operate as efficiently as possible, producing the greatest output of wanted goods and services for the least input of scarce labor, capital, and material. If the revenues to the owners of the factors of production are equitably redistributed to the customers of the producing firms through a democratic decision process, it would be impossible to improve the life of any member of the system without harming the life of another member, because the system would have reached Pareto Optimality. Consequently, the social responsibility of the managers of the producing firms is to maximize profits and leave the redistribution of economic benefits to the political process.

PRAGMATIC OBJECTIONS TO ECONOMIC THEORY

The usual objections to microeconomic theory are pragmatic in nature, based upon very obvious problems in our national society, and they generally include the three issues discussed by Professor Velasquez in the statement quoted earlier in this chapter.

Exclusion of Segments of Society. It is alleged that the minorities and the poor, because they lack ownership of any of the factors of production beyond their unskilled labor, receive inadequate income to participate in the product markets and consequently cannot maximize their own satisfactions in any meaningful way. The microeconomic response is quite obvious: "We grant you that this happens, but it is the fault of the political process and not of the economic system. You develop logically attractive political decision rules for the more equitable division of the benefits, and we will work to economically maximize the production of those benefits within market and resource constraints."

Presence of Injurious Practices. It is also alleged that managers of productive firms, because of an excessive concern with maximizing profits, have permitted or even encouraged some practices that are injurious to some members of society through workplace dangers or environmental pollution, or that are destructive to the market system through purchase bribes or employment discrimination. Here, the response of most economists would be that these problems occur, but that they would not occur under the strict application of the theory. Let us look at five of these claimed moral problems and their presumed theoretical solutions.

Purchase bribes. Personal payments to influence purchase decisions are evidently common overseas, and not unknown within the United States. In an efficient market, however, bribes would be futile; they would raise the cost function by an amount equivalent to the payment so that nonbribing competitors would have an obvious price advantage. The microeconomic response is obvious: Insist that purchase decisions be open and subject to public comparison of the bids to ensure the selection of the lowest-priced proposal to supply needed goods and services. The lowest-priced proposal would necessarily come from a nonbribing competitor.

Process pollutants. Many industrial processes result in toxic residues and inert materials as by-products, which are either discharged as air or water pollutants or buried as liquid or solid wastes. The toxic by-products have an obvious social cost, both immediate and long term. The microeconomic response has been clearly stated many times: Companies should recognize these nonfactor costs that are external to the productive process and include them in the pricing function. It might be expected, were these external costs accurately computed, that investments in proper disposal equipment would become clearly beneficial for the firm, or if they were fully included in the price, the product would become overly expensive for the customer to buy. Under either alternative, the amount of pollution would be substantially reduced.

Workplace hazards. It would appear that many of the mechanical hazards of industrial processing have been eliminated. Forty years of state and federal labor laws have removed most of the unprotected belts, open gearing, and nonshielded presses. Chemical risks still remain, however, and physiological and psychological problems will probably always be a part of mass manufacturing, due to the repetitive nature of the tasks and the time constraints of the process. The microeconomic response to workplace hazards is similar to that for process pollutants: The nonfactor costs of production should be recognized and included in the final price. Certainly, if the market is to operate efficiently to allocate resources within the society, customers have to pay the full costs of production, not partial costs subsidized by the physical or mental health of the workers.

Product dangers.   The press has recently reported numerous instances of unsafe products, particularly in the automobile industry. Gas tanks poorly located, radial tires poorly fabricated, and automatic transmissions poorly designed have all been mentioned, together with such nonautomotive products as hair dryers (containing asbestos), teddy bears (containing sharp objects), and packaged foods (containing nonnutrients). I think it is safe to assume that the economic response would be that a product offered for sale within a competitive market should perform the function for which it was designed, and that many of the reported failures and hazards come from decisions to differentiate products in slight or artificial ways to avoid the discipline of price competition. Whatever the cause of product failures and hazards, the costs of improper design are now being charged back against the manufacturing firms through liability suits and jury awards. It can be assumed that product safety will soon be improved as a result of objective economic analysis.

Minority employment.   Racial or sexual discrimination in employment, in an efficient labor market, would be self-defeating; a workforce limited to young or middle-aged white males would raise the cost of labor in the productive function and provide the nondiscriminating employer with a cost advantage. It is assumed in economic analysis that all groups are equal in performance capabilities. Training might be needed to justify that assumption, but the microeconomic response would be that training to correct social injustices should be provided as a public investment, determined by the political processes. Cost–benefit analysis would—in the view of most economists—assuredly show an economic return on that investment, as well as a social gain.

Absence of Competitive Markets.   Lastly, it is often claimed that the product markets for consumer goods and services are not price competitive because of oligopolistic (dominance by a limited number of large companies) practices among the producing firms serving those markets. Companies have become much larger recently, doubtless due to economies of scale and scope in production and distribution, while products have become more "differentiated," marked by slight distinctions in performance and design but supported by heavy promotion. The dominance of large firms in each market, and the inability of customers to judge the relative worth of products in those markets, is said to lead toward "administered" rather than competitive prices. Administered pricing, where the price level is set by the company to provide a set return above costs without reference to either supply or demand, of course destroys the efficiency of the market. The economic response, however, is very simple: "Oh, we grant you that market structures are not truly competitive, and that market processes are not actually efficient under current conditions. However, no one is advocating limited competition or inadequate information. Public policy changes to restrict competitor size and to ensure consumer information are needed to reestablish the discipline of the market."

THEORETICAL OBJECTIONS TO ECONOMIC THEORY

Economic theory is awesomely complete. There are few operating decisions in business to which it could not be applied—from hiring workers, purchasing supplies, and borrowing money to selecting technologies, establishing capacities, and setting prices. Likewise, there are few ethical problems to which microeconomic theory is not applicable, whether purchase bribes, process pollutants, workplace hazards, product dangers, or racial discrimination. It is very difficult to say, "Here is a managerial decision or action with definite ethical implications that is not included in the theory."

Economic theory is also enviably unified. All the managerial decisions and actions work together, through a system of explicit relationships, to create a socially desirable goal: maximum output of the wanted goods and services at a minimum input of the scarce material, capital, and labor. It is very difficult to say, "Here is a managerial decision or action following microeconomic theory that does not lead to a socially beneficial outcome."

Where does this discussion lead us? Are we forced to accept economic theory as an ethical system of belief for business management because of the complete and unified nature of the paradigm? Should we always act to maximize profits, as long as we are truthful, honest, and competitive, and use the concept of Pareto Optimality as the means of resolving our moral concerns? Or, is there a theoretical problem with that paradigm?

Most noneconomists are intuitively distressed by the proposal that business managers have no moral responsibilities to other members of society, outside of fiduciary duties to a small circle of corporate owners. Most noneconomists are equally distressed by the proposal that business managers are governed by no moral requirements of behavior beyond adhering to personal standards of honesty and truthfulness, observing legal statutes for contracts and against collusion, and computing accurate costs for personal harms and social dangers. Why is this distressing, and what are the arguments against the microeconomic model that can be expressed on a theoretic rather than a pragmatic or intuitive basis? There are two major arguments: One pertains to the assumptions about human nature and the second centers on the beliefs about human worth that are part of economic theory.

Assumptions about the Nature of Human Beings

The economic model is utilitarian; that is, it is a philosophical system of belief that focuses on outcomes rather than duties, with the understanding that larger outcomes are invariably better than lesser ones. Utilitarianism has often been roughly translated as "the greatest good for the greatest number." The economic model follows this doctrine. It takes the position that the ultimate end is the greatest general good, and it defines that good as the maximum benefits of consumer products and services at the minimum costs of labor, capital, and material. The problem, as with all utilitarian theories, is that the distribution of the benefits and the imposition of the costs may be unjust. Consequently, it is necessary to add a political process to the economic paradigm to ensure justice in the distribution of benefits and the imposition of costs.

But, "justice" is defined in the theory as a democratically determined pattern of distribution and imposition. This pattern does not follow a rule such as to each person equally, or to each according to his or her need, to his or her effort, to his or her contribution, to his or her competence, or even to his or her ownership of the factors of production. Instead, the pattern varies with the collective opinions of the members of society. This requires all members of society to be generously concerned with the charitable distribution of social benefits and the considerate imposition of social costs at the same time as they are selfishly concerned with the personal maximization of material goods and services in the product markets and of financial wages, rents, and interest payments in the factor markets.

I think that we can safely say that human nature exhibits both selfish and generous traits. We can doubtless go further and accept that human beings can perform selfish and then generous acts alternately. But it would seem an extreme assumption to believe that people can concurrently be generously attentive to others in all political decisions and selfishly attentive to themselves in all economic activities, and never confuse the two roles. The microeconomic model would appear to be based upon an exceedingly complex and unlikely view of the nature of human beings.

Assumptions about the Value of Human Beings

The microeconomic model is impersonal, for it requires that everyone be treated as a means to an end and not as an end in and of himself or herself. Customers for goods and services are people who maximize material satisfactions as a means of determining product demand curves. Owners of land, capital, and labor are people who maximize financial revenues as a means of determining factor-supply curves. Company managers are people who maximize corporate profits as a means of balancing market demands and factor supplies. No one acts as an individual human being, pursuing personal goals that move beyond economic outcomes to personal desires for liberty, opportunity, dignity, and respect.

This denial of worth can be seen particularly clearly in the position of the manager of the firm, who must act solely as an agent for the financial interests of the stockholders. What does this do to managers' self-esteem and self-respect? How can they live worthwhile lives when always being treated as a means to other people's ends or, perhaps even worse, when always treating other people as means to their own ends? Even though the society as an economic system may have achieved Pareto Optimality with maximal benefits at minimal costs, does the individual develop any sense of dignity and pride? The microeconomic model would appear to be based upon an exceedingly low and narrow view of the worth of human beings.

Where does this discussion of the moral content of economic theory lead us? There would seem to be two major conclusions. If we look at economic theory as a structured pattern of relationships explaining the optimal uses of scarce material, capital, and labor to produce the optimal numbers of consumer goods and services, then it is a logically complete and intellectually satisfying view of the world. But, if we look at economic theory as the sole means of reaching a decision when confronted with a moral problem—a problem in which some individuals and groups will be hurt or harmed, or have their rights ignored or abridged—then it seems incomplete because of the unlikely assumptions about human nature and the unsuited beliefs about human worth. Most people want something more out of life than just being automated participants in a consumption–production cycle.

We have to respect the theory—particularly with the provisions that all markets must be competitive and all costs must be included—but we have to add to it. We have to add the legal requirements and ethical duties that are further means of resolving moral problems in ways that will be understandable to all because they appeal to the nature and worth of all. The next two chapters will look specifically at the moral claims of those two doctrines—legal requirements and ethical duties—as a further means of determining what is "right" and "just" and "proper" in the decisions and actions of business management.

CASE 2–1

Susan Shapiro

Susan Shapiro had an undergraduate degree in chemistry from Smith College, a master's degree in chemical engineering from M.I.T., three years' service as a sergeant in the Israeli army, and an MBA from the University of Michigan. The following is a nearly verbatim account of her experiences during the first month of employment with a large chemical company in New York.

We spent about three weeks in New York City, being told about the structure of the company and the uses of the products, and then they took us down to Baton Rouge to look at a chemical plant. You realize that most of the MBAs who go to work for a chemical company have very little knowledge of chemistry. There were 28 of us who started in the training program that year, and the others generally had undergraduate degrees in engineering or economics. I don't know what you learn by looking at a chemical plant, but they flew us down South, put us up at a Holiday Inn, and took us on a tour of their plant the next day.

As part of the tour, we were taken into a drying shed where an intermediate chemical product was being washed with benzine and then dried. The cake was dumped in a rotating screen and sprayed with benzine, which was then partially recovered by a vacuum box under the screen. However, the vacuum box technology is out of date now, and never did work very well. Much of the solvent evaporated within the shed, and the atmosphere was heavy with the fumes despite the "open air" type of construction.

Benzine is a known carcinogen; there is a direct, statistically valid correlation between benzine and leukemia and birth defects. The federal standard is 10 parts per million, and a lab director would get upset if you let the concentration get near 100 parts for more than a few minutes, but in the drying shed it was over 1,000. The air was humid with the vapor, and the eyes of the men who were working in the area were watering. I was glad to get out, and we were only in the drying shed about three minutes.

I told the foreman who was showing us around—he was a big, burly man with probably 30 years' experience—that the conditions in the shed were dangerous to the health of the men working there, but he told me, "Lady, don't worry about it. That is a sign-on-job (a job to which newly hired employees are assigned until they build up their seniority so that they can transfer to more desirable work). We've all done it, and it hasn't hurt any of us."

That night, back at the motel, I went up to the director of personnel who was in charge of the training program and told him about the situation. He was more willing to listen than the foreman, but he said essentially the same thing. "Susan, you can't change the company in the first month. Wait awhile; understand the problems, but don't be a troublemaker right at the start."

The next morning everybody else flew back to New York City. I stayed in Baton Rouge and went to see the plant manager. I got to his office by 8:00, and explained to his secretary why I wanted to see him. He was already there, at work, and he came out to say that he was "up against it that morning" and had no time to meet with me. I said, "Fine, I'll wait."

I did wait, until after lunchtime. Then he came up to me and said he didn't want to keep tripping over me every time he went in and came out of his office, and if I would just go away for awhile, he would promise to see me between 4:30 and 5:00.

It was 5:15 when he invited me to "come in and explain what has you so hot and bothered." I told him. He said that he certainly knew what I was talking about, and that every year he put a capital request into the budget to fix the problem, but that it always came back rejected—"probably by some MBA staff type" were his words—because the project could not now show an adequate return on investment, and because the present process was technically "open air" and therefore, not contrary to OSHA regulations.

I started to explain that OSHA never seemed to know what it was doing— which is true, in my opinion—but he stopped me. He said he was leaving to pick up his family because his daughter was playing in a Little League baseball game at 6:30, and then they would have supper at McDonald's. He said I could go along, if I didn't mind sitting next to his five-year-old son "who held the world's record for the number of consecutive times he has spilled his milk in a restaurant." He was a very decent man, working for a very indecent company.

I told him I would go back to New York, and see what I could do. He did wish me "good luck," but he also asked me not to get him personally involved because he thought that "insisting upon funding for a project that won't meet targeted rates of return is a surefire way to be shown the door marked exit in large black letters." "The senior people up there are going to tell you that it's legal," he continued, "and you know, unfortunately, they're going to be right." (Verbal statement of Susan Shapiro, a disguised name, to the case writer)

Class Assignment. What would you do in this situation? If you decide that she should continue her campaign to change the benzine drying process, prepare a presentation that you believe she should make to the "senior executives up there who are going to tell you that it's legal." If you decide that she should stop her campaign, be ready to convince her that is the best thing to do over the long term for everyone, not just for the workers assigned to the drying shed. One of the concepts of this course is that you have to be able to logically convince other people that your recommendation is "right" by arguing from the basic principles of what is best for society. There are three of these basic principles:

- *Economic benefits.* Always take the action that generates the greatest profits for the company because this will generate the greatest benefits for the society, provided that all markets are fully competitive, all customers are fully informed, and all external and internal costs are fully included.

- *Legal requirements.* Always take the action that most fully complies with the law because the law in a democratic society represents the combined moral standards of all the people within that society, provided it can be shown that the self-interests of the various groups have been truly combined in the formulation process.

- *Ethical duties.* Always take the action that you (1) would be willing to see widely reported in national newspapers; (2) that you believe will build a sense of community among everyone associated with the action; (3) that you expect will generate the greatest net good; (4) that you would be willing to see others take in situations in which you might be the victim; (5) that does not harm the "least among us; and (6) that does not interfere with the right of everyone to develop their skills to the fullest.

CASE 2–2

World Bank and the Export of Pollution

The World Bank is a transnational organization that provides funding for economic development projects throughout the world. It was started in 1946 to help in the rebuilding of Europe following the Second World War, with 14 member nations led by the United States. By 1990 it had grown to 125 member nations, and the focus had shifted to assisting Third World countries in their efforts to escape from poverty. It grants loans to governmental agencies and public institutions to build the physical infrastructure needed for global modernization.

The World Bank is not small. It has $30 billion in basic equity capital, subscribed by the member nations, but it can also borrow much greater amounts from capital markets in New York, London, Frankfurt, Singapore, and Tokyo at reduced rates because all of their borrowings are guaranteed by the member nations. The bank then loans those funds at increased rates for development projects that appear to hold the promise of economic progress for the recipient country. About one-third of those loans are for hydroelectric dams, power plants, and transmission lines to generate electricity. Another third are for roads, railroads, bridges, port facilities, and pipelines to extend transportation. The last third are for rural irrigation systems to improve agriculture, urban water and sewer projects to improve health, and factory modernization programs to improve productivity.

The World Bank is headquartered in Washington, D.C. Voting power among the member nations is proportional to their capital subscriptions, and consequently the Board of Directors is dominated by Western countries. Many of the upper-level employees are American citizens. In 1991 the chief economist at the World Bank was Lawrence Summers, who had previously been a professor of economics at Harvard. In December of that year he sent the following memorandum to some colleagues and friends:

> Just between you and me, shouldn't the World Bank be encouraging *more* migration of the dirty industries to the LDCs [less developed countries]? I can think of three reasons:
>
> 1. The measurement of the costs of health-impairing pollution depends on the foregone earnings from increased morbidity and mortality. From this point of view a given amount of health-impairing pollution should be done in the country with the lowest cost, which will be the country with the lowest wages. I think the economic logic behind dumping a load of toxic waste in the lowest wage country is impeccable and we should face up to that.

2. The costs of pollution are likely to be non-linear as the initial increments of pollution probably have very low cost. I've always thought that under-populated countries in Africa are vastly under polluted; their air quality is probably inefficiently low compared to Los Angeles or Mexico City. Only the lamentable facts that so much pollution is generated by non-tradable industries (transport, electrical generation) and that the unit transport costs of solid waste are so high prevent world-welfare-enhancing trade in air pollution.

3. The demand for a clean environment for aesthetic and health reasons is likely to have very high income-elasticity. The concern over an agent that causes a one-in-a-million change in the odds of prostate cancer is obviously going to be much higher in a country where people survive to get prostate cancer than in a country where under-5 mortality is 200 per thousand. Also, much of the concern over industrial atmospheric discharge is about visibility-impairing particulates. These discharges may have very little direct health impact. Clearly trade in goods that embody aesthetic pollution concerns could be welfare-enhancing. While production is mobile the consumption of pretty air is a non-tradable.

The problem with the arguments against all of these proposals for more pollution in LDCs (intrinsic rights to certain goods, moral reasons, social concerns, lack of adequate markets, etc.) could be turned around and used more or less effectively against every Bank proposal for liberalization [of trade]. (Hausman and McPherson, *Economic Analysis and Moral Philosophy*, Cambridge: Cambridge University Press, 1996, p. 9)

This memo to friends and colleagues was somehow obtained by *The Economist*, a British news magazine with a worldwide audience. Its publication, in the words of Hausman and McPherson, "caused an uproar" and as a result, in the words of an author to be quoted later, environmentalists "went ballistic." Many people apparently were offended by the blatantness of the proposal to export pollution-causing processes to Third World nations where they would do less harm in monetary terms. They would do less monetary harm, Summers argued, because people's lives were worth far less in those low wage countries (human life was valued as the discounted sum of the annual earnings to be expected by each individual over time), and because amenities ("pretty" air and attractive views) were far less appreciated. Some of the subsequent letters to the editor, and to Professor Summers, were said to be vitriolic. There was, however, also substantial and forthright support from other economists:

Economics is the science of competing preferences. Environmentalism goes beyond science when it elevates matters of *preference* to matters of *morality*. A proposal to pave a wilderness and put up a parking lot is an occasion for conflict between those who prefer wilderness and those who prefer parking. In the ensuing struggle, each side attempts to impose its preferences by manipulating the political and economic systems. Because one side must win and one side must lose, the battle is hard-fought and sometimes bitter. All of this is to be expected.

But in the 25 years since the first Earth Day, a new and ugly element has emerged in the form of one side's conviction that its preferences are Right and the other side's are Wrong. The science of economics shuns such moral posturing; the religion of environmentalism embraces it.

Economics forces us to confront a fundamental symmetry. The conflict arises because each side wants to allocate the same resource in a different way. Jack wants his woodland at the expense of Jill's parking space and Jill wants her parking space at the expense of Jack's woodland. That formulation is morally neutral and should serve as a warning against assigning exalted moral status to either Jack or Jill.

The symmetries run deeper. Environmentalists claim that wilderness should take precedence over parking because a decision to pave is "irrevocable." Of course they are right, but they overlook the fact that a decision *not* to pave is *equally* irrevocable. Unless we pave today, my opportunity to park tomorrow is lost as irretrievably as tomorrow itself will be lost. The ability to park in a more distant future might be a quite inadequate substitute for that lost opportunity.

A variation on the environmentalist theme is that we owe the wilderness not to ourselves but to future generations. But do we have any reason to think that future generations will prefer inheriting the wilderness to inheriting the profits from the parking lot? This is one of the first questions that would be raised in any honest scientific inquiry.

Another variation is that the parking lot's developer is motivated by profits, not preferences. To this there are two replies. First, the developer's profits are generated by his customer's preferences; the ultimate conflict is not with the developer but with those who prefer to park. Second, the implication of the argument is that a preference for a profit is somehow morally inferior to a preference for a wilderness, which is just the sort of posturing that the argument was designed to avoid.

It seems to me that the "irrevocability" argument, the "future generations" argument, and the "preferences not profits" argument all rely on false distinctions that wither before honest scrutiny. Why, then, do some environmentalists repeat these arguments? Perhaps honest scrutiny is simply not a part of their agenda. In many cases, they begin with the postulate that they hold the moral high ground, and conclude that they are thereby licensed to disseminate intellectually dishonest propaganda as long as it serves the higher purpose of winning converts to the cause.

* * * * *

In the current political climate, it is frequently taken as an axiom that the U.S. government should concern itself with the welfare of Americans first; it is also frequently taken as an axiom that air pollution is always and everywhere a bad thing. You might, then, have expected a general chorus of approval when the chief economist of the World Bank suggested that it might be a good thing to re-locate high-pollution industries to Third World countries. To most economists, this is a self-evident opportunity to make not just Americans but everybody better off. People in wealthy countries can afford to sacrifice some income for the luxury of cleaner air; people in poorer countries are happy to breathe inferior air in exchange for the opportunity to improve their incomes. But when the bank economist's observation was leaked to the media, parts of the environmental community went ballistic. To them, pollution is a form of sin. They seek not to improve our welfare, but to save our souls. (Landsburg, *The Armchair Economist: Economics and Everyday Life*, New York, Free Press, 1993, pp. 224–227)

Class Assignment. What is your view? Should polluting industries that affect both human health and environmental quality be exported to poorer countries where people's lives and preferences are less valued? For that matter, should wilderness areas be paved with asphalt for parking lots as long as their operations will be profitable? Remember, you must be able to defend your position, whether "yes" or "no." How would you argue either for or against Professor Summers, Professor Landsburg, or both?

CASE 2–3

Green Giant and the Move to Mexico

The Green Giant Company is a food products firm that specializes in canned and frozen vegetables. Started as the Minnesota Valley Canning Company in 1903, it was one of the earliest to adopt a memorable advertising character, the Jolly Green Giant who, together with his friend Little Sprout, appeared first in magazines and then on radio and eventually television. The company's name was changed in 1950 to reflect the popularity of the advertising symbol and slogan.

Green Giant was also one of the first to adopt the new technology of freezing rather than canning vegetables, which helped greatly to preserve their taste and texture. Growth was steady during the 1950s and 60s, and the company expanded from southern Minnesota to central California where there was a much longer growing season. A large facility for freezing fresh vegetables was built at Salinas, California, about 120 miles south of San Francisco, in 1964.

The Green Giant Company was acquired, in a friendly takeover, by the Pillsbury Company of Minneapolis, Minnesota, in 1978. Pillsbury produced flour, baking products, and packaged cake/cookie/brownie mixes. The food industry segments of the combined firms did not overlap, so the acquisition gave Pillsbury a much broader product line with customer appeal and a much larger output with economies of scale and scope.

In 1987, Pillsbury itself was acquired, in an unfriendly takeover, by the Grand Metropolitan Company of Great Britain. Grand Metropolitan produced alcoholic beverages and owned strings of pubs and betting parlors in England, Scotland, and Wales. It was said that the senior executives of that company were concerned about the decline in the consumption of alcoholic beverages as watching television at home replaced the traditional British practice of going out in the evening for a pint of beer and a game of darts at the neighborhood pub. They were determined to enter the consumer products market, and picked Pillsbury because they felt that those products, frozen fresh vegetables and packaged baking mixes, would fit other social changes, such as the growing employment of women outside the home, that were then taking place in Britain.

Pillsbury and Green Giant, together, were acquired by Grand Metropolitan when the Pillsbury stockholders agreed to accept a payment of $5.6 billion. Soon after the acquisition was completed, executives at Green Giant were told that they must increase the profits at that division "substantially" to help pay off debt arising from the acquisition. The executives at Green Giant were reminded that Grand Metropolitan's style of management had always been characterized as "a light but firm hand upon the throat." Failure to increase profits quickly and substantially, it was inferred, could have severe career implications.

The problem with increasing profits either quickly or substantially in the canned and frozen vegetable industry is that these products have become close to commodities, with little brand recognition or consumer loyalty. Green Giant had the best-known trademark in the industry and held the largest market share, but it still controlled only 14 percent of total industry sales. The remaining 86 percent was held by Birdseye, Del Monte, Dole, Heinz, and "house brands" produced for the various supermarket chains. Further, the per capita consumption of frozen vegetables in the United States was steady, not growing, and canned vegetable consumption was falling as fresh produce was brought from distant nonseasonal growing regions by direct truck or even air shipment. Consequently there was little opportunity to raise sales through consumer advertising or to increase prices through product differentiation.

It was possible, however, to decrease costs by moving from California to Mexico. Green Giant had, since 1984, operated a small freezing plant in Irapuato, Mexico. Irapuato is in central Mexico, 500 miles south of the U.S.–Mexico border. The plant had been built in this area because the hot, sunny climate and dry, fertile soil produced excellent crops of cauliflower and broccoli year round, given adequate water for irrigation. Green Giant had drilled a number of deep wells and found adequate water.

The growing, processing, and packaging of frozen vegetables for export to the United States from Mexico also turned out to be very inexpensive. The average wage in Irapuato was 65 cents per hour. The average wage in Salinas, California, was $7.50 per hour. There were, of course, additional costs for transportation of the finished products north to the United States and for supervision of the untrained workers in Mexico, but the overall impact upon the profits of Green Giant could be very substantial and very quick if all of the California operations were moved to Mexico. It was estimated that such a move would save Green Giant $13,200 per worker per year.

In 1988, soon after the acquisition of Green Giant and Pillsbury by Grand Metropolitan, there were 1,400 workers working in the company's processing plants in the Salinas area. Salinas was a small city, almost totally dependent upon agricultural products for its livelihood. The prosperity of Silicon Valley, only 70 miles to the north in San Jose and Sunnyvale, had never reached Salinas primarily, it was said, because the population lacked the high degree of education needed for high-technology electronics manufacturing.

The question, in 1988, was whether Green Giant should move all of its growing, processing, and packaging operations from Salinas to Iraputao. There were a number of factors that would impact this decision beyond the obvious savings in costs:

1. The gain of jobs and the resulting industrial development would be welcomed in Irapuato. Even though Green Giant paid only 65 cents per hour, this was still above the minimum wage for the area, set by the government at 55 cents per hour. People had lined up to get the early jobs offered at Green Giant—or Gigante Verde as the company was known locally—and it was expected that the same thing would happen if all 1,400 jobs were moved to the area. Mexican unions had tried, but failed, to organize the workers.

   > Unfortunately, their employees are very happy. We can make no progress. (Statement by Antonio Mosqueza, union organizer, quoted in the *San Jose News*, June 16, 1991, p. 6)

2. The loss of the jobs, and the resulting unemployment, would be devastating to Salinas. It was expected that the economy of the area would remain agricultural, due to the excellent soil and weather conditions, but most of the jobs actually growing and harvesting the vegetables were considered to be too hard—bending and stooping under a very hot sun—for the people who had worked in the processing plants for Green Giant, many for the nearly 30 years the company had operated in Salinas. Most of the vegetables grown in the area would be shipped fresh to consumers in the rest of the country. There would be few job opportunities for the laid-off plant workers.

   > We helped Green Giant make their millions, and what will we be left with? Aching backs and twisted fingers. (Statement by Green Giant employee, quoted in *San Jose News*, June 16, 1991)

3. The movement of operations from Salinas to Irapuato would have substantial environmental impacts upon the area. Central Mexico is an arid region. Water is in short supply. Green Giant has drilled wells over 450 feet deep to get adequate amounts of clean water for washing and blanching (lightly boiling for about 30 seconds) the vegetables. With increased production following the move it was expected that the deep wells would dry up the 20-foot and 30-foot wells of the local population, who

would then be forced to get water for cooking and washing from the river. No money was available for a municipal water system that would extend beyond the commercial center of the town. The river water could not—according to U.S. law—be used for processing vegetables destined for export to the United States because it is polluted by bacteria in untreated sewage from towns that are farther upstream and by pesticides that are in the runoff from the agricultural fields.

> Green Giant and the U.S. government are both saying that the river water is not good enough for those of us who are so fortunate as to live in the United States, but that it is plenty good enough for Mexicans. (Verbal statement of environmental activist contacted by the case writer)

4. The movement of operations from Salinas to Irapuato would also have some social impacts upon the area. It can be assumed that Green Giant will pay taxes on their property in Mexico, though at a rate below that paid previously in California. These taxes will help to pay for needed improvements in the educational system and the physical infrastructure of the community. It can also be assumed, however, that converting about 6,000 acres of land from growing corn and beans—the local subsistence crops—to growing broccoli and cauliflower for export will increase prices for corn and beans and thus increase the local cost of living.

> Mexico does not have an efficient distribution system for food from one region to another. People are dependent upon what is grown locally. Water and food, of course, are the two most basic needs of life. Green Giant is going to take both of them. (Verbal statement of environmental activist contacted by the case writer)
>
> Green Giant is operating in a socially conscious way. We pay above the minimum wage. We provide health care for our employees. We are willing to work with the community in the construction of a water system and sewage plant. Whether you or anybody else likes it or not, Green Giant has set an example for others to follow. (Statement of Terry Thompson, vice president of Pillsbury, quoted in *San Jose News*, June 16, 1991, p. 6)

5. The movement of operations from Salinas to Irapuato will, lastly, have an economic impact upon both countries. The jobs, though manual, repetitive, and dull, will be the first step in industrialization. Some of the workers will have to be selected and trained in machine repair, quality control, cost accounting, and workforce supervision. The wages, though low, will bring increases in living standards and the start of a middle class. The United States will benefit from the export of goods designed for that middle class and from improved competitiveness in the world economy, as low cost labor in Mexico can be combined with capital and technology in the United States to counter firms from Japan and Southeastern Asia who are making extensive use of the low-cost labor in parts of the Orient.

> Everyone benefits from freer trade. Mexico will export more to the U.S. The U.S. will export more to Mexico. Both countries will do what they are good at doing; this is the doctrine of comparative advantage, and the standards of living in each country will rise over time. (Statement of financial economist contacted by the case writer)

The emerging global company is divorced from where it produces its goods. It has no heart, and it has no soul. It is a financial enterprise designed to maximize profits. Many of the people who inhabit it may be fine, upstanding human beings, but the organization has its own merciless logic. (Statement of labor economist, quoted in *San Jose News*, June 16, 1991, p. 6)

Class Assignment.   Put yourself in the position of the president of Green Giant in 1988. What action would you recommend, and why? If you decide to move, how would you explain your decision to the plant worker quoted above who said, "We helped Green Giant make their millions, and what will we be left with? Aching backs and twisted fingers"? If you decide not to move, how would you explain your decision to the senior executives at Grand Metropolitan who have demanded a "substantial and quick" increase in profits and have told you that their management style emphasizes a "light but firm hand upon the throat"? Lastly, do you truly believe—as the labor economist quoted above explained—that there is a "merciless logic" to all managerial decisions, despite the presence of "fine, upstanding human beings" within the organization?

CHAPTER 3

Moral Analysis and Legal Requirements

We are concerned in this book with ethical dilemmas: decisions and actions faced by business managers in which the financial performance (measured by the revenues, costs and profits generated by the firm) and the social performance (stated in terms of the obligations to the individuals and groups associated with the firm) are in conflict. These are the moral problems in which some individuals and groups to whom the organization has some form of obligation—employees, customers, suppliers, distributors, creditors, stockholders, local residents, national citizens and global inhabitants—are going to be hurt or harmed in some way while others are going to be benefited and helped. These are also the moral problems in which some of those individuals or groups are going to have their rights ignored or even diminished while others will see their rights acknowledged and perhaps expanded. The question is how to decide: how to find a balance between financial performance and social performance when faced by an ethical dilemma, and how to decide what is "right" and "just" and "fair" as the solution to the underlying moral problem.

In Chapter 1 it was suggested that you first recognize the moral impacts—the mixture of outcome benefits and harms, and the contrast between rights exercised and denied—and compare those impacts to the moral standards of the various individuals and groups who will be associated with or affected by the managerial decision or action. People's moral standards are bound to differ due to differences in their religious and cultural traditions and in their economic and social situations. Everyone will not view the same issues in the same way. To get widespread understanding, and hopefully agreement, you have to address the moral concerns of all of those involved. It was suggested that you do this in stages. Firstly, clearly state the moral problem in a way that explicitly recognizes the concerns of each of those individuals and groups, and then examine their concerns though the analytical methods of economic outcomes, legal requirements and ethical duties. This approach will enable you to explain your moral solution in a way that will be understandable, and hopefully acceptable, to all. Explanation to reach agreement, in the view of this text, is fully as important as decision to reach closure. This approach has been portrayed as a graphic, which is repeated in Figure 3–1 on the following page:

FIGURE 3–1

Analytical Process for the Resolution of Moral Problems

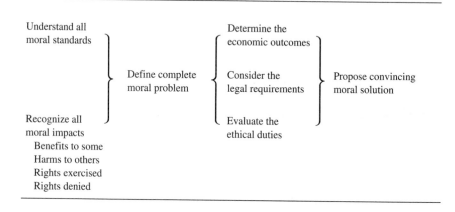

Understand all
moral standards

Recognize all
moral impacts
  Benefits to some
  Harms to others
  Rights exercised
  Rights denied

Define complete
moral problem

Determine the
economic outcomes

Consider the
legal requirements

Evaluate the
ethical duties

Propose convincing
moral solution

In Chapter 2 we looked at economic outcomes as a means of determining what is "right" and "just" and "fair" in order to resolve an ethical dilemma and reach an understandable and perhaps acceptable moral solution. Economic outcomes are not just the financial consequences of the company's decision or action for the firm. Instead, they are the financial consequences of that decision and action for all the members of the full society due to the economic relationships that exist between a producing firm, the product markets, and individual consumers on the demand side, and the factor markets and factor owners on the supply side. The political processes "in the middle" connect those two sides. According to economic theory, those relationships should distribute the benefits and harms of the corporate decision or action throughout society in a way that reflects everyone's utility preferences for both product purchases and factor sales, while the political processes should ensure that no one is left out. The result is greater output at lesser input for the full society, with that output distributed and that input allocated by impersonal market forces, supervised by impartial political processes. This condition, known as Pareto Optimality, should benefit all the members of the society.

The conclusion of Chapter 2 was that maximizing economic outcomes for the full society, and distributing those outcomes by impersonal markets, is a legitimate way of beginning to consider the moral problems of management. It is not, however, a complete and conclusive way of considering those problems. All of the product and factor markets have to be competitive and all of the external and internal costs have to be included, of course, but something more is still needed. That something more is a greater recognition of the nature and a fuller understanding of the worth of individual human beings. People don't live just to be product purchasers, factor sellers, and output determiners; they want something more in terms of justice, liberty, dignity, and respect. Part of that something more will be addressed in this chapter through the analytical method of legal requirements.

The analytical method of legal requirements can be summarized very simply in the statement that everyone should always obey the law. The law in a democratic society can be said to represent the minimal moral standards of that society, and those minimal moral standards should recognize the nature and understand the worth of individual human beings. You may or may not agree with the extent of those standards or the degree of that recognition and understanding, but you cannot really fault a person who obeys the law. You may feel that a person within an organization who faces a complex moral problem in which some people are going to be harmed and harmed badly, or have their rights eroded and eroded harshly, should go beyond the law. That person, however, may disagree with you. He or she may say, "We plan to optimize returns for our firm and benefits for our society. If you don't like that outcome, get together with a majority of your fellow citizens and pass a new law, which more fully recognizes the nature and understands the worth of other people, and we will obey the provisions of that new law. But, until that happens please do not lecture us on the superiority of your moral standards. We see nothing wrong with what we are doing, and evidently other people don't either for what we are doing is currently legal and approved by a majority of the population."

This "always obey the law and be fully legal in your actions" method of moral analysis has a lengthy historical basis. Thomas Hobbes (1588–1679) was the originator of the proposal that the sole moral obligation of men and women was to obey the law, or the supreme governmental authority that sets the law. It is necessary to recognize that Hobbes lived during the end of the Middle Ages in England. This was a time of intellectual ferment as the feudal class structure was breaking down into a more open and equal society, but it was also an era of rebellion, conflict, and crime. Homes of the nobles had to be protected by deep moats and strong walls. Travels of the merchants had to be escorted by armed guards. Hobbes explained that this was a natural outcome of every person looking after his (at this time there was little gender equality, and consequently an added "or her" would have been considered superfluous) self-interests. This, he said, led to a presence of chaos, a lack of security, and a block to progress. There are four major points in his reasoning:

- *Equal ability.* Men, he wrote, are equals in their strength of body and mind despite their differences in class and position. Equality of ability leads to an equality of ambition, and therefore to a constant struggle by everyone for material gain and personal safety.

- *Continual war.* The individual struggles eventually become a war, and here there is a famous quotation: "And such a war as is every man against every man." This war, he wrote, was continual like bad weather, not intermittent like a shower.

- *Depressed economy.* This continual war where "every man is enemy to every man" resulted in a lack of security, and the lack of security led to a decline in industry, and here again there is a famous quotation: "and the life of man, solitary, poor, nasty, brutish, and short."

- *Proposed solution.* To stop this continual war, Hobbes said it is necessary to think of a "state of nature," a free association of equal individuals living before any self-serving institutions were put in place. He proposed that those people would reach two "Natural Laws":

> Men who are engaged in a continual war, to gain the benefits of an enforced peace, will seek it by all means available to them.
> The only means available to them is for all men to surrender all rights to a central authority who will establish peace by force and decree.

What does all this mean for the analytical method of legal requirements and the understood solution of moral problems? At the simplest level, the proposal from Hobbes comes across as the rule that everyone should always obey the law because it is in everyone's self-interest to have a stable and orderly society even though they have to give up their rights to obtain that stability and order. This, essentially, is very similar to the analytical method of economic outcomes in which Friedman proposed that everyone should always act to maximize returns because it is in everyone's self-interest to have a productive and efficient society. In Friedman's economic argument, you may not like the products that are produced or the resources that are consumed, but to get productivity and efficiency you have to accept them. In Hobbes's legal stance, you may not like the laws that are generated, particularly when those laws are established by autocratic dictums on the part of a governmental authority rather than by a democratic vote through the full society, but to avoid continual war once again you have to accept them. At this level, both the economic outcomes and legal requirements for a society are based upon the enlightened self-interests of members of that society.

At a more complex level, however, the proposal from Hobbes emerges as the legal requirement that all laws should reflect what people living in a state of nature would accept as the governing rules of society. This is not enlightened self-interest. This is impartial self-interest. This is the idea of the "Social Contract"; it is a very important and basic concept in moral analysis and needs to be further explained.

If you were to take 100 people, somehow separated from all prior economic, political, and social institutions, and put them on an island, would that society be idyllic or chaotic? Let us assume that it would be idyllic as long as there was enough food, fuel, clothing, and shelter for everyone. But suppose there was a shortage; then what would happen? You might well have the war of "every man against every man" that Hobbes predicted.

A "contractarian"—that is, a person who believes in the analytical worth of the concept of the Social Contract—would argue that whatever agreement those 100 people would make to stop the conflict and end the shortage would be the most rigorous definition you could find as to what was "right" and "just" and "fair" for that society at that time. This would then form a legal requirement for every member of that society to follow for the maintenance of their society and the production and distribution of their goods.

The contractarian would say that the people on the island, being free and equal but facing a shortage, would first discuss the distribution of benefits, the allocation of harms, the recognition of rights, and the imposition of wrongs. The agreement they then reached would have to be unanimous to be effective —one person holding out would make the agreement nonbinding in any Natural Law sense. This agreement would be totally without self-interest because people would not know their self-interest, and completely in the interests of the full society. It would be the way in which members of that society should distribute their benefits and harms, and should allocate their rights and wrongs, for this would be the way that had been determined by all to be best for all.

Obviously, you cannot put 100 people who are ignorant of their position in society on an island and record their decision on the distribution of the benefits and harms, and the allocation of rights and wrongs, that they would consider to be "right" and "just" and "fair." But, you can imagine what would happen if you put everyone involved in a managerial dilemma—those benefited and those harmed, those with rights recognized and those with rights denied—in a room under conditions in which they did not know what position they held. They could be executives, employees, customers, suppliers, distributors, creditors, owners, or local residents. If they did not know what position they held they would not know how they would be affected. If they did not know how they would be affected, they would not know their self-interests. They would then discuss the situation and attempt to find a solution that would be "fair" to all for they would not know where within that "all" they would find themselves. This is the Social Contract concept that is also known as the "Veil of Ignorance." If no one knows what position they hold within an extended organization facing a moral problem, then they will not know how they will be affected by the various decisions or actions that are possible. Consequently, any resolution to that problem those people reach must be without known self-interest, and thus in the community interests of the citizens rather than the self-interests of the individuals.

The primacy of community interests is the reason that the concept of the legal requirements—always obey the law—can be used as a method of moral analysis. The idea is that there is a set of rules, established by the full society, that recognize those community interests. Why not, then, fall back upon those rules when faced with a conflict between the financial performance of an organization and the social performance of that organization? Why not let the law decide, particularly in a democratic society where the argument can easily be made that the rules within the law represent the collective moral judgments made by members of the full society? Why not follow these collective moral judgments instead of trying to establish our individual moral opinions?

There are numerous examples of laws that do reflect collective moral judgments. Almost everybody within the United States would agree that unprovoked assaults are wrong; we have laws against assault. Almost everybody would agree that toxic chemical discharges are wrong; we have laws against pollution. Almost all of us would agree that charitable giving is right; we have no laws against charitable giving. Instead, we have laws—provisions within the tax code—that encourage gifts of money, food, and clothing to the poor and to organizations that work to help the poor. The question of this chapter is whether we can use this set of rules—often complex, occasionally obsolete, and continually changing—to form "right" and "just" and "fair" decisions when faced with a choice between our financial gains and our social obligations.

Numerous attorneys and business executives believe that you can base ethical decisions and actions on the requirements of the law. These people would say that if a law is wrong, it should be changed, but that until it is changed it provides a meaningful guide for action. It provides this guide for action, they would add, because each law within a democratic society represents a combined moral judgment by all the members of our society on a given issue or problem. They will concede that you and I might not agree personally with the combined judgment on a particular issue. But, they would add, if managers follow the law on that issue, those managers cannot truly be said to be wrong in any ethical sense since they are following the impartial moral standards of the majority of their peers.

How do we respond to those claims? And if it is not possible to respond logically and convincingly, are we forced to accept those claims that the rule of law should be determinant in resolving moral problems even though some people may be hurt or harmed, or have their rights ignored or restricted, in ways that they believe to be unfair? I think that it is necessary first to define the law, so that all of us will recognize that we are discussing the same set of concepts, and then to examine the processes that are involved in formulating the law. This examination will be generally the same as in Chapter 2, "Moral Analysis and Economic Outcomes," in which we looked at market forces as the determinants for managerial decisions in ethical dilemmas. However, legal theory is much less complete than economic theory and there are numerous alternative hypotheses that will have to be considered. First, however, let us define the law and expand on what is meant by the rule of law.

DEFINITION OF THE LAW

The law can be defined as a consistent set of universal rules that are widely published, generally accepted, and usually enforced. These rules describe the ways in which people are required to act in their relationships with other people within a society. They are requirements to act in a given way, not just expectations or suggestions or petitions to act in that way. There is an aura of insistency about the law; it defines what you *must* do.

These requirements to act, or more generally requirements *not to act* in a given way—most laws are negative commandments, telling us what we should not do in given situations—have a set of characteristics that were mentioned briefly above. The law was defined as a consistent, universal, published, accepted, and enforced set of rules. Each of those terms needs to be further defined:

- *Consistent.* The requirements to act or not to act have to be consistent to be considered part of the law. That is, if two requirements contradict each other, both cannot be termed a law, because obviously people cannot obey both.

- *Universal.* The requirements to act or not to act also have to be universal, or applicable to everyone with similar characteristics facing the same set of circumstances, to be considered part of the law. People tend not to obey rules that they believe are applied only to themselves and not to others.

- *Published.* The requirements to act or not to act have to be published in written form so that they are accessible to everyone within the society to be considered part of the law. Everyone may not have the time to read or be able to understand the rules, which tend to be complex due to the need to precisely define what constitute similar characteristics and the same set of circumstances. However, trained professionals—attorneys—are available to interpret and explain the law, so that ignorance of the published rules is not considered to be a valid excuse.

- *Accepted.* The requirements to act or not to act in a given way have to be generally obeyed. If most members of the society do not voluntarily obey the law, too great a burden will be placed on the last provision, that of enforcement.

- *Enforced.* The requirements to act or not to act in a given way have to be enforced. Members of society have to understand that they will be compelled to obey the law if they do not choose to do so voluntarily. People have to recognize that if they disobey the law, and if that disobedience is noted and can be proven, they will suffer some loss of convenience, time, money, freedom, or life. There is, it was said, an aura of insistency about the law; there is also, or should be, an aura of inevitability: It defines what will happen if you don't follow the rules.

This set of rules that are consistent, universal, published, accepted, and enforced—what we call law—is supported by a framework of highly specialized social institutions. There are legislatures and councils to form the law; attorneys and paralegal personnel to explain the law; courts and agencies to interpret the law; sheriffs and police to enforce the law. These social institutions often change people's perception of the law because the institutions are obviously not perfect.

The adversarial relationships within a trial court often seem to ignore the provisions of consistency and universality and to focus on winning rather than on justice. The enforcement actions of the police also often seem to be arbitrary and to concentrate on keeping the peace rather than maintaining equity. Let us admit that enforcing the law, on the street, is a difficult and occasionally dangerous task. Police do not always act in the interests of the full society. Let us also admit that interpreting the law, in the court, is a complex and frequently tempting activity. Attorneys, also, do not always act in the interests of the full society. But we are looking at the law as an ideal concept of consistent and universal rules to guide managerial decisions, not as a flawed reality.

THE LAW AS COLLECTIVE MORAL STANDARDS

If the law is viewed in ideal terms as a set of universal and consistent rules to govern human actions and management decisions within society, the question is whether we can accept these rules—flawed though they may be by pragmatic problems in interpretation and enforcement—as representing the collective moral judgments of members of our society. If we can, then we have the standards to guide managerial decisions and actions even though these standards may be at a minimal level. If we cannot accept the set of rules as representing the collective moral judgment of our society, then we will have to look elsewhere for our standards. In considering the possible relationship between moral judgments and legal requirements, there would seem to be three conclusions that can be reached fairly quickly:

Considerable Overlap

The requirements of the law overlap to a considerable extent but do not duplicate the probable moral standards of society. Clearly, a person who violates the federal law against bank robbery also violates the moral standard against theft. And it is easy to show that the laws governing sexual conduct, narcotics usage, product liability, and contract adherence are similar to the moral beliefs that probably are held by a majority of people in our society. I think that we can agree that in a democratic society, the legal requirements do reflect many of the basic values of the citizens, and that there is an area of overlap between the law and morality as shown in Figure 3–2.

But the area of overlap is not complete. There are some laws that are morally inert, with no ethical content whatever. The requirement that we drive on the right-hand side of the road, for example, is neither inherently right nor inherently wrong; it is just essential that we all agree on which side we are going to drive. There are also some laws that are morally repugnant. Until the early 1960s, some areas of the United States legally required racial discrimination (segregated education, housing, and travel accommodations), and slavery was legally condoned just 100 years earlier. Finally, there are some moral standards that have no legal standing whatever. We all object to lying, but truthfulness is not required by law except in a court, under oath, and in a few other specific instances such as employment contracts and property sales.

People who believe in the rule of law and accept legal regulations as the best means of governing human conduct within society would respond by saying that it is not at all clear that racial segregation was deplored by a majority of the population prior to 1962, or even that slavery was considered unconscionable before 1862. In a much lighter vein, concerning lying, they might even claim that most people have become accustomed to, and perhaps are amused by, a reasonable lack of truthfulness in advertising messages and political discourse. Moral standards, they would say, are difficult to determine, and we must be careful not to infer that our standards represent those held by a majority of the population.

Negative Injunctions

The requirements of the law tend to be negative, while the standards of morality more often are positive. In the law, we are forbidden to assault, rob, or defame each other, but we are not required to help people, even in extreme situations. There is no law, for example, that we must go to the aid of a drowning child. Here, we do have a situation where the moral standards of the majority can be inferred, for doubtless 99.9 percent of the adult population within the United States would go to the aid of a drowning child, to the limit of their ability. People who support the rule of law, however, would say that this instance does not indicate a lack of relationship between moral standards and legal requirements; it only indicates the difficulty of translating one into the other when a positive compassionate or charitable act is needed. How, they would question, can you define in consistent and universal terms what is meant by assistance, the characteristics of the person who is to provide that assistance, and the circumstances under which it will be required? This, they would conclude, is just another illustration that the law represents the minimum set of standards to govern behavior in society and that actions beyond that minimum have to come from individual initiative, not legal force.

FIGURE 3–2 _____

Overlap between Moral Standards and Legal Requirements

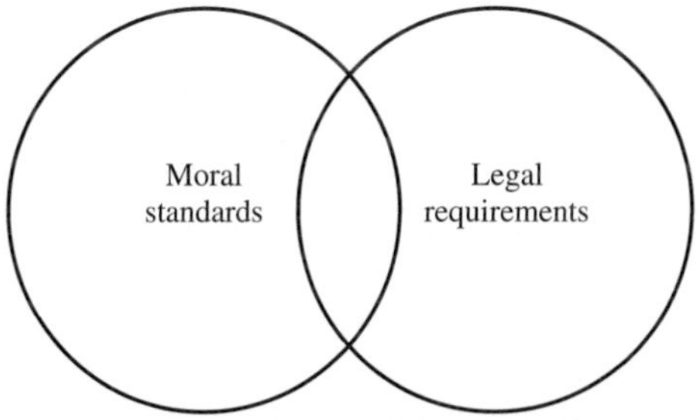

Lengthy Delays

The requirements of the law tend to lag behind the apparent moral standards of society. Slavery, of course, is the most odious example, but sexual and racial discrimination, environmental pollution, and foreign bribery can all be cited as moral problems that were belatedly addressed by legislation. Advocates of the rule of law would say, however, that the evidence of a delay between apparent moral consensus and enacted legal sanctions does not necessarily indicate a lack of relationship between legal requirements and moral standards. It only serves to confirm that relationship, they would claim, for laws controlling discrimination, pollution, and bribery were eventually passed.

None of these arguments—that legal requirements are not fully consistent with moral standards (they overlap rather than duplicate), or that the legal requirements appear in different forms (negative rather than positive) and at different times (sequential rather than concurrent) than moral standards—seems truly decisive. None of these arguments really helps to determine whether a given legal requirement does indeed represent a collective moral judgment by members of a specific society and consequently can serve as means to analyze the managerial decisions and actions of a company within that society. We can easily say that the law does not represent our moral judgment in a given situation, but how can we say that the law in that instance does not represent the moral judgment of a majority of our peers? For that, I think, we have to follow through the process by which our society has developed the law as a universal and consistent set of rules to govern human conduct.

FORMATION OF THE LAW: PROPOSED STAGES

Law is obviously a dynamic entity, for the rules change over time. Think of the changes that have occurred in the laws governing employment, for example, or pollution. This is essentially the same point that was made previously, that there seems to be a time lag between changes in moral standards and changes in legal requirements. Actions that 20 years ago were considered to be fully legal—such as racial and gender discrimination in hiring, or the discharge of chemical wastes into lakes and streams—are now clearly illegal. The question is whether these changes in the law came from changes in the moral standards of a majority of our population through social and political processes, and consequently whether the law does represent the collective moral standards of our society. The social and political processes by which the changing moral standards of individual human beings are alleged to become institutionalized into the formal legal framework of society are lengthy and complex, but a simplified version is shown in graphic form in Figure 3–3.

There are four stages in the proposed formation of explicit legal requirements through the inclusion of collective moral standards. These are the stages of (1) individual persons, (2) small groups, (3) formal organizations, and

FIGURE 3-3

Process by which Individual Norms, Beliefs, and Values Are Institutionalized into Law

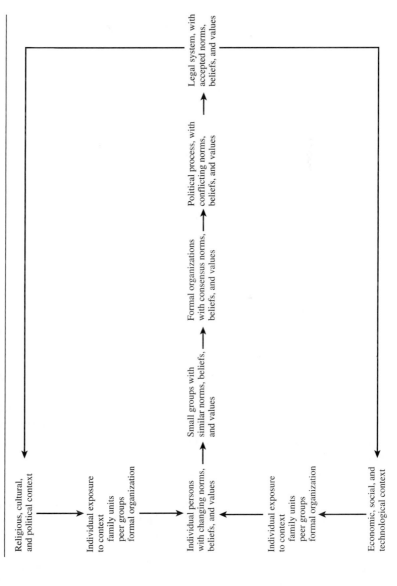

(4) political institutions. Each will be addressed in sequence. Some of the information about the first stage has been covered in an earlier chapter, but it is repeated here for emphasis and understanding.

Formation of the Law: Individual Persons

As Chapter 1 described, each individual within society has a set of goals, norms, beliefs, and values that together form his or her moral standards. Goals, also as described in that chapter, are what we want out of life. They include material possessions (cars, homes, boats, and vacations), lifestyle preferences (security, position, leisure, and power), personal goods (family, friends, health, and respect) and social aims (justice, equality, a clean environment, and a world at peace). Clearly these goals differ between people. Equally clearly they influence the norms, beliefs, and values that those individuals hold, and consequently the moral standards that they profess and allegedly the laws that they wish to see enacted.

Norms, once more as described in the earlier chapter, are criteria of behavior. They are the ways an individual expects others to act when faced with given situations. Foreign students from certain Asiatic countries, for example, bow slightly when addressing a university professor; the bow is their norm or expectation of behavior given that situation. University faculty members within the United States are generally somewhat annoyed when this occurs; their norm or expectation of behavior in that situation is considerably less formal and generally more egalitarian. The depth of the bow and the degree of annoyance both decline over time as the expectations of behavior on both sides are modified through learning.

Another example of a norm of behavior is far less facetious and much more relevant to the discussion of moral standards and the law. Most people expect that others, when they meet them, should not cause them injury. Norms are expectations of the ways people ideally should act, not anticipations of the ways people really will act. A person who holds a norm against assault and robbery—as most of us do—will not ordinarily walk down a dark street in the warehouse district of a big city at three in the morning; he or she feels that people should not assault and rob each other, not that they will not do so.

Norms are expectations of desired behavior, not requirements for that behavior. This is the major difference between a norm and a law; the norm is not published, may not be obeyed, and cannot be enforced except by the sanctions of a small group whose members hold similar norms and use such penalties as disapproval or exclusion. Norms also are often neither consistent nor universal. The person who actually commits a crime in the warehouse district at three in the morning, feeling it permissible to assault and rob someone else given his or her situation and need upon one night, doubtless would feel outraged and unfairly treated if assaulted and robbed in the same place and at the same time the following night. Norms are just the way we feel about behavior; often they are neither logically consistent nor universally applied because we have never thought through the reasons we hold them.

Beliefs are criteria of thought; they are the ways an individual expects other people to think about given concepts and to support specific norms. I believe in participatory democracy, for example, and I expect others to recognize the worth of that concept and support my norm of free elections. You may believe in environmental preservation and expect other people to recognize the importance of that idea and support your norm against burying harmful chemicals.

Beliefs are different from norms in that they involve no action—no overt behavior towards others—just an abstract way of thinking that tends to support an individual's goals and norms. Asiatic students who bow to American professors believe, it is alleged, in a hierarchical society based upon age, not position, with definite gradations between older faculty and younger students. People who hold the norm that others should not assault and rob them, even on darkened streets and in deserted neighborhoods, generally believe in the worth of human beings and the preservation of personal property. In one last example, the norm that a company should not bury toxic wastes in leaking 55-gallon drums is associated with beliefs about the public benefits of a clean environment and the adverse effects of chemical pollution upon family health.

Values, the fourth and last of this pattern of personal criteria that together form the moral standards of an individual, are the rankings or priorities that a person establishes for his or her goals, norms, and beliefs. Most people do not consider that all their goals, norms, and beliefs are equal in importance; generally there are some that seem much more important than others. The important goals, norms, and beliefs are the ones that a person "values," or holds in high esteem.

Values, of course, are often controversial. Why? Because a goal, norm, or belief that one person holds in high esteem can conflict with a different goal, norm, or belief that another person holds in equally high esteem. Generally there will be little accommodation or compromise because each person attaches great importance to his or her goals of what people should want to achieve, to his or her norms of how people should want to act, and to his or her beliefs of why people should want to accept his or her goals and norms. We live in a pluralistic society, with numerous cultural traditions, and in a secular nation, with no accepted or endorsed religious doctrines; consequently we have to live with the fact that goals, norms, beliefs, and values will differ among individuals. These differences can and do lead to conflicts. Similarities, however, can and do lead to associations. Those associations are important in the formation of the small groups that allegedly affect the formation of the law.

Formation of the Law: Small Groups

People with similar goals, norms, beliefs, and values tend to associate with each other. This is partially the result of those similarities; we all like to be with other people who tend to accept our views on the important issues of life. But it is also partially the result of the influence of our religious and cultural traditions and our economic and social situations upon our goals, norms, beliefs, and values. We also all like to associate with others who tend to share our traditions and situations. These associations, over time, lead to the formation of small and informal groups of like-minded individuals.

These small and informal groups of like-minded individuals do, through a process called accretion of power, have an apparent though delayed and indirect impact upon the legal requirements in a democratic society. People with closely similar goals, norms, beliefs, and values and from nearly identical traditions and situations tend to rely upon the groups to which they belong to forward their views and respect their backgrounds in their interactions with the larger formal organizations and political institutions.

It has to be admitted that these tendencies towards conformity can—and frequently do—lead to exclusion and discrimination. This, we will find, is one of the reasons that the legal requirements of a society cannot be said to be fully based upon the moral standards of all of the members of that society. There frequently has been some ostracism of people who hold diverse standards. But it also has to be admitted that these small and informal groups of people who share parallel views and compatible backgrounds do wield considerable influence through social and political processes upon the viewpoints of organizations and the requirements of societies. Groups of people, even though their numbers are small and their structures informal, are generally more powerful in changing organizational policies and social laws than are single individuals.

There are exceptions to this "groups are more powerful than individuals" dictum, of course. Some individuals are particularly articulate. Some individuals are exceptionally adept. And some individuals are unusually charismatic. But in general it can be said that coherent groups generate greater influence on organizational policies and social laws than do independent persons, for most of us are not "particularly articulate," "exceptionally adept," or "unusually charismatic."

Formation of the Law: Large Organizations

Small, informal groups are usually part of much larger formal organizations. These larger formal organizations can be of many different types: business firms, labor unions, political parties, charitable agencies, religious institutions, and veterans' associations. They all share—and this is the reason for the "formal" classification—accepted goals, stated policies, and structured positions. People know why they exist or claim to exist, how they act or claim to act, and who's in charge or claims to be in charge. There are exceptions here too, of course. The accepted goals of some organizations tend to get lost over time. The stated policies ("policies" are explicit statements as to what should be done in given situations) tend to get forgotten, and the structured positions ("structure" refers to the hierarchical ranking, or authoritative power, of those positions) tend to become ignored. But, generally the goals, the policies, and the positions are dominant in the management of large formal organizations.

The small informal groups that are part of each large and formal organization tend to come into conflict with each other over their distinctive goals, norms, beliefs, and values. Over time the larger organizations and the small groups either achieve an acceptable compromise on these issues and their resultant standards, or split into smaller organizations that can achieve such a compromise. There are alternative theories on the means by which this compromise is formed: autocratic decision, bureaucratic adjustment, coalition bargaining, or collective choice. Doubtless all these methods are employed to different degrees in different organizations, but the outcome that can be observed is that many organizations do eventually display a culture of shared goals, norms, beliefs, and values that do lead to accepted standards. Organizations that display such a coherent culture—and remember that these are not just business firms; they include labor unions, political parties, charitable agencies, religious groups, and industrial associations as well—tend to have considerable power in the political institutions that formulate the laws and establish the legal requirements of the society.

Formation of the Law: Political Institutions

The political institutions—governmental units at federal, state, and local levels—are the means by which the goals, norms, beliefs, and values, and the resultant moral standards, of private individuals, small groups, and larger organizations are formalized into law. The political process by which this transmission occurs can, once again, be seen basically as a means of resolving conflict. Organizations, groups, and individuals obviously have different opinions on what should be achieved in the future (goals), what should be done now (norms), what should be the supporting rationale (beliefs), what should be the order of priority (values), and what are the standards that should be applied (morals). These different views have to be reconciled into a consistent, universal, published, accepted, and enforced set of rules (the definition of the law) to be effective. This is—or should be—the function of the political institutions.

Again, there are alternative theories on the ways by which this is done: presidential leadership, institutional compromise, congressional bargaining, and constituent pressure. The terms would differ at the federal, state, and local levels, but the process doubtless remains approximately the same. The important issue is that all of the participants in this process are influenced by votes, surveys, contributions, reports, messages, and—to some extent— threats from private individuals, small groups, and large organizations. The accretion of power means that the groups are more effective than the individuals, and the organizations more effective than the groups, in wielding this influence.

The actual process by which laws are enacted represents a complex series of interactions. Doubtless no one except a member of Congress or a representative in one of the state legislatures fully appreciates the extent and time demands of the formal hearings, office meetings, and committee reports, with their constant interruptions. There are also informal exchanges that occur in hallways, parking lots, and evening receptions, marked by both open efforts to summarize opinions from the general voters expressed in personal letters, telephone calls, and media reports, and closed efforts to include viewpoints of the special interests reinforced by campaign contributions. All of these help to form the opinions of the legislators. It is easy to be cynical when thinking of the political process, particularly when the high cost of election campaigns is considered and the need to raise money to finance those campaigns is included, but it is difficult to invent a better process than representative democracy.

CONCLUSIONS ON LEGAL REQUIREMENTS AS A METHOD OF MORAL ANALYSIS

The question now is whether this sequence of private individuals to small groups to large organizations to political institutions, lengthy and complex though it may be, truly does serve to combine the personal moral standards of our population, slowly and gradually, into the universal legal requirements of our society. That is, does the law actually represent the collective moral judgment of our citizens, or does this cumulative process break down at some point? The proposal that the law of a democratic society does indeed represent the collective moral judgment of the citizens of that society is certainly appealing. However, there would seem to be five major problems in the transfer from individual moral standards to universal legal requirements through the various stages of the social and political process:

- *Inadequate information.* The goals, norms, beliefs, and values, and consequently the moral standards, of the members of society may be based upon a lack of information relative to issues of importance. Many people in southern Quebec may have been unaware of the impact of the huge hydroelectric generating projects— described at the beginning of the first chapter of this book—upon the people of northern Quebec. Many people in the United States may be unaware of the magnitude of the toxic waste disposal problem; I certainly do not know the amount or the impact of that waste upon human health and the natural environment. It is difficult for personal moral standards to influence the law if some information is missing.

- *Incomplete participation.* The moral standards of some members of society may not be included in the formation of the small groups that subsequently influence the formal organizations and the legal institutions. People with similar goals, norms, beliefs, and values and from identical religious/cultural traditions and economic/social situations tend to become associated in small groups, but those similarities and identities also tend to exclude some members of society from different traditions and alternative situations. Goals, norms, beliefs, and values lead to conflicts as well as to associations. It is difficult for personal moral standards to influence the law if some individual viewpoints are excluded.

- *Inconsistent representation.* The moral standards of some groups within society may not be fully represented in the consensus of the formal organizations that subsequently influence the legal institutions. Many organizations do share goals, norms, beliefs, and values, but there is no evidence that each group within the organization has equal influence in determining that consensus. This can be seen in the goals, norms, beliefs, and values of many nonprofit organizations such as hospitals and universities; the standards of the professional personnel—the physicians and the faculty—often seem to predominate. It is difficult for personal moral standards to actively influence the law if some group standings are given prominence.

- *Inconsistent formulation.* The moral standards of some organizations within society may not be equally considered in the agreements of the political institutions that result, or should result, in the formulation of the law. This is the same point that was made above in shaping the consensus of an organization, though on a much larger scale. There is no guarantee that all organizations have equal influence, or even equal influence weighted by size or need, in determining the final provisions of the law. This can be seen in much tax legislation; certain organizations always seem to be favored. It is difficult for personal moral standards to eventually influence the law if some organizational considerations are preferred.

- *Inconclusive composition.* The moral standards of individuals, groups, organizations, and institutions that make it through the social and political processes that allegedly formulate the law are often incompletely or imprecisely stated and have to be supplemented by judicial court decisions or administrative agency actions. This can be seen in both product liability cases and equal employment reviews; the meaning and the application of legal requirements frequently have to be clarified outside of the legislative procedures. It is difficult for personal moral standards to influence the law if some provisions are interpreted by governmental bodies that intentionally are independent of those standards.

What can we say in summary? We can observe that there obviously is some overlap between the moral standards and the legal requirements of our society. The federal law against robbery and the moral standard against stealing serve as an example. And we can see that some changes in the goals, norms, beliefs, and values of individual members of society have eventually been reflected by changes in the law. The Foreign Corrupt Practices Act and the Federal Equal Employment Act are examples here. But we will have to admit that there is no direct relationship in all instances. The social and political processes by which the law is formulated are too complex and too cumbersome—and perhaps too subject to manipulation—for changes in people's goals, norms, beliefs, and values to be directly translated into changes in that set of universal and consistent rules that we call law. Consequently, we cannot view this set of rules as representing the collective moral judgments of our society, and therefore we cannot rely totally on this set of rules when confronted by an ethical dilemma.

Legal requirements can serve as a guide to managerial decisions and actions, but as in the case of economic outcomes, they are not enough. They don't include the full range of personal goals, norm, beliefs, and values and consequently—once again, as in economic outcomes—don't represent the true nature and actual worth of individual human beings. Legal requirements are useful. They provide an approximation of that nature, and they approach that worth by recognizing the value of liberty, opportunity, dignity, and respect. We need something more. In the next chapter we will look at the fundamental norms and absolute values of normative philosophy as a third possible means of providing that "something more."

CASE 3–1

Sarah Goodwin

Sarah Goodwin was a graduate of an MBA program on the West Coast. She had majored in marketing, was interested in retailing, and had been delighted to receive a job offer from a large and prestigious department store chain in northern California. The first year of employment at this chain was considered to be a training program, but formal instruction was very limited. Instead, after a quick tour of the facilities and a welcoming speech by the president, each of the new trainees was assigned to work as an assistant to a buyer in one of the departments. The intent was that the trainees would work with five or six buyers during the year, rotating assignments every two months, and would make themselves "useful" enough during those assignments so at least one buyer would ask to have that person join his or her department on a permanent basis.

Buyers are critical in the management of a department store. They select the goods to be offered, negotiate purchase terms, set retail prices, arrange displays, organize promotions, and are generally responsible for the operations of the departments within the store. Each buyer acts as a profit center, and sales figures and profit margins are reported monthly to the senior executives. In this particular chain, the sales and profits were calculated on a "per square foot of floor space occupied by the department" basis, and the buyers contended, generally on a friendly basis, to outperform each other so that their square footage would be expanded. The buyers received substantial commissions based upon monthly profits.

Sarah's first assignment was to work for the buyer of the gourmet food department. This was a small unit at the main store that sold packaged food items such as jams and jellies, crackers and cookies, cheese and spreads, candies, and the like, most of which were imported from Europe. The department also offered preserved foods, such as smoked fish and meats, and some expensive delicacies, such as caviar, truffles, and estate-bottled wines. Many of the items were packaged as gifts, in boxes or baskets with decorative wrapping and ties.

Sarah was originally disappointed to have been sent to such a small and specialized department, rather than to a larger one that dealt with more general fashion goods, but she soon found that this assignment was considered to be a "plum." The buyer, Maria Castellani, was a well-known personality throughout the store; witty, competent, and sarcastic, she served as a sounding board, consultant, and friend to the other buyers. She would evaluate fashions, forecast trends, chastise managers ("managers" in a department store are the people associated with finance, personnel, accounting, or planning, not merchandising), and discuss retailing events and changes in an amusing, informative way. Everybody in the store seemed to find a reason to stop by the gourmet food department at least once during each day to chat with Maria. Sarah was naturally included in these conversations, and consequently she found that she was getting to know all of the other buyers and could ask one of them to request her as an assistant at the next rotation of the assignment.

For the first five weeks of her employment, Sara was exceptionally happy, pleased with her career and her life. She was living in a house on one of the cable car lines with three other professionally employed women. She felt that she was performing well on her first job and making sensible arrangements for her next assignment. Then, an event occurred that threatened to destroy all of her contentment:

> We had received a shipment of thin little wafers from England that had a crème filling flavored with fruit: strawberries and raspberries. They were very good. They were packaged in foil-covered boxes, but somehow some of them had become infested with insects.

> We did not think that all of the boxes were infested because not all of the customers brought them back. But some people did, and obviously we could not continue to sell them. We couldn't inspect the packages and keep the ones that were not infested because there were too many—about $9,000 worth—and because we would have had to tear the foil to open each box. Maria said that the manufacturer would not give us a refund because the infestation doubtless occurred during shipment, or even during storage at our own warehouse.

> Maria told me to get rid of them. I thought that she meant for me to arrange to have them taken to the dump, but she said, "Absolutely not. Call [name of an executive] at [name of a convenience store chain in southern California]. They operate down in the ghetto and can sell anything. We've got to get our money back."

> I protested, but Maria told me, "Look, there is nothing wrong with this. The people down in the ghetto have never had luxury food items of this nature. These wafers will be sold very cheaply, and for most of the people who buy them it will be an opportunity to try something really good. Only a few people will get an infested box. They won't be very happy, but down in the ghetto they expect that when they see a low price on an expensive product. They make the choice. We don't." (Verbal statement of Sarah Goodwin, a disguised name, to the case writer)

Class Assignment.   What would you do in this situation? You can either ship the wafers or not. If you decide to ship the wafers, then be prepared to explain your action to the three housemates who probably will have the same initial reaction that Sarah had. If you decide not to ship the wafers, then be prepared to explain your action firstly to Maria and—if not successful there—to a senior executive in the department store chain to whom you might appeal.

CASE 3–2

Johnson Controls and Gender Equality

Lead and other heavy metals have a known and harmful effect upon a fetus if absorbed into a mother's body even in very minimal amounts prior to or during pregnancy. Companies with industrial processes that require the use of these heavy metals have normally taken the position that they would bar women of childbearing age from employment on the production line. The problem, from the point of view of the women involved, was that those jobs tended to be highly skilled and highly paid. Most of the actual assembly work in these semihazardous industries has been automated in recent years, and consequently the employment opportunities now are in quality control, machine maintenance, and laboratory analysis.

Young women who started in nonhazardous work areas at entry level pay would eventually find their way to promotion blocked because they were barred from those skilled positions. Johnson Controls, a major manufacturer of lead-acid batteries for automobiles required evidence of surgical sterilization before women under age 55 could be employed in the areas there those batteries actually were made. Offended by that company rule, and encouraged by other sex discrimination cases, a group of female employees at Johnson Controls sued the company. The case eventually reached the Supreme Court, which in 1991 ruled that employers could not bar women of childbearing age from certain jobs because of the potential risk to a possible child:

> "Women as capable of doing their jobs as their male counterparts may not be forced to choose between having a child and having a job," the high court said in an opinion written by Justice Harry Blackmun. . . ."If an employer fully informs the woman of the risk and the employer has not acted negligently, the basis for holding an employer liable seems remote at best." (*The Wall Street Journal,* March 21, 1991, p. B1)

Companies using lead and other heavy metals in their production processes were not reassured, however, by that last statement of Justice Blackmun. The question of legal liability, it was felt, would gradually evolve about the definitions of "acting negligently" and "informing fully." The Occupational Safety and Health Administration (OSHA) had no standards for permissible exposure of heavy metals to a fetus, and it was expected that the government would take at least three to five years to develop those standards, which could then be applied retroactively. In the meantime, if a child were born with birth defects to a worker exposed as part of her job to heavy metals, even if the worker had insisted upon that job as one of her legal rights, it was felt probable that a jury would view the situation with considerable sympathy and grant a substantial award.

Further, even if a woman acknowledged that she had been duly warned about the general dangers, she could still claim that she had not been told about any specific defect that might occur. And, the child in later years could sue for damages, claiming that he or she had not been able to participate in the original decision affecting his or her rights and health.

Assume that you are a manager employed by the lead-acid battery division of Johnson Controls, an attorney advising that division, or a member of any of the other professions that might reasonably be expected to provide medical advice or technical assistance. Assume that the manufacturing and marketing of lead-acid batteries is a globally competitive industry, with numerous foreign firms that generally are susceptible to fewer environmental regulations and to lower work safety requirements. Assume that Johnson Controls has been able to maintain its market position and financial return despite that foreign competition by means of extensive investments in factory automation.

Assume that 3,000 people are currently employed at three plants. Only 15 percent of those employees are women of childbearing age; they work in secretarial and support positions, segregated from the actual production processes, but both the percentage and the exposure can be expected to increase rapidly following the Supreme Court decision as more women apply for the higher-paid jobs directly involved with manufacturing. Assume that you believe the present production process to be safe; the company currently monitors the level of lead in the bloodstream of all workers, male and female, and this level is substantially below existing industry standards. Assume that you have no data on the probability of harm to a fetus associated with those existing standards, and that you probably cannot get that data due to the prior exclusion of women from the relevant workforce. Assume lastly that you have only three choices:

- Close all three plants and shift all manufacturing overseas where legal claims for reproductive health would be minimal at best, and probably not recognized by local courts. There would be charges against company earnings for closing the plants and greatly increased expenses for transportation and communication, but profits over the long term could be expected to increase about 25 percent due to lower wage rates.

- Continue to operate all three plants at present locations with present safety standards. Attempt to quickly move women who become pregnant to nonhazardous jobs, and gather data on the incidence of birth defects. Profits would neither increase nor decrease until legal suits were won or lost in court, and even then the chances of birth defects and the costs of legal settlements might be less than currently feared.

- Continue to operate all three plants at present locations, but with greatly heightened safety standards. Adopt the "clean-room" technology of the electronics industry, with zero tolerance for lead in the bloodstream. Clean-room technology is expensive, however, and profits could be expected to decrease 50 to 60 percent even with substantial wage concessions negotiated with the workers.

Class Assignment. You may select any of the three alternatives, but assume that your recommendation will be challenged by others within the firm. One of the concepts of this course is that you have to be able to logically convince others that your recommendation is "right" by arguing from the basic principles as to what is best for society. There are three of these basic principles:

- *Economic benefits.* Always take the action that generates the greatest profits for the company because this will generate the greatest benefits for the society, provided that all markets are fully competitive, all customers are fully informed, and all external and internal costs are fully included.

- *Legal requirements.* Always take the action that most fully complies with the law for the law in a democratic society represents the combined moral standards of all of the people within that society, provided it can be shown that the self-interests of the various groups have been truly combined in the formulation process.

- *Ethical duties.* Always take the action that you (1) would be willing to see widely reported in national newspapers; (2) that you believe will build a sense of community among everyone associated with the action; (3) that you expect will generate the greatest net good; (4) that you would be willing to see others take in situations in which you might be the victim; (5) that does not harm the "least among us"; and (6) that does not interfere with the right of everyone to develop their skills to the fullest.

CASE 3–3

H. B. Fuller and the Sale of Resistol in Central America

Resistol is a fast-drying, solvent-based liquid adhesive used to glue paper, cardboard, wood, leather, plastic, rubber, and textile products. In essence it is

---

SOURCE: This is a shortened version of an earlier case written by Professors Norman Bowie and Stefanie Lenway, both of the Carlson School of Management at the University of Minnesota, and is used with their permission.

an industrial-strength form of the familiar airplane glue or rubber cement, with the properties of rapid set, strong adhesion, and water resistance.

Resistol is widely used in Central and South America by the small shoe and clothing manufacturers, leather workers, wood workers, carpenters, and repair shops that are typical of the region. It is also widely used by individual customers for the quick repair of shoes, clothing, and household goods. It is easily available from industrial suppliers in large containers and from retail shops in small tubes. The easy availability is a large part of the problem.

Fumes from the solvent in Resistol are a hallucinogenic, and street children in four of the poorest countries of Central America—Guatemala, Honduras, Nicaragua, and El Salvador—have started using those fumes as a mood-altering drug:

> They lie senseless on doorsteps and pavements, grimy and loose limbed, like discarded rag dolls.

> Some are just five or six years old. Others are already young adults, and all are addicted to sniffing a commonly sold glue that is doing them irreversible brain damage.

> Roger, 21, has been sniffing Resistol for eight years. Today, even when he is not high, Roger walks with a stagger, his motor control wrecked. His scarred face puckers with concentration, his right foot taps nervously, incessantly, as he talks.

> Since he was 11, when he ran away from the aunt who raised him, Roger's home has been the streets of [Tegucigalpa] the capital of Honduras, the second poorest nation in the western hemisphere after Haiti.

> Roger spends his time begging, shinning shoes, washing car windows, scratching together a few pesos a day, and sleeping in doorways at night.

> Sniffing glue, he says, "makes me feel happy, makes me feel big. I know that it's doing me damage, but it's a habit I've got, and a habit's a habit. I cannot give it up even though I wish to."

> No one knows how many of Tegucigalpa's street urchins seek escape from the squalor and misery of their daily existence through the hallucinogenic fumes of Resistol. No one has spent the time and money needed to study the question.

> But, one thing is clear, according to Dr. Rosalio Zalava, head of the Health Ministry's Department of Mental Health, "These children come from the poorest slums of the big cities. They have grown up as illegal squatters in very disturbed states of mental health, tense, depressed, aggressive."

> "Some turn that aggression on society, and start stealing. Others turn it on themselves, and adopt self-destructive behavior."

> But, he understands the attraction of the glue whose solvent, toluene, produces feelings of elation. "It gives you delusions of grandeur, you feel powerful, and that compensates these kids for reality, where they feel completely worthless, like nobodies." (InterPress News Service, July 16, 1985, p. 1)

Resistol is manufactured by H. B. Fuller Company of St. Paul, Minnesota, a specialty chemical company frequently confused with the better-known but much smaller Fuller Brush Company. The adhesive is marketed in Central America by Kativo Chemical Industries, S.A., a wholly owned subsidiary of H. B. Fuller.

Traditionally the H. B. Fuller Company has given regional executives in foreign subsidiaries a great deal of autonomy to respond quickly to currency fluctuations, political changes, and market needs. When the story quoted above appeared in the Honduran newspapers under the title "Los Reistoleros" (the users of Resistol), Humberto "Beto" Larach, the manager of Kativo's Adhesive Division, quickly informed the editors that Resistol was not the only substance abused by Honduran street children and that the image of the manufacturer was being damaged by taking a prestigious trademark as a synonym for drug abusers. He threatened to sue the newspaper for defamation of character.

Senor Larach felt strongly that the glue-sniffing problem was not caused by the solvent in the product, but by the poverty of the region, for which he and H. B. Fuller were not responsible. He recommended to the St. Paul office that no action be taken to change the formulation or the distribution of the product. It was possible, for example, to use a much less volatile solvent that would decrease the hallucinogenic effect of the fumes but would also lengthen the drying time of the adhesive. Senor Larach said that in Third World countries most industrial supply firms and retail stores would stock only one brand of a product and that if the product specifications were changed in an unsatisfactory way the users would demand that their suppliers switch brands to a readily available competitor with the desired qualities. Resistol at the date of the case was by far the dominant quick-setting adhesive sold in the region, with a market share over 80 percent, but competitive products were readily available from companies in both France and West Germany.

Senor Larach also explained that reducing the volatility of only the solvent of the adhesive sold through the retail stores (that is, keeping the adhesive sold through industrial suppliers at full "industrial" strength) would not solve the problem either. The street children currently obtained the glue in small tubes from the retail stores and in small jars from adults who either bought it through the industrial suppliers or stole it from the industrial users.

In 1986 a Peace Corps volunteer in Honduras, disturbed by the situation and angered by what he perceived as a lack of response on the part of Kativo, formed a committee of local religious and social leaders to attempt to reduce the use of the drug by the street children. The first act of this committee was to petition the government to pass a law dictating that allyl isothiocyanate (also known as "oil of mustard") be added to all quick-setting adhesives sold in the country to prevent their abuse. Allyl isothiocyanate is a chemical that irritates the mucous membranes of the upper respiratory tract; it can also cause burns to the eyes and skin. When used in full strength it is the "mustard gas" that caused horrendous casualties in World War I. Members of the committee had no intention that the chemical be used in full strength in Resistol; they conceded, however, that its presence even in diluted form would make the adhesive unpleasant to apply in normal industrial and consumer use but felt that situation was better than its continued misuse by children. During the 1970s allyl isothiocyanate had been added to airplane glue in the United States to prevent a similar form of abuse.

The Peace Corps volunteer in Honduras also started a letter-writing campaign directed both to the senior executives at H. B. Fuller and to the trust officers and pension managers who held much of that company's common stock. The letters were accompanied by photographs of the street children, translations from news accounts, statements by the local clergy, and invitations to visit the region and observe the situation.

The senior executives at H. B. Fuller commissioned a study by a large international consulting firm, which reached seven major conclusions:

1. Oil of mustard is not only a skin and lung irritant; prolonged exposure even in diluted form can cause nausea, dizziness, headaches, and asthma.

2. No less hallucinogenic solvent is readily available that will not severely detract from the present quick-setting, high-adhesion, and water-resistant qualities of the product.

3. No less harmful additive is readily available that will both decrease the use of the adhesive as a street drug and maintain the present desirable product qualities.

4. It would be possible to search for a less hallucinogenic solvent or a less harmful additive, but the search would be expensive and no guarantee of success could be offered.

5. Sales of Resistol in Central America amounted to over $12 million per year; profits were not listed in the report released to the public but they were assumed to be high.

6. Sales of Resistol in Central America were thought to be important to the industrial development of the region. Water-based adhesives are used in Europe, the United States, and Japan, but these require microwave dryers and presses for curing. Those dryers and presses are not available in Central America due to their capital cost.

7. Sales of Resistol in Central America were thought to be related to the sales of paint (the major product of both H. B. Fuller and Kativo); that is, if the suppliers and retailers purchased industrial adhesives from other sources they were likely to purchase industrial finishes from those sources as well. Paint sales by Kativo were over $50 million per year.

In 1987, two events occurred that forced the senior executives at H. B. Fuller to address directly the problem of Resistol sales in Central America. First, the National Assembly of Honduras passed a law mandating the use of allyl isothiocyanate in all solvent-based adhesives sold in that country. Senor Larach, however, reported that the National Assembly had included no mechanism for enforcement of the law, that he had been assured by members of the Assembly that the law had been passed to placate the committee's religious and social leaders, and that there was no intent to enforce it. Senor Larach also said that the National Assembly was likely to be dissolved in the near future (which would overturn all laws passed during its recent session) as part of the political instability that troubled the region.

Second, the president of H. B. Fuller Company received a telephone call from the editor of the largest statewide newspaper in Minnesota. The editor explained that his daughter was a member of the Peace Corps in Central America, and had complained that "a company in St. Paul is selling a product that is literally burning out the brains of children down here." The editor also said that the paper had sent a reporter to Honduras and planned to run a story on the allegation if true, and that the call from the editor was a courtesy to alert the executives at H. B. Fuller and enable them to "tell their side of the story if they wished to."

Class Assignment. You are president of H. B. Fuller Company. What would you do? If you wish to stop the production, change the formulation, or alter the distribution of Resistol in Central America, do realize that—as the case describes—there were be severe marketing consequences? Current customers apparently like the product "as is" and Senor Larach reports that they will respond to any changes by simply buying less of it. If your decision is likely to result in revenue—and consequently profit—decreases, be prepared to explain that decision to members of the board of directors. If your decision is to continue the production and marketing of Resistol with no changes in formulation or distribution, then be prepared to explain that decision to readers of the "largest statewide newspaper in Minnesota." One of the essential concepts of this course is that you have to be able to logically convince other people that your recommendation is "right" by arguing from the basic principles as to what is best for society. There are three of these basic principles:

- *Economic benefits.* Always take the action that generates the greatest profits for the company because this will generate the greatest benefits for the society, provided that all markets are fully competitive, all customers are fully informed, and all external and internal costs are fully included.

- *Legal requirements.* Always take the action that most fully complies with the law for the law in a democratic society represents the combined moral standards of all the people within that society, provided it can be shown that the self-interests of the various groups have been truly combined in the formulation process.

- *Ethical duties.* Always take the action that you (1) would be willing to see widely reported in national newspapers; (2) that you believe will build a sense of community among everyone associated with the action; (3) that you expect will generate the greatest net good; (4) that you would be willing to see others take in situations in which you might be the victim; (5) that does not harm the "least among us"; and (6) that does not interfere with the right of everyone to develop their skills to the fullest.

CHAPTER 4

Moral Analysis and Ethical Duties

We are concerned in this book with ethical dilemmas: decisions and actions faced by business managers in which the financial performance (measured by the revenues, costs, and profits generated by the firm) and the social performance (stated in terms of the obligations to the individuals and groups associated with the firm) are in conflict. These are the moral problems in which some individuals and groups to whom the organization has some form of obligation—employees, customers, suppliers, distributors, creditors, stockholders, local residents, national citizens, and global inhabitants—are going to be hurt or harmed in some way while others are going to be benefited and helped. These are also the moral problems in which some of those individuals or groups are going to have their rights ignored or even diminished while others will see their rights acknowledged and often expanded. The question is how to decide—how to find a balance between financial performance and social performance when faced by an ethical dilemma, and how to decide what is "right" and "just" and "fair" as the solution to the underlying moral problem. The first chapter of this text suggested a formal analytical process for the resolution of these complex moral problems.

The analytical process described in Figure 4–1 proposed three alternative means of resolving these moral problems that mix benefits and harms and contrast the recognition and denial of rights. Let us assume that you want to reach a solution with which you can feel comfortable and believe to be as "right" and "just" and "fair" as possible. But, let us also assume that you further want to reach a solution with which the other people associated with or affected by the problem can likewise feel comfortable, and agree to be as "right" and "just" and "fair" as possible. The argument of this text is that explaining your decision to reach an agreement on moral problems is fully as important as making your decision to reach a closure on those problems. How can you both make and explain your decision? There are three methods of analysis that should help you to decide and others to understand. They are summarized, once again, very briefly below:

- *Economic outcomes,* based upon impersonal market forces. This methodology was described in Chapter 2. The belief is that a manager should always act to maximize product revenues and minimize factor costs, given that all markets are competitive and all costs are included. The underlying rationale is that each firm is connected to the product markets and factors markets of the society, and individuals within the society can thus decide what products they most want to buy and what factors they least want to keep. Under those conditions, personal decisions on what is best for the individual should aggregate into market decisions as to what is best for the society. As we saw in the earlier chapter, however, there are both practical and theoretical problems with that approach. The most telling problem is that it does not fully recognize the nature nor completely value the worth of individual human beings as expressed by their needs for liberty, opportunity, dignity, and respect. It certainly helps to know the economic outcomes to the society, but something more is needed.

- *Legal requirements,* based upon impartial social and political processes. This methodology was described in Chapter3. The belief is that a manager should always obey the law, despite disagreements with some provisions of that law, for the law can be said to represent the collective moral standards of the members of our society. Each member has a set of goals, norms, beliefs, and values that are primarily derived from his or her religious and cultural traditions and his or her economic and social situations. Combined, those goals, norms, beliefs, and values form his or her moral standards. The moral standards of each individual are gradually aggregated into the legal requirements of the society through impartial social and political processes that move from informal groups to formal organizations to legal institutions. Again, there are both practical and theoretical problems with this approach; the most telling is that it does not combine all traditions and all situations equally, and some are excluded. It certainly helps to know the legal requirements of the society, but once again something more is needed.

FIGURE 4–1

Analytical Process for the Resolution of Moral Problems

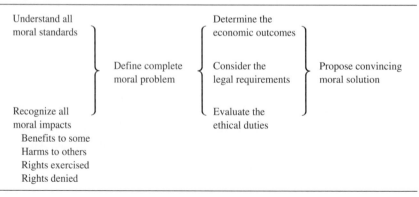

- *Ethical duties,* based upon rational thought processes. This methodology will be described in the current chapter. Essentially the belief is that a manager should always act in accordance with a set of objective norms of behavior or universal statements of belief that are "right" and "just" and "fair" in, of, and by themselves. The norms and beliefs that all of us hold intuitively are based upon our religious and cultural traditions and our economic and social situations. They are subjective and personal; they vary between people. But there are some norms and beliefs that can be said to be objective and universal, to be based upon reason rather than emotion. These can be considered to be "right" and "just" and "fair" in, of, and by themselves because they can be logically seen to lead to a "good" society in which everyone will have liberty, opportunity, dignity, and respect. This is "moral reasoning": logically working from an objective and universal first principle through to a decision on the ethical duties we owe to others. There are some problems here also; though perhaps not as serious as in the other two approaches. Moral reasoning does recognize the nature and value the worth of human beings as expressed by their needs for liberty, opportunity, dignity, and respect.

Moral reasoning—logically working from an objective and universal first principle through to a decision on the ethical duties we owe to others—requires an understanding of normative philosophy. It is not possible to summarize normative philosophy in a single chapter just as, quite frankly, it is not really possible to summarize economic relationships or social/political processes in a single chapter. But, it is possible to convey some of the basic concepts and methods, provided the reader is interested and willing to think about them. I assume that you are interested and willing to think about these issues or you would not have gotten this far.

DEFINITION OF NORMATIVE PHILOSOPHY

Philosophy is the study of thought and conduct. Normative philosophy is the study of proper thought and conduct; that is, how we should think and behave. Normative philosophers have been looking at these issues of proper behavior for more than 2,400 years, since the time of Socrates, who lived from 470 to 399 B.C. They have attempted to establish a logical thought process, based upon an incontrovertible first principle, that would determine whether an act is "right" or "wrong," "just" or "unjust," "fair" or "unfair." They have not been successful–otherwise all that would be needed would be to quote the sources and state the findings—but many of their concepts and methods can be used to expand the earlier concepts of economic outcomes and legal requirements. All hard ethical choices are compromises, between financial needs and social responsibilities in the case of a business firm, between material wants and personal duties in the case of an individual. Normative philosophy provides some help in making those compromises, but that help is not as extensive as one might wish. Here, however, is an introduction to the normative philosophy of morality and ethics.

First, there is a difference between morality and ethics. Morality refers to the standards of behavior by which people are judged, and particularly to the standards of behavior by which people are judged in their relationships with others. A person in the midst of a desert, isolated from everyone else, might act in a way that was immature, demeaning, or stupid, but he or she could not truly be said to have acted immorally since that behavior could have no impact upon others, unless it were to waste water or some other resource needed by travelers in the future.

Ethics, on the other hand, encompasses the system of beliefs that supports a particular view of morality. If I believe that a person should not smoke in a crowded room, it is because I have accepted the research findings of most scientists and the published statements of the Surgeon General that tobacco smoke is harmful to health. My acceptance of those findings is my ethic for that particular situation. Ethics is normally used in the plural form because most people have a system of interrelated beliefs rather than a single opinion. This difference between morality and ethics is easy to remember if one speaks of moral standards of behavior and ethical systems of belief, and I will use those terms in this discussion.

THE CONCEPT OF ETHICAL RELATIVISM

The next issue to be addressed in this description of the techniques of moral reasoning is that of ethical relativism. The question here is very basic: Are there objective universal principles upon which one can construct an ethical system of belief that is applicable to all groups in all cultures at all times? Moral standards of behavior differ between groups within a single culture, between cultures, and between times. This is obvious. For example, within the contemporary United States, moral standards for decisions on environmental protection differ between the leaders of public interest groups and the executives of major industrial corporations. It is probable that these standards of environmental protection would differ even more greatly between the United States and Third World countries, or between the contemporary period and the late nineteenth century.

The ethical systems of belief supporting the moral standards of behavior also differ; each group, in each country, in each time period, can usually give a clear explanation of the basis for its actions. To continue the earlier example, representatives of natural resource interest groups can provide a perfectly logical reason for their support of a prohibition upon logging in old growth forests. It preserves the recreational opportunities for future generations, they would say. Managerial personnel from a natural resource company can offer an equally logical reason for their opposition to such a prohibition. We need the building materials for present-day housing, they would claim. Both sides base their arguments on a system of beliefs as to what is best for the national society, but unfortunately those beliefs differ. I think we can all agree that among the most irritating aspects of the debate over ethical issues such as environmental protection are the attitudes of personal self-righteousness and the implications of opponent self-interest that seem to pervade all these discussions. Both sides assume that their systems of belief are so widely held, and so obviously logical, that their opponents have to be small-minded and illiberal. They do not recognize the legitimate differences that can exist between ethical systems as to what is "right" or "just" and "fair" for the society.

The question in ethical relativism is not whether different moral standards and ethical beliefs exist; they obviously do, and we all have experiences to confirm that fact. The question is whether there is any commonality that overrides the differences. In the mixed chorus of competing moral standards and diverse ethical systems, can we discern any single principle that unifies them all? Or are we left with the weak and unsatisfactory conclusion that all ethical systems are equally valid, and that a person's choice has to be relative to his or her religious and cultural traditions and economic and social situations? If all ethical systems are equally valid, then no firm moral judgments can be made about individual behavior, and we are all on our own to do as we like to others, within economic limits and legal constraints.

Fortunately, there is one principle that does seem to exist across all groups, cultures, and times and that does form part of every ethical system: the belief that members of a group do bear some form of responsibility for the well-being of other members of that group. There is disagreement about the size of those groups and the nature of those responsibilities, but there is widespread recognition that men and women are social beings, that cooperation is necessary for survival, and that some standards of behavior are needed to ensure that cooperation. In one of the most famous statements in normative philosophy, Thomas Hobbes (1588–1679) argued (as was explained previously in Chapter 3) that if everyone acted on the basis of his or her own self-interest and ignored the well-being of others, life would be "solitary, poor, nasty, brutish, and short."

People in all cultures, even the most primitive, do not act solely for their own self-interest, and they understand that standards of behavior are needed to promote cooperation and ensure survival. These standards of behavior can be either negative—it is considered wrong to harm other members of the group—or positive—it is considered right to help other group members—but they do exist and can be traced in both sociological and anthropological studies. Consequently, the important question in moral relativism is not whether your moral standards are as good as mine; it is whether your moral standards that help other members of society are as good as mine that help other members of society.

That second question is very different from the first; it forces both of us to justify our standards relative to a principle that does extend over groups, cultures, and times. We can say that our definitions of what is "right" differ, and we can each act in accordance with those definitions and believe that we are morally correct. Yet the way in which we determine what is "right" has to be exactly the same, and has to come down to the benefit for our mutual society.

That "benefit" is not necessarily material. It includes the achievement of economic outcomes, the observance of legal requirements *and the attainment of greater cooperation and cohesion.* This latter benefit is the input of normative philosophy into ethical analysis and the determination of moral standards.

The fact that there can be two different moral standards, both of which can be considered to be "right," is confusing to many people. Let me try to clarify this apparent paradox with an example. We will use what I assume will be the familiar example of low-level corruption among South American import customs officials. Let us say that I am from Brazil, one of the countries in South America in which this problem is endemic, and I believe it is morally acceptable to pay small bribes to the customs agents in order to expedite import clearance and shipment to the customer. You, on the other hand, are from the United States, and you find the practice to be morally unacceptable. We differ, though I work for you, in the same company, I don't dwell on the differences.

You come to Brazil; together we shepherd an important shipment through customs. You return to New York and tell your friends at lunch, "I had to pay." They are shocked, or would be if South American customs officials were not so notorious. I have dinner with friends that night, and tell them, "The man didn't want to pay." They are shocked, or would be if North American business practices were not often thought to be so bizarre. Both of us are right, as long as we base our standards on what we believe to be best for society. I think, "Customs agents need the money; our government sets their salary assuming that they make a small percentage." You think, "The system would work better if everyone were much more honest." Both of our standards are based upon what we believe to be best for our society; consequently both are "right."

Now, if we had the time and wanted to make the effort, we could search for a universal principle that would help us to define what we meant by "best" for our society. And if we could measure that "best" in the achievement of economic outcomes, the observance of legal requirements and the attainment of social cooperation, then we might be able to agree on which of our standards was more "right." We can't measure those goods in any comparable sense so we can never really resolve that question. *But, we can come close.*

What I am trying to explain, using this illustration, is that two different moral standards can both be believed to be "right." That is not the same thing as saying that the two different moral standards actually are "right." We have to accept the proposition that we bear some responsibility for other members of our society or life becomes very "solitary, poor, nasty, brutish, and short," for us as well as for others. That responsibility becomes the absolute upon which our ethical systems are based. The difficulty comes in defining the exact terms of that responsibility. That is the function and goal of normative philosophy. Normative philosophy can't do this, but once again *it can come close* because it does focus on the inherent human desires for justice, liberty, dignity, and respect.

This is somewhat in the nature of an aside, but the question of moral relativism—whether moral standards are valid across groups and cultures and times, or whether moral standards just depend upon religious/cultural traditions and economic/social situations—is sometimes applied to business firms. Albert Carr, in a famous article in the *Harvard Business Review* titled "Is Business Bluffing Ethical" (January–February, 1968) suggested that business was a "game" in which different rules apply than in everyday life. It was a game, he said, similar to poker in which no one expected the truth to be fully spoken or agreements to be completely honored. The game players know that some evasions are permitted in company statements; hearers have to be vigilant. The game players also know that some compromises can be made in company products; buyers have to be wary. There are rules that limit the evasions and compromises, but those rules are set by the players themselves and are not fully understood by the public.

It is not difficult to find evidence of this "game" approach to business. Company–union wage negotiations are seldom examples of verisimilitude. Public accountants would not be needed if all financial figures were accurately reported. There is a reason that gas pumps and grocery scales are inspected by a public agency and sealed to prevent tampering. The pictures of a product on the outside of a box frequently do not match the reality of the product on the inside of that box.

What do you think of this view of management as a game, in which almost any act is permitted that the other side does not detect and offset? This is a game in which the rules are set by the players, using their moral standards, which they then claim are "fully as good as anyone else's." How would you argue against this view? This text would suggest that you first come back to the objective and universal absolute that everyone has some responsibility for the well-being of other members of society. This is a moral standard that has been exhibited by every other culture at every other time.

Then, you should question whether the moral standards evidenced in the management as a game approach would benefit society—as measured by the achievement of economic outcomes, the observance of legal requirements, and the realization of social cooperation—as much as the moral standards of a different "tell the truth and don't compromise on quality" approach. It would strike me that the answer to that question was clear. We have to justify our moral standards by showing how they benefit society, not by saying that they benefit us.

Let us say that you accept the basic premise that both you and I bear some form of responsibility for other people within our society, and that our society cannot continue to exist without some standards of behavior between individuals, groups, organizations, and institutions that would benefit all of society. The question then becomes, how do we determine what those standards of behavior should be? We all have an intuitive understanding of what we believe to be "right" and "wrong." The problem is that we don't know exactly how to classify our own actions and those of our neighbors.

The universal recognition that we owe something to other people within our society and should be bound by some objective concept of "right" and "wrong" in our behavior to those people has to be made operational. That is, we have to establish some consistent analytical method to classify our actions as "right" or "wrong." If we can't, it's not for lack of trying. As mentioned before, intellectual history over the past 2,400 years has been filled with attempts to justify subjective and individual moral standards of behavior through objective and universal ethical systems of belief, or "principles." None work perfectly, but six major systems do have a direct relevance to managerial decisions: Eternal Law, Personal Virtue, Utilitarian Benefit, Universal Duty, Distributive Justice, and Personal Liberty.

THE PRINCIPLE OF ETERNAL LAW

The principle of Eternal Law can be summarized in the statement that we should act in the way that our Creator wanted us to act, with kindness and compassion towards others. Many church leaders and some philosophers (Thomas Aquinas and Thomas Jefferson among them) believe that there is an Eternal Law, incorporated in the mind of God, apparent in the state of Nature, revealed in the Holy Scripture or Sacred Writing of each religion, and immediately obvious to any man or woman who will take the time to study either nature or the Scripture and Writings. Thomas Jefferson, really the first of the secular humanists, believed that the truths of this law were "self-evident," in his famous phrase, that the rights were "inalienable," and that the duties could easily be derived from the rights. If people had rights to "life, liberty and the pursuit of happiness," then they had obligations to ensure those rights for others, even if this meant revolution against the British Crown. Religious leaders tend to emphasize the revealed source of the truth more than the reasoned nature, but they also believe that the state of the Law is unchanging, and that the rights and duties are obvious: If we are Loved, then we must love others. This reciprocal exchange is summarized in Christian theology by the Golden Rule: Do unto others as you would have others do unto you.

What is wrong with Eternal Law or Natural Law, interpreted by either religious leaders or normative philosophers, as the basis for an ethical system in management? Nothing, except for the number of interpretations. No two Natural Law theorists, and very few religious writers, have ever been able to agree on the exact provisions of the revealed or reasoned truth. Each religion provides moral standards for its members, and many of the members observe those standards in daily life, but the standards differ between groups, and there is no way to determine which one is "right" or "just" or "fair" for the full society.

Even the Golden Rule, that simple, elegant, sensible guide to life, somehow can't be applied universally. If you were a wealthy man or woman, you would probably want to be able to retain your wealth, and you would be willing to let others retain their wealth as well. If I were a poor person, I would want others to share their benefits and income, and I in turn would be willing to share the little I had. Religious rules of conduct tend to be situation dependent; that is, our interpretation of them seems to vary with our personal circumstances. This may happen because most of our religious injunctions for moral behavior were developed many years ago in an agricultural society that had greater equality between individuals but lesser liberty for each person. The rules are not easily applied in an industrialized and global society where those conditions are exactly reversed.

Let me at this point add that the Golden Rule is not limited to Christianity. It is found in the sacred writings of almost all of the world's religions. The following is a very brief listing, in alphabetical order to ensure no preference or bias, of these totally sensible but not fully applicable statements:

- *Buddhism* (religious creed and ethical system of central and eastern Asia, founded about 460 B.C.). "Harm not others with that which pains yourself."

- *Confucianism* (ethical system added to the existing Chinese religious creed about 510 B.C.). "Loving kindness is the one maxim which ought to be acted upon throughout one's life."

- *Hinduism* (traditional religious creed and social system of the Indian subcontinent). "This is the sum of duty: do nothing to others which if done to you would cause you pain."

- *Islam* (religious creed of western and southeastern Asia, founded about 630 A.D.). "Not one of you is a believer until you wish to everyone what you love for yourself."

- *Judaism.* "What is hurtful to yourself, do not do to others. That is the whole of the Torah, and the remainder is but commentary. Go and learn it."

- *Taoism* (religious creed and philosophic system of northern China, founded about 550 B.C.). "Regard your neighbor's gain as your gain, and regard your neighbor's loss as your loss."

THE PRINCIPLE OF PERSONAL VIRTUE

The principle of personal virtue can be summarized in the statement that we should act in ways that convey a sense of honor, pride, and self-worth. We don't necessarily have to be kind and compassionate to others. We don't necessarily have to be concerned about the rights or benefits of others who are in some way beneath us on any economic, social, or political scale. We do, however, have to be honest, truthful, courageous, temperate, and high-minded. Why? Because the goal of human existence is the active, rational pursuit of excellence, and excellence requires those personal virtues.

The "rational pursuit of excellence"—a goal also often termed "knowledge of the good"—is the basis of ancient Greek philosophy. If you commit those two phrases firmly to your memory, all of the rest of the teachings of Socrates, Plato, and Aristotle will be absolutely clear to you.

2,400 years ago in Athens those three men began to address questions of duties and justice, and they laid the foundation for the Western approach to both politics and ethics. Why in Athens, and why at that time? Greece is a mountainous peninsula, with limited agricultural land suitable for growing grain, but the climate is warm and mild, ideal for olives, grapes, and livestock. There were easy sea routes along the coast to Egypt, then the granary of the Eastern Mediterranean. Egypt had surplus wheat and barley for export, but needed olive oil and wine. A very prosperous trade developed between the two regions. The defeat of the invading Persian army at Marathon in 490 B.C. brought a period of peace in Greece that lasted for 140 years, a time that came to be know as the "Golden Age" of Athens.

Conflicts between the nobles (the ex-warriors), the merchants (the ex-sailors) and the citizens (the current residents) brought an interest in government within Athens. An interest in government brought schools to teach first rhetoric (how to talk to the assembled groups), and then logic (how to convince the assembled groups). An interest in logic led to the question, "What is the good life?"

Socrates (470–399 B.C.) addressed this question, "What is the good life," for both individuals and societies (which, at the time, meant city-states such as Athens). Socrates wrote nothing, yet Plato recorded Socrates' discussions with other Athenians in the form of a set of dialogues soon after the death of the older man, and these can be assumed to be his thoughts if not his words.

The goal of Socrates was to develop the "first rule for a successful life." Successful then meant happy; it would probably now be translated as contented and prosperous. There could be no happiness in the pursuit of pleasure, Socrates continued, or the ownership of property, unless you knew how to use each one of those well. Knowledge of the "good" was then the goal of life. But, knowledge of the "good" came from both the goodness/badness of the character and the wisdom/foolishness of the intellect. It was necessary to develop both so that everyone (nobles, merchants, and citizens) would recognize the "good" both for themselves (ethics) and for their society (politics). Ethics and politics were synonymous in Greek thinking; you could not have one without the other.

Plato (427–347 B.C.) focused on politics, on the need to have a "good" society in order to have a "good" life. He wrote *The Republic,* in which he focused on the concept of justice. Athens at the time, like the other city-states on the Greek peninsula, was divided into statesmen (the leaders of the citizens; they were men of thought), nobles (the warriors, who were men of courage), and merchants (the sailors, who were men of discretion). You needed all three for a "good" (again, contented and prosperous) society. "Justice" was said to be the harmonious union of all three groups of citizens, with each group excelling at what they did best and with no group interfering with the activities of any of the others.

Aristotle (384–322 B.C.) focused on ethics, on the need to have "good" men (and women, though women were not emphasized in the Greek philosophy nearly as much as in the Greek literature of the period) in order to have a "good" society. The goal of a society, he wrote, has to be happiness for all of the citizens. But, what is happiness? Not pleasure, wealth, or fame. People are reasoning animals, he wrote, and thus happiness has to be associated with reason. Given that the active use of reason leads to excellence, then happiness has to be the pursuit of excellence. But excellence can occur on a number of different dimensions, such as openness, honesty, truthfulness, temperance (moderation), friendliness, courage, modesty, and pride. If everyone would strive for excellence on those dimensions, then all of the elements in the diverse society—statesmen, warriors, and merchants, each with different goals, activities, and interests—would work well together.

This ethical principle that "we should be open, honest, truthful, moderate, and proud" of what we do can be translated into very modern terms. Would you be willing to have your decisions and actions relative to a moral problem in which some people are going to be hurt or harmed in some way reported on the front page of a national newspaper, or portrayed on the evening portion of a national news broadcast?

What is the problem with the ethical principle of personal virtue? Being "open, honest, truthful, moderate, and proud" in reality is not enough. Some people can be "open, honest, truthful, moderate, and proud" of decisions and actions that may seem to the rest of us to have been exploitive, mean, and self-centered. But, these very specific dimensions of personal virtue do provide a different perspective from which to view complex moral problems, and they do seem to help in deciding when the question is, "What is the right thing to do?"

THE PRINCIPLE OF UTILITARIAN BENEFITS

The principle of Utilitarian Benefits can be summarized in the statement that we should attempt to create the greatest net benefits for society. This is termed a teleological approach in normative philosophy. It places complete emphasis upon the outcome, not the character or intent, of individual actions. *Teleology* is derived from a Greek term that means outcome or result, and some of the most influential philosophers in the Western tradition—including Jeremy Bentham and J. S. Mill—have held that the moral worth of personal conduct can be determined solely by the consequences of that behavior. That is, an act or decision is "right" if it results in benefits for people, and it is "wrong" if it leads to damages or harm; the objective obviously is to create the greatest degree of benefit while incurring the least amount of damages or harm.

The benefits can vary. Material benefits are not the only ones that count, though they are certainly a good starting place for the calculations, but friendships, knowledge, health, and the other satisfactions we all find in life should be included as well. Think in terms of satisfactions, not pleasures; focusing on pleasures can lead to a very hedonistic and self-centered approach. The aggregate satisfactions or benefits for everyone within society have to be considered.

The benefits are not all positive. There are negative costs and adverse outcomes associated with each action, and they have to be included to establish a balance. The negative costs and adverse outcomes include pain, sickness, death, ignorance, isolation, and unhappiness. The aggregate harms or costs have to be considered, and then a balance of the net consequences can be computed.

This teleological ethical system—focusing on net consequences, not on personal characteristics or individual intentions—is termed Utilitarianism, a moral philosophy originated by Jeremy Bentham (1748–1832), a British thinker. The name of the philosophy is derived from the word *utility,* which had an 18th-century meaning that referred to the degree of usefulness of a household object or a domestic animal. That is, a horse could be said to have a utility for plowing beyond the cost of its upkeep. Utility has this same meaning, and this same derivation, in economic theory; it measures our degree of preference for a given good or service relative to price. In Utilitarian theory, it measures our perception of the net benefits and harms associated with a given act.

Utilitarianism is obviously close to the economic concept of cost–benefit analysis, particularly as the benefits are not to be confused with expediency and have to be calculated for the long-term consequences as carefully as for the short-term outcomes. Utilities, both benefits and costs, have to be computed equally for everyone. My satisfactions, and my costs, cannot be considered to be more important in some way than your satisfactions and your costs. The decision rule that is then followed is to produce the greatest net benefits for society; an act is "right" if, and only if, it produces greater net benefits for society than any other act possible under the circumstances. There are, of course, problems in measuring net benefits—the combination of positive and negative outcomes associated with the act—but mathematical precision is not required; we can approximate the outcomes and include them in our calculations.

Utilitarianism differs from the economic concept of cost–benefit analysis in that the distribution of the costs and benefits has to be included as well. That is, these are net benefits to society, and each individual within the society has to be considered equally and treated equally in the distribution. "The greatest good for the greatest number" takes precedence in Utilitarian theory over "The greatest good for a smaller, more elite number" in cost–benefit analysis. Of course, in full economic theory—as discussed in Chapter 2—the allocation of costs and the distribution of benefits are controlled by impersonal market forces.

To save time and to avoid the need to compute the full consequences of every decision and action, most Utilitarians recommend the adoption of simplifying rules. These rules, such as "always tell the truth" or "never renege on a contract," can be logically shown to lead to beneficial outcomes in all foreseeable cases, but the basis for the rules remains the balance of positive and negative consequences for the full society that comes from every act or decision.

What is wrong with Utilitarianism? Not very much, except for the possibility of exploitation. In the vast majority of cases, where no one is going to be hurt very badly, and particularly where it is possible to use financial equivalents for both the costs and the benefits, it is a familiar and useful form of analysis. But, there is always the possibility of justifying benefits for the great majority of the population by imposing sacrifices or penalties on a small minority. Utilitarianism fails because in reality it is two principles: greatest good and greatest number. At some point in our decision processes on important matters, these two principles come into conflict, and then we have no single means of determining what is the "right" or "best" or "proper" act. Utilitarian Benefits fails as a determinant of moral actions because it is impossible to balance the benefits awarded to the majority against the harms imposed upon a minority.

THE PRINCIPLE OF UNIVERSAL DUTIES

The ethical principle of Universal Duties can be summarized in two statements. Both, as you will soon see, are felt to have exactly the same meaning. You can't apply one to a moral problem without also applying the other, but the two formulations are thought to help in understanding the single principle. The first statement is, "Take no action that you would not be willing to see that others, faced with the same or an equivalent situation, should also be free or even forced to take." The second statement is, "Treat each person as an end in himself or herself, worthy of dignity and respect, never as a means to your own ends."

This is a deontological approach to managerial ethics. In essence, it is the reverse of teleological theory. *Deontology* is derived from another Greek term; it refers to the duties or obligations of an individual. This ethical principle states that the moral worth of an action cannot be dependent upon the outcome because those outcomes are so indefinite and uncertain at the time a decision to act is made. Instead, the moral worth of an action has to depend upon the intentions of the person making the decision or performing the act. If I wish the best for others, then my moral actions are praiseworthy, even though I happen to be an ineffectual and clumsy individual who always seems to be breaking something or hurting someone. It is assumed that we are not all clumsy and ineffectual people, and therefore that good intentions will normally result in beneficial outcomes.

Personal intentions can be translated into personal duties or obligations because, if we truly wish the best for others, then we will always act in ways to ensure those beneficial results, and those ways become duties that are incumbent upon us rather than choices that are open to us. It is our duty to tell the truth. It is our duty to adhere to contracts. It is our duty not to take property that belongs to others. Truthfulness, legality, and honesty can be logically derived from the basic principles of all ethical systems. In deontological theory they are the duties that we owe to others, while in teleological theory they are the actions that bring the greatest benefit to others.

Our personal duties are universal, applicable to everyone, and consequently much of deontological theory is also termed Universalism, just as large portions of teleological theory are called Utilitarianism. The first duty of

Universalism is to treat others as ends and not as means. Other people should be seen as valuable ends in and by themselves, worthy of dignity and respect, and not as impersonal means to achieve other people's ends. No actions can be considered to be "right" in accordance with personal duty if they disregard the ultimate moral worth of any other human being.

Immanuel Kant (1724–1804) proposed a simple test for personal duty and good will, to eliminate self-interest and self-deception and to ensure regard for the moral worth of others. The test is to ask yourself whether you would be willing to have everyone in the world, faced with similar circumstances, forced to act in exactly the same way. This is the Categorical Imperative; *categorical,* of course, means absolute or unqualified, and the precept is that an act or decision can be judged to be "right" and "just" and "fair" only if everyone must, without qualification, perform the same act or reach the same decision, given similar circumstances.

Kant starts with the simple proposition that it is unfair for me to do something that others don't do or can't do or won't do. This is not because the total effect upon society might be harmful if everyone took the same action, such as refusing to pay taxes. That would be a utilitarian doctrine based upon outcomes rather than a universal precept based upon duties. Instead, all of us owe others the duty of acting logically and consistently. I have a "will," or a view of the way I want the world to be, and my views must be consistent or I would have a "contradiction in wills," which would not be fair to others given my duty to act logically and consistently. That is, I should pay taxes not because if everyone else did not pay taxes the government would collapse and there would be chaos. Instead, I should pay taxes because I want a world of law and order, and therefore I must also want to provide the financial support for that law and order. Law and order and taxes are right for me if, and only if, they are right for everyone else—that is, if they are "universalizable." Kant can be understood as an attempt to tie moral actions to rational decisions, with rationality defined as being based upon consistent and universal maxims. Moral standards, according to Kant, are characterized by logical consistency.

The two formulations by Kant—(1) to act only in ways that I would wish all others to act, faced with the same set of circumstances, and (2) always to treat other people with dignity and respect—can be viewed as a single injunction. The first version says that what is morally right for me must be morally right for all others. Everyone is of equal value. If this is so, then no person's rights or benefits should be subordinated to anyone else's rights or benefits. If that is so, then we must treat all people as free and equal in the pursuit of their interests, which means that they must be ends, worthy of dignity and respect, rather than means to our own ends.

Universal Duties, particularly when supported by the Categorical Imperative test, is a familiar and useful guide to moral behavior. The common law is a form of Universalism: Everyone, faced with a just debt, should pay that debt and no one, needing money, should rob banks. Company policies that have a legal or ethical content are usually Universalist: All personnel managers, in considering promotions and pay increases, should include length of service as well as individual ability; and no product manager, in setting prices, should contact competitors or agree to trade constraints.

What is wrong with the principle of Universal Duties? It is a useful method of moral reasoning, but there are no priorities and there are no degrees. I might will that law and order be absolute, with no opposition to the government outside of the formal electoral process, while you might prefer greater personal freedoms. I might will that everyone pay taxes at 7 percent of their annual income, while you might believe that a graduated income tax would be more equitable. The principle of Universal Duties is another ethical system that seems to depend upon the situation of the individual for interpretation. Even the more basic formulation of the Categorical Imperative to treat each other as moral objects, worthy of dignity and respect, provides very limited help. It is difficult to treat others as ends and not as means all the time, particularly when so many people do serve willingly as means to our personal ends: Storekeepers are means of procuring our dinners; customers are means of earning our livelihoods; employees are means of staffing our factories. Both formulations of the Categorical Imperative have to be filled in with either Utilitarian Benefits (I should want some rule to be a universal law if the consequences of its adoption would be beneficial to others) or with Personal Virtues (I should want some rule to be universalized if I can be open, honest, truthful, and proud of its adoption). But, those additives have to come from outside the formal Universal Duty concepts.

THE PRINCIPLE OF DISTRIBUTIVE JUSTICE

The principle of Distributive Justice can be summarized in one simple statement: Never take any action that would harm the least among us, those with least income, education, wealth, competence, influence, or power. We don't have to help those people in the lower ranks of our society to any great extent; we just should never harm them.

None of the three classical theories—Personal Virtues, Utilitarian Benefits, and Universal Duties—can be used to judge all moral actions under all circumstances, and consequently two modern ethical systems have been developed based upon the primacy of a single concept rather than the advocacy of a single rule. The first of these, the principle of Distributive Justice, has been proposed by John Rawls, a member of the Harvard faculty. It is explicitly based upon the primacy of a single concept: justice. Justice is felt to be the first value of social institutions, just as truth is the first value of belief systems. Rawls explained that our beliefs, no matter how useful and complete, have to be rejected or revised if they are found to be untrue. In the same fashion our norms, no matter how efficient or accepted, must be reformed or abolished if they are found to be unjust.

Professor Rawls proposes that society is an association of individuals who cooperate to advance the good of all. Therefore society and the institutions within it are marked by conflict as well as by collaboration. The collaboration comes about since individuals recognize that joint actions generate much greater benefits than solitary efforts. The conflict is inherent because people are concerned by the just distribution of those benefits. Each person prefers a greater to a lesser share and proposes a system of distribution to ensure that greater share. These distributive systems can have very different bases: to each person equally, or to each according to his or her need, to his or her effort, to his or her contribution, or to his or her competence. Most modem economic systems make use of all five principles: Public education is, theoretically, distributed equally, while welfare payments are on the basis of need, sales commissions on the basis of effort, public honors on the basis of contribution, and managerial salaries on the basis of competence.

Professor Rawls believes that all of these assorted distributive systems are unjust. He suggests that the primacy of justice in the basic structure of our society requires greater equality. Free and rational persons, he suggests, would recognize the obvious benefits of cooperation and, concerned about the just distribution of those benefits, would accept social and economic inequalities only if they could be shown to result in compensating benefits for everyone. "Everyone," particularly, should include the least advantaged members of our society: poor, unskilled, and with native intelligence but little education or training. According to Rawls, I would not object to your having more of the social and economic benefits of cooperation than I do, but I would not work hard, beyond the minimum level of effort required to maintain my present standard of living, just so that you could have more. I would want to share in that "more," or—at the very least—I would want to be assured that I would not lose the little I already had.

It is not hard to find evidence of this attitude within our society, so the theory of Distributive Justice does appear to have considerable empirical support. Professor Rawls, however, starts not with our society, but with society in a "natural state." This is the Veil of Ignorance existence at the beginning of time when people were still ignorant of the exact nature of the differences among them, when no one knew who was the most talented, the most energetic, the most competent or—for that matter—the most grasping. What reciprocal arrangement, he asks, would people under those conditions make for the just distribution of the benefits produced by their cooperation? This is the familiar idea of the Social Contract, and the basic question is, What principles would free and rational persons, concerned with furthering their own interests yet wishing to maintain the cooperative efforts of all, adopt as defining the fundamental terms of their association?

They would not select absolute equality in the distribution of benefits, Professor Rawls argues, because they would recognize that some of them would put forth greater efforts, have greater skills, develop greater competencies, and so on. They would not agree to absolute inequality based upon effort, skill, or competence because they would not know who among them had those qualities and who lacked them, and consequently who among them would receive the greater and the lesser shares. Instead, they would develop a concept of conditional inequality, where differences in benefits had to be justified, and they would propose a rule that those differences in benefits could be justified only if they could be shown to result in compensating benefits for everyone. "Everyone," once again, would have to include the least advantaged members of society. That is, the distribution of income would be unequal, but the inequalities would have to work for the benefit of all, and they could be shown to work for the benefit of all if it was obvious that they helped in some measure the least advantaged among us. If those people were helped in some small measure, or at least stayed the same, then it would seem clear that everyone else benefited to some greater extent, and then everyone would cooperate to produce even larger benefits.

Distributive Justice can be expanded from an economic system for the distribution of benefits to an ethical system for the evaluation of behavior in that acts can be considered to be "right" and "just" and "fair" if they lead to greater cooperation by all members of our society. What are the problems with this concept of distributive justice? It is entirely dependent upon an acceptance of the proposition that social cooperation provides the basis for all economic and social benefits. Individual effort is downplayed, if not ignored. We all recognize that some organized activities would never take place unless some one individual was willing to take the risks and responsibilities of starting and directing those activities. That individual effort is ignored in Distributive Justice: It forms the basis, however, for the sixth and last ethical principle to be discussed.

THE PRINCIPLE OF CONTRIBUTIVE LIBERTY

The principle of Contributive Liberty can be also be summarized in one simple statement. Never take any action that would interfere with the rights of everyone—not just the poor, the uneducated and the weak—to develop their skills to the fullest. We don't have to help people. We just can never interfere with their attempting to help themselves.

The theory of Contributive Liberty (the phrase is my own, developed to contrast with Distributive Justice) is an ethical system proposed by Robert Nozick, also currently a member of the Harvard faculty. This system is another based upon the primacy of a single value, rather than a single rule, but that value is liberty rather than justice. Liberty is thought to be the first requirement of society. An institution or law that violates individual liberty, even though it may result in greater happiness and increased benefits for others, has to be rejected as being unjust for all.

Professor Nozick agrees that society is an association of individuals, and that cooperation between those individuals is necessary for economic gain, but he would argue that the cooperation comes about as a result of the exchange of goods and services. The holdings of each person, in income, wealth, and the other bases of self-respect, are derived from other people in exchange for some good or service, or are received from other people in the form of a gift. An existing pattern of holdings may have come about through application of any of the principles of distribution. These would be (1) to each equally, or to each according to (2) need, (3) effort, (4) contribution, or (5) competence. The patterns of holdings can be changed by transfers and those transfers by exchange or gift can be considered to be "just" as long as they are voluntary. Nonvoluntary exchanges or gifts, based upon the use of social force or other coercive means, would clearly be unjust.

Contributive Liberty can be expanded from essentially a market system for the exchange of holdings to an ethical system for the evaluation of behavior as long as individuals are allowed to make informed choices among alternative courses of action leading towards their own welfare. Those choices could be considered to be "right" and "just" and "fair" as long as the same opportunities for informed choices were extended to others. Justice, then, depends upon equal opportunities for choice and exchange, not upon equal allocations of wealth and income. What is wrong with this concept of liberty? It is based upon a very narrow definition of liberty that is limited to the negative right not to suffer interference from others; there may also be a positive right to receive some of the benefits enjoyed by others. That is, the right to life is certainly the right not to be killed by your neighbors, but it may also include the right to continue living through access to some minimal level of food, shelter, clothing, and medical assistance. And, it is assumed that the food, shelter, clothing, and medical assistance are produced through personal initiative, not through social cooperation.

CONCLUSIONS ON THE PRINCIPLES OF NORMATIVE PHILOSOPHY

There are six major ethical systems, as summarized in Figure 4–2. They do not outwardly conflict with each other. An action such as lying that is considered "wrong" in one ethical system will generally be considered "wrong" in all others, but these ethical systems cannot be reconciled into a single logically consistent whole. Eventually conflict will arise over the primacy of the alternative norms and beliefs. Each ethical system expresses a portion of the truth. Each system has adherents and opponents. And each, it is important to admit, is incomplete or inadequate as a means of judging the true moral content of managerial decisions and actions.

FIGURE 4–2

Summary of Beliefs and Problems in the Five Major Ethical Systems

	Nature of the Ethical Systems of Belief	*Problems in the Ethical Systems of Belief*
Eternal Law	Moral standards are given in an Eternal Law, which is revealed in writings or apparent in nature and then interpreted by religious leaders or humanist philosophers. The belief is that everyone should act in accordance with the interpretation of the Law.	There are multiple interpretations of the Law, but no method to choose among them beyond human rationality, and human rationality needs an absolute principle or value as the basis for choice.
Personal Virtue	Moral standards are applied to the character of the person taking an action or making a decision. The principle is that everyone should act in a way in which they can be open, honest, truthful, and proud.	Some people can feel proud and be willing to be open, honest, and truthful about actions that many other people believe to be absolutely "wrong."
Utilitarian Benefits	Moral standards are applied to the outcome of an action or decision. The principle is that everyone should act to generate the greatest benefits for the largest number of people.	Immoral acts can be justified if they provide substantial benefits for the majority, even at an unbearable cost or harm to the minority; an additional principle or value is needed to balance the benefit–cost equation.
Universal Duties	Moral standards are applied to the intent of an action or decision; the principle is that everyone should act to ensure that similar decisions would be reached by others, given similar circumstances.	Immoral acts can be justified by persons who are prone to self-deception or self-importance, and there is no scale to judge between "wills." Additional principle or value is needed to refine the Categorical Imperative concept.
Distributive Justice	Moral standards are based upon the primacy of a single value, which is justice. Everyone should act to ensure a more equitable distribution of benefits, for this promotes individual self-respect, which is essential for social cooperation.	The primacy of the value of justice is dependent upon acceptance of the proposition that an equitable distribution of benefits ensures social cooperation.
Contributive Liberty	Moral standards are based upon the primacy of a single value, which is liberty. Everyone should act to ensure greater freedom of choice, for this promotes market exchange, which is essential for social productivity.	The primacy of the value of liberty is dependent upon acceptance of the proposition that a market system of exchange ensures social productivity.

The major implication for managers of this listing is that there is no single system of belief, with rationally derived standards of moral behavior or methods of moral reasoning, that can guide executives fully in reaching "proper" ethical decisions when confronting difficult moral problems. A moral problem, to repeat the earlier definition and sharpen the present discussion, is one that will harm others in ways that are beyond their own control. A decision to introduce a new brand of chocolate cake mix has no moral dimensions since others within the society are perfectly free to buy or to ignore the product. But a decision to close the plant producing the cake mix, or to use a high-cholesterol shortening in the production of that mix, or to ask for government help in shutting off imports competitive to that mix, would have a moral content. Those actions do have an impact upon others. A product manager, faced let us say in an unlikely but perhaps not totally unrealistic problem of imported cake mixes from a foreign country that has very low wage rates and very high government subsidies, has to respond, and each response has moral implications. Lowering production means cutting employment; reducing the cost means compromising the quality; and requesting government help means endorsing restrictions.

There is no single system of belief to guide managers in reaching "proper" ethical decisions to difficult moral problems, but this does not mean that all of us are on our own, to do as we like in our decisions and actions that affect others. We do have obligations to other people. We cannot ignore those obligations. The difficulty comes in identifying our obligations and then in evaluating our alternatives, with no single set of moral standards to guide us.

What should we do? Instead of using just one ethical system, which we must admit is imperfect, we have to use all six systems and think through the consequences of our actions on multiple dimensions. Is this decision one of which we can be open, honest, truthful, and proud, or do we have to hide it and hope that no one notices? Is this action kind and compassionate, and does it lead to a greater sense of community, of brotherhood/sisterhood? Does this decision or action result in greater benefits than damages for society as a whole, not just for our organization as part of that society? Is this decision self-serving, or would we be willing to have everyone else take the same action when faced with the same or similar circumstances? We understand the need for social cooperation; will our decision increase or decrease the willingness of others to contribute? We recognize the importance of personal freedom; will our decision increase or decrease the liberty of others to act?

Moral reasoning of this nature, utilizing all six ethical systems, is not simple and easy, but it is satisfying. It does work. It works particularly well when combined with the economic outcomes and legal requirements forms of analysis. That combination, and its organizational consequences, will be the topic of Chapter 5, "Why Should a Business Manager Be Moral?"

CASE 4–1

The Good Life at RJR Nabisco

RJR Nabisco was formed June 1, 1985, as a result of a merger between R. J. Reynolds Tobacco Company and National Brands Corporation. National Brands was itself the result of an earlier merger between National Biscuit Company (crackers and cereals) and Standard Brands (packaged foods).

The products of RJR Nabisco are generally well known. They include Camel, Doral, Salem, Vantage, and Winston cigarettes; Ritz, Premium, and Triscuit crackers; Oreo, Chips Ahoy, and Fig Newtons cookies; Fleischmann's and Blue Bonnet margarine; Shredded Wheat and Cream of Wheat cereals; Planters peanuts, Life Savers mints, Baby Ruth candy bars, Royal gelatins, Del Monte canned fruits, Grey Poupon mustard, and Milk-Bone dog food. The sales of the consumer products of RJR Nabisco have steadily increased since the merger, helped by the strong cash flows from the tobacco products. It is said that cigarettes and pipe tobacco are ideal "cash cows"; that is, they have high margins and steady sales in a mature market and consequently provide excess cash that can be used for other corporate purposes. The excess cash provided by the cigarettes was used at RJR Nabisco to promote the food products, which in turn achieved high margins on expanding sales in a growth market. The profits of RJR Nabisco expanded even more rapidly than did sales. The simplified income statement below shows this growth in million of dollars.

	1985	1986	1987	1988
Sales revenues	$11,622	$15,102	$15,766	$16,956
Cost of goods sold	6,024	7,920	8,221	16,956
S & A expenses	3,646	4,842	4,991	5,322
Financial costs	380	660	848	577
Income taxes	662	718	527	893
After-tax profits	$ 910	$ 962	$ 1,179	$ 1,393

The steady tobacco cash flows and the expanding corporate profits funded a lifestyle at the corporate headquarters of RJR Nabisco that was described in a national newspaper as "a monument of free-spending, nouveau-riche excess" (*The Wall Street Journal*, January 4, 1990, p. B1).

Executives were very well paid. Mr. F. Ross Johnson, the chairman and chief executive officer, received $3.5 million in 1988. The next 31 persons (whose salaries were published in total, not individually, in the 10K annual report for that year) received an average of $458,000 each. These salaries may seem low when read in later years; they were considered to be munificent in 1988.

Executives also received numerous "perks." All of the senior managers at corporate headquarters, and many of the functional and technical people at the divisional offices, were given an allowance of $10,000 a year for estate planning, tax assistance, and investment counseling. Everyone at the managerial rank received at least one country club membership and was given at least one company car. Executives could select their own country club and their own car model. Some managers received multiple club memberships; Mr. Johnson held the record with over 24 club memberships spread across the country. Some managers selected very luxurious cars; the record here was a special Mercedes Benz said to have cost over $200,000.

Office decorations at the corporate headquarters matched the managerial salaries, perks, and cars. *The Wall Street Journal* reported that Mr. Johnson's office included a $51,000 vase, a $36,000 table, and a $100,000 rug (Ibid.).

Expensive furnishings even extended to the corporate jet hangar at the Atlanta airport. The RJR Nabisco jet hangar was not a sheet metal building of the type that is commonly seen at airports. Instead, it was a three-story building of tinted glass, surrounding by $250,000 in landscaping. A visitor entered through a tall open atrium, with a roof made of glass panels, floors laid in Italian marble, and walls paneled with Dominican mahogany. In the pilots' lounge and control room were $600,000 in furniture and $100,000 in paintings and statuary.

RJR Nabisco employed 36 pilots and co-pilots and maintained 10 corporate jets in a fleet commonly known as either the RJR Air Force or Air Johnson. The pilots and planes were used to carry managers to workday meetings and inspection tours, of course, but they were also used to bring sports figures, entertainment stars, and elected officials to Atlanta for weekend outings. The sports figures and entertainment stars were paid to be representatives for the company but spent much of their time playing golf and socializing with the senior executives:

> [Mr. Johnson] took excellent care of them, paying more for occasional public appearances than for an average senior vice president: [Don] Meredith got $500,000 a year, [Frank] Gifford $413,000 plus a New York office and apartment, golfer Ben Crenshaw $400,000 and golfer Fuzzy Zoeller $300,000. The king was Jack Nicklaus, who commanded $1 million a year. (Bryan Burrough and John Heylar, *Barbarians at the Gate: The Fall of RJR Nabisco,* New York: Harper & Row, 1990, p. 95)

It was said that many of the representatives for RJR Nabisco did very little "representing." Jack Nicklaus, for example refused to make more than six appearances a year, and he didn't like to play golf with RJR Nabisco's largest customers or meet with them at the evening cocktail parties and dinners.

> Then there was the O. J. Simpson problem. Simpson, the football star and sports announcer, was being paid $250,000 a year but was a perennial no-show at RJR

events. So was Don Mattingly of the New York Yankees who also pulled down a quarter million. Johnson didn't care. Subordinates took care of those and other problems. He was having a grand time. "A few million dollars," he always said, "are lost in the sands of time." (Ibid., 95)

Class Assignment.   Is this lifestyle of the senior executive officers at a major U.S. corporation "right" or "wrong" in your opinion? Should it be continued, or should it be stopped? Be prepared to support your belief; don't just say "yes, it's o.k. to continue" or "no, it should be stopped" in class and then remain silent. Why is the lifestyle "right," or why is it "wrong"? This text has emphasized the following method of analysis to justify your decisions:

1. What groups benefited from the corporate lifestyle?

2. What groups were harmed by the corporate lifestyle?

3. What groups were able to exercise all of their rights under the "good life"?

4. What groups were denied some of their rights under the "good life"?

5. How should you express the moral problem (if you think that this situation constitutes a moral problem) so that each of the individuals and groups will believe that you fully recognize and completely understand their particular problems and concerns?

6. What are the economic benefits? The rule is that you should always take the action that will generate the greatest profits for the company because this will also generate the greatest benefits for the society, provided it can be shown that all markets are fully competitive, all customers are fully informed, and all external and internal costs are fully included.

7. What are the legal requirements? The rule here is that you should always take the action that most fully complies with the law because the law in a democratic society represents the minimal moral standards of all of the people within that society, provided it can be shown that the goals, norms, beliefs, and values of all of the various individuals, groups, and organizations have been equitably considered in the formulation process.

8. What are the ethical duties? The rules here are that you should always take the action that you (1) would be proud to see widely reported in national newspapers; (2) believe will build a sense of community among everyone associated with the action; (3) expect will generate the greatest net social good; (4) would be willing to see others take in similar situations in which you might be the victim; (5) believe does not harm the "least among us"; and (6) think does not interfere with the right of everyone to develop their skills to the fullest.

9. What is your decision, and how would you explain that decision to the other individuals and groups that are going to be affected by your decision or action?

CASE 4–2

The Leveraged Buyout of RJR Nabisco

On October 15, 1988, the stock of RJR Nabisco was selling at $56 per share. The company was a conglomerate, put together during the period 1978 to 1985 by means of mergers of R. J. Reynolds (cigarettes and other tobacco products), Standard Brands (coffee, tea, margarine, candy, wine, and liquor), the National Biscuit Company (cookies, crackers, and breakfast cereals), and Del Monte Corporation (canned goods).

On October 20, Ross Johnson, the chairman and chief executive officer of RJR Nabisco, announced an offer to "take the company private" at $75 per share. Taking the company private meant that RJR Nabisco, supported by the investment firm Shearson Lehman Brothers, was offering to buy back, from the existing shareholders, all of the common stock of the company. The assets of the company were to be pledged as security for the bank loans and corporate bonds needed to pay for that common stock, in a process known as a "leveraged buyback." The company would then be restructured, which meant that new common stock would be sold to the members of the corporate management team and the partners in the investment banking firm who had arranged the buyback. The new common stock would not be publicly traded on one of the stock exchanges but would be privately held by the investors. Consequently, the complete process was termed "taking a company private through a leveraged buyout or leveraged buyback."

How exactly does a leveraged buyout (an offer to purchase all of the stock by an outside group of "raiders") or a leveraged buyback (an offer to purchase all of the stock by an inside group of managers) work? It is easiest to explain the complete process as a series of steps:

1. The investor group, whether outside raiders or inside managers, puts up approximately 10 percent of the purchase price in cash, using either their own resources or those of an investment bank. Investment banks have traditionally been willing to commit their capital to facilitate a buyout or buyback because they receive substantial fees for advising on the transaction, substantial commissions for the eventual sale of the corporate bonds, and a substantial portion of the equity of the restructured firm.

2. Then the investor group, relying on the assets of the company as collateral, borrows 30 percent to 40 percent of the purchase price from a syndicate of commercial banks. Commercial banks have traditionally been willing to commit their capital to finance a buyout or buyback because they hold allegedly secure collateral for the loan amounts and they receive substantial fees for the loan commitments.

3. Finally, the investment bank, acting either by itself or as a member of a syndicate of other investment banks, raises the balance of 50 percent to 60 percent of

the purchase price through the sale of high-risk "junk" bonds to savings and loan institutions, mutual bond funds, and investment pension trusts. The savings and loans, mutual funds, and investment trusts have traditionally been willing to invest their capital in these bonds because they receive much higher interest rates than could be obtained in more normal investments.

4. The existing stockholders, including arbitrageurs who buy in anticipation of the price rise that almost inevitably follows a buyout or buyback offer, are paid the bid price of the stock. The stockholders are not forced to sell. They "tender" their stock, or promise to make it available in the event that the buyback or buy-out is completed. The buyback or buyout is completed when a substantial majority of the stockholders (the actual percentage required by law varies from state to state) have tendered their shares.

5. After the buyout or buyback is completed, selected portions of the company are sold in order to repay the bank loans (known as "bridge" loans due to the short amount of time they are expected to be in effect). The company is then owned by the members of the investor group and the partners of the investment bank and is financed by the junk bonds. The high interest charges of the junk bonds continue, of course, and usually no dividends are paid on the common stock in order to use all of the available cash flow to service the debt and repay the bonds. The available cash flow is usually increased by eliminating the luxuries and "perks" of management, and frequently, though not inevitably, by cutting employment, reducing research and development (R&D), closing plants, and halting capital improvements. Once the junk bonds have been repaid, the company can be "taken public" again through a public issuance and sale of the stock on one of the major stock exchanges. Very large profits can be made by the members of the investment group and the partners of the investment bank when (and if) the company can be successfully taken public.

The actual buyout or buyback process is usually not as direct, simple, or straightforward as has been described. Once the first offer has been made, the company is considered to be "in play." Other investor groups make higher offers. Other investment banks propose different terms. Arbitrageurs and private investors buy and sell legally on the public rumors (or illegally on the "inside" information) of higher bids and/or unavailable financing. "Unavailable financing," of course, means that a prior bid that had been considered legitimate must be taken off the market, and the next lower bid becomes the probable price for the buyout or buyback.

In the particular case of RJR Nabisco, Ross Johnson made the initial offer of $75 per share on October 20, 1988. Mr. Johnson said that despite the best efforts of his management team, the price of the stock had remained depressed at $56 per share for a number of years, and he wanted to "increase value for the shareholders."

On October 24, Kohlberg Kravis Roberts (a private banking firm and buyout specialist) bid $90 per share. The firm said that the stock of RJR Nabisco was obviously worth much more than the $75 per share offered by Mr. Johnson and questioned his motives in making the original offer at "such an unrealistic figure."

On November 4, Mr. Johnson and Shearson Lehman Brothers increased their bid to $92 per share. They claimed, in making the new offer, that Kohlberg Kravis Roberts wanted only to "break up" the company (divide it into its basic product divisions of tobacco, coffee, tea, etc.) and sell off those pieces to the highest bidder, which often meant to a foreign firm wishing to enter the U.S. market. Mr. Johnson, on the other hand, said that only "poorly performing" divisions would be sold under his restructuring plan.

On November 5, a spokesperson for Kohlberg Kravis Roberts released to the press an internal document from RJR Nabisco that detailed the agreement between the company and Shearson Lehman Brothers. It was not explained how Kohlberg Kravis Roberts had obtained the copy, though it is frequently assumed in investment banking arrangements of this nature that a dissatisfied member of the management team or an excluded person in the investment bank has sold the document, for very substantial amounts of cash.

The document stated that Ross Johnson and "six to nine other executives" (the other executives were not named, and it was unclear why the number might vary) would receive 8.5 percent of the stock in the new company at the successful completion of the buyback. The balance of the stock was to go to the partners at Shearson Lehman Brothers and to a series of wealthy private investors and university endowment funds that were providing the original 10 percent of the purchase price and (in small amounts, as a "sweetener") to some of the savings and loans, mutual funds, and pension trusts that were expected to purchase the junk bonds.

The stock percentage allocated to Mr. Johnson and his fellow executives was to increase to 20 percent, provided "certain conditions were met." These conditions involved the sale of over 50 percent of the divisions of the company, both those that were classified as "poorly performing" and others that were operating profitably, by certain times and at certain figures, in order to rapidly repay all of the bridge loans and some of the junk bonds.

The 8.5 percent of the stock in the company allocated to Mr. Johnson and his fellow executives was to be purchased for $20 million in total (not $20 million from each executive). The company was to provide an interest-free loan of $20 million to the group in order to facilitate that purchase. The additional stock, if the certain conditions were met, was to be provided as a "bonus."

The amounts of stock, which were to go to other Shearson Lehman Brothers partners, wealthy private investors, university endowment funds, and junk bond purchasers, were large and apparently promised a return of 35 percent to 50 percent per year upon the investment, but these amounts and returns were common in leveraged buyouts and buybacks and raised no concerns among members of the financial community.

The amounts of stock, which were to go to Mr. Johnson and the "six to nine other executives," were considered to be unprecedented by people within the financial community. If RJR Nabisco were valued at the most recent offer of $92 per share for all of the stock in the firm, then the company as it currently existed was worth $22 billion. Granted that the stock to be issued to Mr.

Johnson and the small group of other executives would be in the restructured firm, after the issuance of junk bonds, it still had to be assumed that the $92 bid price represented Mr. Johnson's accurate valuation of the worth of the company's assets. Mr. Johnson and "six to nine other executives" were to be given stock worth $1.87 billion and were required to invest only $20 million in the form of a non-interest-paying loan from the company. If the "certain conditions" of the buyback were met, that small group would receive additional stock worth $2.53 billion as a "bonus," for a total of $4.40 billion. Members of Congress and representatives of the media expressed both shock and outrage.

On November 7, a spokesperson for Frostman Little, a private investment bank, said that the very large amounts of capital being used to compensate members of management indicated that the value being placed upon RJR Nabisco was still too low and announced a new offer of $97 per share. Frostman Little, a relatively small investment bank, said that it was financially supported by Procter & Gamble, Castle & Cook, and Ralston Purina, all large manufacturers and marketers of packaged consumer goods and food products. It seemed obvious to members of the financial community that arrangements had already been made by Frostman Little for the purchase of the nontobacco divisions of RJR Nabisco by those manufacturers and marketers and that, consequently, the $97 bid approached an accurate valuation for the firm.

On November 16, Ross Johnson and Shearson Lehman Brothers raised their bid to $100 per share and announced that the package of compensation for the senior executives had been "misunderstood" and was being rescinded. It was not stated exactly what compensation arrangements would be made to replace that original "package." It was known that Kohlberg Kravis Roberts was planning to rebid before the final deadline of November 23, and it was thought that Frostman Little might do so also.

Ross Johnson and the partners at Shearson Lehman Brothers realized that they would have to submit another bid, higher than their current offer of $100 per share, to defeat the other contestants. They had invited Salomon Brothers, a very large investment banking firm with expertise in selling junk bonds, to participate in the bidding process. The participants in that process began to gather shortly after 9:00 in the morning of November 23 to set the price and terms of the final bid, which was due at the offices of Skadden Arps (attorneys for RJR Nabisco) at 5:00 that afternoon.

The problem was to select a number, above $100 per share, that would just barely exceed the final bids from the other competitors. Those final bids, of course, were unknown. Consequently, the selection process became a guessing game. No one wanted to name a specific figure and become personally responsible for the eventual success or failure of the largest buyout in the history of the merger movement. Everyone wanted someone else to name that figure and assume that responsibility. For six hours, interrupted by telephone calls to and from friends, informants, and experts, the investment bankers and company executives alternatively considered and then avoided talking about the size of the final bid in an aura of increasing urgency and concern. *The Wall Street Journal* (January 4, 1990, p. B1) reported that these supposed sophisticated discussions of financial market economics were punctuated with cries of "Let's get on with it," "Christ, we need a *** number," "If you don't make up your minds soon, we'll have no bid at all," and "Can you believe this? I can't believe that this is happening."

Just after 3:00, a number was selected, apparently at random (no one ever claimed responsibility). The number was $114 per share. That figure had to be entered into the formal bid, a six-inch-thick package of cash flows, pro forma statements, repayment schedules, loan guarantees, and interest rates, all of which were influenced by this final price for the company. Across Manhattan, at commercial banks, law offices, and accounting firms, the numbers were computed and telephoned or faxed to the 87th floor office of Shearson Lehman Brothers where the bid package was being assembled. At 4:20, four attorneys were ordered into a cab with the incomplete bid package and a portable telephone; they were to write in final numbers during the trip to the law offices of Skadden Arps, where the bid was due precisely at 5:00.

Traffic in Manhattan is never light, and this was a Friday afternoon when it is traditionally very heavy. The cab was soon stopped in traffic. It was obvious that the bid would be not delivered to the law offices on time. The four attorneys bolted from the cab and sprinted along the sidewalks in a desperate effort to reach Skadden Arps before 5:00:

> When [the] breathless group reached Skadden Arps, their path was blocked by a throng of photographers and television cameras. The newsmen, spotting the portable phone, crowded around and began shouting questions. The attorneys plunged like fullbacks through the assemblage and into the lobby.
>
> As Truesdell [leader of the group] and his three companions spilled from the elevator on the upper floor, their way was blocked by an enormous security guard. A minute later, Truesdell was escorted into the reception area where, exhausted, he handed over a binder containing the group's bid.
>
> [He] looked at his watch. It was 5:01. The largest takeover bid in corporate history was late. He prayed no one would notice. (Bryan Burrough and John Helyar, *Barbarians at the Gate: The Fall of RJR Nabisco*, New York: Harper & Row, 1990, p. 401)

On November 29, the board of directors of RJR Nabisco announced that it would recommend to the stockholders of the company that they accept the new bid from Kohlberg Kravis Roberts at $109 per share. The bid from Ross Johnson and Shearson Lehman Brothers (the one that had arrived at 5:01 on November 23) at $114 was rejected. Complex tax reasons were given for the rejection of the higher offer, but it was widely believed that the original bid at $75 per share, which was now considered to have been far too low, and the compensation package, which had always been considered to have been far too high, were also responsible. Ross Johnson retired from the company he had tried to purchase with a "golden parachute" said to be worth $56 million.

Mr. Johnson obviously benefited from the leveraged buyout of RJR Nabisco, even though he had lost in the bidding process. Who else benefited and who was harmed, and what were the extent of those benefits and harms? The balance of the case will discuss those two issues.

It is difficult to tell exactly the extent of benefits and harms in most leveraged buyouts because the published information is so limited. Once a company has been "taken private," the owners no longer have a requirement to file quarterly financial reports. And the reports they do file are not truly comparable to those of the earlier firm because so many of the divisions have been sold. It is possible, however, to make some estimates of benefits and harms based upon "rules of thumb" that are generally accepted in the financial community. Using those rules of thumb, it can be said that the following groups probably will receive reasonably substantial benefits from the leveraged buyout of RJR Nabisco:

1. Members of investor groups can receive huge returns. The actual rate of return depends upon the ability of the investor group to quickly sell some of the divisions, cut many of the expenses, and repay much of the debt before it takes the company public once again. The usual rule for a successful buyout is a compound return of 35 percent to 50 percent per year for the five years needed to prepare the company for the public sale. For RJR Nabisco, this would mean a profit of $11.2 billion to $18.9 billion, given an original investment by Kohlberg Kravis Roberts and others of $2.5 billion (10 percent of the total price).

2. Company stockholders also do very well. RJR Nabisco stockholders, including the arbitrageurs who purchased shares only after the first hint of the takeover attempt, were paid $109 per share for stock that had been selling on the open market at $56 per share just five weeks previously. It is said that more than 500 residents of Durham, North Carolina, where the original R. J. Reynolds Tobacco Company had been headquartered and run in paternalistic fashion until the merger with Nabisco, became instant millionaires as a result of stock they had received years earlier as employee benefits. Company stockholders in total received $12.15 billion above the prior market value of the stock as a result of the leveraged buyback.

3. The investment banks receive fees for providing takeover advice and commissions for arranging the sale of corporate junk bonds. The usual rule is that 1.5 percent of the final price goes to the investment banks on the winning side. Kohlberg Kravis Roberts had retained Wasserstein Perella, Morgan Stanley, and Drexel Burnham Lambert to assist in the takeover. It is estimated that they received $375 million. The investment banks on the losing side receive far less; it is thought that Shearson and Salomon Brothers shared about $25 million.

4. Merger and acquisition attorneys receive fees both to assist and to fight takeovers. The usual rule is 1 percent of the final price. It is estimated that all of the law firms involved in the RJR leveraged buyout (including Davis Polk whose attorneys sprinted along the sidewalks of Third Avenue to reach the filing location on time) received $250 million.

5. Commercial banks receive fees to commit the funds needed for the secured loans in the buyout. The usual rule is 0.7 percent of the final price, even though the commercial banks finance only 30 percent to 40 percent of the cost and the rest is raised through the sale of junk bonds. The purchasers of the junk bonds can be

further compensated by receiving portions of the equity as "sweeteners." These sweeteners cannot be paid to commercial banks, which are forbidden to own the equity of corporate clients, and consequently they receive "commitment fees." The commitment fees from RJR Nabisco were estimated at $175 million.

Who loses when a company is "taken private" through either a leveraged buyout (outside raiders) or a leveraged buyback (inside management)? The accounting is even more difficult here, for it is problematic to express many of the harms or losses in dollar equivalents, but it is generally believed that three major groups share in the downside:

1. The U.S. government loses due to lower tax receipts. The capital gains of the stockholders are of course taxed when their shares are repurchased at the bid price. The interest payments of the company on the bonds and loans used to finance those repurchases, however, are all tax exempt. The interest payments normally are much larger than the capital gains, and consequently tax revenues to the government decline overall. It has been estimated that the federal government will receive $2.5 billion in capital gains taxes from the takeover of RJR Nabisco but will lose $7.5 billion through interest exemptions in the five years following that takeover, for a net loss of $5 billion.

2. The existing bondholders of the company lose due to lower bond rating. The ratings of the existing corporate bonds are downgraded following issuance of the high-risk "junk" debt needed to finance the buyback. The new debt does not take precedence over the existing bonds, but the very large increase in the total amount of debt decreases the creditworthiness of the firm and consequently the credit rating of the existing debt. At RJR Nabisco, the long-term debt on the balance sheet increased from $3.88 billion before the buyout to $19.7 billion afterwards, and the market value of the earlier debt was reduced by over 30 percent. The State Employees Pension Fund of North Carolina, which had been a substantial investor in the bonds of the R. J. Reynolds Tobacco Company before it merged with the National Biscuit Company, lost $620 million. The close similarity of the loss to the pension fund ($620 million) and the gain to the investment banks ($400 million in total) and law firms ($250 million) did not go unnoticed. The state treasurer said in obvious exasperation, "We could have saved everyone a lot of trouble if they had just sent the bills for the bankers and lawyers directly to us, and forgotten about the buyout."

3. The current employees of the company lose due to company restructuring. It is hard to compare employment numbers and wage/salary payments before and after a leveraged buyout or buyback because so many of the divisions are sold and consequently are no longer included in the database. It has always been assumed that most of the employees stay with those divisions under the new ownership, but recent evidence seems to indicate that this assumption about continued employment within disposed divisions may not be warranted as duplicate offices and plants are consolidated and redundant positions are eliminated. It is usually estimated that 20 percent of the employees in the retained divisions are discharged or asked to take early retirement as a result of the cost-savings moves. RJR Nabisco had 120,334 full-time employees prior to the leveraged buyout; if the 20 percent figure is applied to the retained and disposed

divisions equally, the number of people adversely affected by the leveraged buyout would be 24,100.

Class Assignment.   It has been claimed that leveraged buyouts and buybacks create financial value for the shareholders and for society. In the instance just described of the leveraged buyout of RJR Nabisco by Kohlberg Kravis Roberts, that claim would appear to be true. The benefits of the transaction have been estimated to total $24,165 million, the harms only $5,520 million:

Benefits:	Investor group profits	$11,200 million
	Company stockholders	12,140 million
	Investment banks	400 million
	Attorneys and law firms	250 million
	Commercial banks	175 million
	Total	$24,165 million
Harms:	Government tax losses	$ 5,000 million
	Existing bondholders	520 million
	24,100 employees discharged	not estimated
	Total	$ 5,520 million

Was this leveraged buyout of a major U.S. corporation "right" or "wrong" in your opinion? Be prepared to support your belief; don't just say "yes" or "no" in class and stop. Why was it "right" or why was it "wrong"? This text has emphasized the following method of analysis:

1. What groups benefited from the leveraged buyout?
2. What groups were harmed by the leveraged buyout?
3. What groups were able to exercise all of their rights during the leveraged buyout?
4. What groups were denied some of their rights during the leveraged buyout?
5. How should you express the moral problem (if you think that this situation constitutes a moral problem) so that each of the individuals and groups will believe that you fully recognize and completely understand their particular problems and concerns?
6. What are the economic benefits? The rule is that you should always take the action that will generate the greatest profits for the company because this will also generate the greatest benefits for the society, provided it can be shown that all markets are fully competitive, all customers are fully informed, and all external and internal costs are fully included.
7. What are the legal requirements? The rule here is that you should always take the action that most fully complies with the law because the law in a democratic society represents the combined moral standards of all of the people within that society, provided it can be shown that the goals, norms, beliefs, and values of all of the various individuals, groups, and organizations have been equitably considered in the formulation process.
8. What are the ethical duties? The rules here are that you should always take the action that you (1) would be proud to see widely reported in national newspapers;

(2) that you believe will build a sense of community among everyone associated with the action; (3) that you expect will generate the greatest net social good; (4) that you would be willing to see others take in similar situations in which you might be the victim; (5) that you believe does not harm the "least among us"; and (6) that you think does not interfere with the right of everyone to develop their skills to the fullest.

9. What is your decision, and how would you explain that decision to the other individuals and groups that are going to be affected by your decision or action?

CASE 4–3

Wal-Mart and Expansion into Smaller Towns

Wal-Mart in 1994 was the world's largest retailer, operating a chain of modern discount stores throughout the United States and beginning to expand abroad. It had started as a single shop selling work clothes and household items in Bentonville, Arkansas, in 1969, but grew rapidly to a total of 2,136 stores handling a wide variety of consumer goods at the date of the case. The annual return to the shareholders since the 1980 listing on the New York Stock Exchange has averaged 32 percent; $10,000 invested at that time was worth $487,000 in 1994. The founder, Sam Walton, was known for his "folksy" approach to employees, customers, and stockholders alike. He drove a pickup truck to work through all the years of his company's growth and was the wealthiest person in the United States at the time of his death in 1993.

The success of the Wal-Mart chain has been extensively studied, and it's outstanding financial performance is said to be based upon six strategic concepts that combine to produce large sales volumes and low operating costs at each of the stores:

- Wide selection. The typical Wal-Mart carries 35,000 items, about 35 percent more than the number handled by other discount chains such as K-mart or national retailers such as Sears.

- Low pricing. The typical Wal-Mart has a price structure that is 5 percent to 8 percent lower than other discount chains, and 15 percent to 20 percent below the national retailers.

- Niche placement. The typical Wal-Mart store is located in a rural community, with very low taxes, wages, and land costs, but then draws upon a large customer base in a 30-mile radius.

- Accurate data. Wal-Mart was the first large retail organization to build an on-line, real-time information system for prompt sales analysis and precise inventory control.

- Direct shipment. Wal-Mart shares its sales and inventory data by store with suppliers, who arrange for direct restocking without intermediate warehousing.
- Central purchasing. Wal-Mart purchases all items for all stores through a central buying unit that offers long-term large-scale contracts in return for very low prices.

The large selections and low prices bring customers from relatively long distances, and consequently Wal-Mart generally develops a strip mall with a large grocery store as the other anchor tenant, and adds fast-food restaurants and specialty shops selling noncompeting items between the two main chains stores to concentrate shoppers at a one-stop location and collect rents from the other merchants. The strip mall is generally built as an interconnected line of single-story concrete block buildings with bare steel truss roofs, filled with 250,000 to 360,000 square feet of packed display shelves and surrounded by 12 to 15 acres of asphalted parking lots and illuminated advertising signs. The resultant mall is huge. It is cheap. It may be unattractive, but it is efficient. And it is often resisted by local people for all four of those reasons.

The resistance is concentrated, of course, among the local merchants in the downtown areas of the local communities who are concerned about their loss of business to the new complex, if it is built. The local merchants are often joined by property owners and vacation visitors who are more worried about the shoddy appearance of the mall and its impact upon their traditional way of life. Together, these groups make the following points in their arguments:

- The downtown section will be "ruined" as the small locally owned stores will be forced to close; they simply cannot compete against Wal-Mart's economies of scale.
- The landscape also will be "ruined"; the large-scale architecture and huge parking lot of the new malls simply don't "look right" in an attractive rural setting
- The vacation appeal may not be ruined, but it certainly will be harmed; people don't want to drive hundreds of miles to find the same urban sprawl they left behind.
- The tax base will be altered; downtown businesses typically pay a large percentage of the town taxes. Once those businesses close the burden shifts to the home owners.
- The job base will also be altered; downtown businesses and vacation resorts provide most of the local employment. Changes here could be disastrous.

The traditional response of Wal-Mart managers has been that they provide lower prices and better selections for local consumers, who are consequently much better off, and that the taxes they pay and the jobs they offer more than make up for whatever taxes and jobs are lost when local businesses close. Wal-Mart does not dispute that local businesses will close; their avowed aim is to dominate local retailing within every area in which they operate. In the few instances where that has not happened, Wal-Mart has simply closed the store and abandoned the mall. Numerous economic studies have confirmed the probable retail dominance; a new Wal-Mart strip mall will generally result in the closing of 35 to 40 local businesses within two to three years, which usually are boarded up rather than replaced. Those same economic studies show that the Wal-Mart strip mall does not quite make up for employment and tax losses, falling about 20 percent to 25 percent behind in both categories, also within the first two to three years.

A number of citizen groups in Petoskey, Michigan, have been particularly adamant in opposing a recently announced plan by Wal-Mart to build a large (360,000 square foot of retail space) mall on 67 acres of farmland the company owns adjacent to Route 131, the southern entrance into town. Petoskey is an old and picturesque village or town situated directly on the shore of Lake Michigan, about 30 miles south of the Straits of Mackinac at the top of the lower peninsula.

Petoskey was originally the site of a trading post and mission school for Indians. Development was slow until the arrival of the railroad in 1870. During the next 25 years Petoskey grew rapidly as a resort area due to the inherent attractiveness of the region, easily reached by lake steamers or passenger trains from Grand Rapids, Kalamazoo, and Chicago. By 1985 there were 24 hotels and boarding houses, together with a thriving business district, all built with distinctive red brick architecture. The Methodist Church, which had run the mission school, converted its property to an educational camp for families and added numerous cottages, lecture halls, concert facilities, and a downtown park along the waterfront. Gas lights installed at this time still operated in 1994. Restaurants and shops were intermingled, and customers tended to stroll the downtown area in the evening in an evocation of earlier days in small town America.

Some factories for food processing—the climate and soil close to the shore have long been known for producing superior fruits and vegetables—and furniture manufacturing using hardwood lumber from the nearby forests were started in the southern part of the town in the early 1900s, but those had mostly closed by the latter half of the century. A very small K-mart had been built in one of the abandoned factories, but Wal-Mart had refused to consider similar remodeling of an existing building as an alternative due to the lack of parking, the inadequate space for product storage, and the inherent inefficiency caused by older, multiple-storied buildings.

Petoskey in 1995 was a prosperous, attractive town with a year-around population of 3,500 people that served as the trading center for Emmet County, which had a permanent population of 23,700 more. There were also 15,200 summer residents who owned property within the county, primarily along the shore, close to Petoskey. The area was almost totally dependent upon tourism during both the summer and winter; numerous golf courses and ski areas had been built close to the lake during the 1960s and 1970s, and these facilities attracted a constant stream of short-term visitors.

Technically it was illegal for Wal-Mart to build upon the farmland that it owned, which had been zoned for farm, residential, or "light" commercial use.

No one had ever anticipated that a large mall might be built on that site, though it was one of the few that was flat enough for commercial construction within the region. The original intent had been that the farmers might want to set up roadside stands to sell vegetables; that was the reason for the lenient zoning restrictions, to make it easier for the local farmers to survive. Courts, however, tended to interpret "light" commercial use broadly, and Wal-Mart was known for aggressive legal tactics, using large numbers of corporate attorneys in continuous hearings, suits, and appeals to simply override opposition. Small towns did not have the resources to oppose that effort. Vermont had successfully opposed Wal-Mart's entry into scenic or historic areas, but zoning restrictions there were both set and upheld by the state, not by the community.

Surveys of the Petoskey and Emmet County population bases have brought mixed results. A market research study conducted by an agency for Wal-Mart found that 47 percent of permanent residents in Petoskey and 62 percent of permanent residents in Emmet County approved of the concept of a new discount store for the obvious reasons: wider selections and lower prices. Among summer residents throughout the area, however, 93 percent opposed the plan. Opposition leaders took photographs of an existing Wal-Mart strip mall in southern Michigan and of the boarded-up central shopping district in that same town five years after the mall opened. They displayed 24-inch by 36-inch enlargements of those photos in the lakeside park of Petoskey under the printed question, "Do you want this urban sprawl in our town?" And they gathered 22,000 signatures opposing the project over just a three-week period.

Class Assignment. You are the Michigan district manager for Wal-Mart. Petoskey is one of the few remaining "untapped" areas in the state; the nearest Wal-Mart stores are 45 to 60 miles away, at Gaylord to the east and Mackinac City to the north. At both locations store closings and the decay of the central business district did follow the introduction of the discount chain; neither, however, is a tourist destination so the impact upon tourism can't really be measured and then applied to Petoskey. You have just received the appeal signed by 22,000 people saying, "Please don't destroy our town; we love it just the way it is." What do you do, and why?

You realize that it will not be easy to find an alternative site near the town. This is an area of steep hills; there is little flat land close to the lake, and much of that has been taken for the numerous golf courses and summer homes. There are a number of suitable sites, large enough for the planned mall and flat enough for the needed construction, inland about 12 miles, but that is the area of lowest population density. Most people in Petoskey and Emmet County, permanent residents and summer visitors alike, live close to the shoreline.

It is one of the prime messages of this course that whatever course of action you decide will create the proper balance of benefits and harms, and of rights and wrongs, you have to be able to explain that decision to everyone affected by it. If you simply say, "It's in our best interests to do this, and we have many more resources and much more power than you do, so we are going to go ahead," you probably will encounter opposition in the future. The text has emphasized the following method of analysis to justify your decisions:

1. What groups will benefit from the expansion into Petoskey?

2. What groups will be harmed by the expansion into Petoskey?

3. What groups will be able to exercise all of their rights under the expansion?

4. What groups will be denied some of their rights under the expansion?

5. How should you express the moral problem (if you believe this to be a moral problem) so that each of the individuals and groups will believe that you fully recognize and completely understand their particular problems and concerns?

6. What are the economic benefits? The rule is that you should always take the action that will generate the greatest profits for the company because this will also generate the greatest benefits for the society, provided it can be shown that all markets are fully competitive, all customers are fully informed, and all external and internal costs are fully included.

7. What are the legal requirements? The rule here is that you should always take the action that most fully complies with the law because the law in a democratic society represents the combined moral standards of all of the people within that society, provided it can be shown that the goals, norms, beliefs, and values of all of the various individuals, groups, and organizations have been equitably considered in the formulation process.

8. What are the ethical duties? The rules here are that you should always take the action that you (1) would be proud to see widely reported in national newspapers; (2) believe will build a sense of community among everyone associated with the action; (3) expect will generate the greatest net social good; (4) would be willing to see others take in similar situations in which you might be the victim; (5) believe does not harm the "least among us"; and (6) think does not interfere with the right of everyone to develop their skills to the fullest.

9. What is your recommendation, and how would you explain that recommendation to the other individuals, groups, and organizations that are going to be affected by your decision or action?

CHAPTER 5

Why Should a Business Manager Be Moral?

We have looked at economic outcomes (Chapter 2), legal requirements (Chapter 3), and ethical duties (Chapter 4) as means of resolving the moral problems of management and found that none are completely satisfactory. None of those analytical methods can give us an answer that we can say with absolute certainty is "right" and "just" and "fair" when attempting to find the proper balance between the financial outputs and the social impacts of a business firm. And none of those analytical methods can give us a means of truly convincing the other people who have been affected by those outputs and impacts that our decision was indeed the "most right," the "most just," and the "most fair" in attempting to reach that balance.

But why is this important? Why should a manager attempt to be moral in his or her decisions and actions? And particularly, why should a manager attempt to convince other people that he or she has reached the "most right," "most just," and "most fair" decision among all of the available alternatives? Perhaps we should all simply resolve not to lie, cheat, or steal, and then begin to look after the interests of the firm that has hired us to the very best of our abilities. Then we could forget about any need to be moral beyond those elementary "don't lie, cheat, or steal" rules, and particularly, we could forget about any need to convince others of the logical nature of our morality. A totally amoral person—one who did not stop to think about the "rightness" and "justness" and "fairness" of his or her decisions but instead concentrated upon profits for his or her employer and benefits for his or herself—might be expected to be far more successful in purely financial terms for both entities over any reasonable period of time. Why should we all not do exactly that?

The answer on one level is that if we want others to worry about whether their treatment of us is "right" and "just" and "fair," then we have to worry about our treatment of them. Reciprocity is the most logical reason for morality. But the world is filled with people who are not logical in the sense of recognizing reciprocity and the need to be consistent. The world is filled with people who might well say, "We'll take our chances on your treatment of us later on, after we try to get what we want now, and if we do indeed get what we want now, then we won't have to worry about your treatment of us later on." How do we react to those people? Do we simply cede to them the first place in financial benefits and managerial positions and hope that eventually they will learn that "what goes around comes around"? That is not a very satisfactory solution for most of the rest of us, who under that rationale would be forced to wait and hope for an eventual solution.

Beyond reciprocity as the reason for our moral actions towards others, however, is—or perhaps ought to be—our concern for the quality of our lives. If we are concerned about the sort of profession we have entered, the sort of organization we have joined, the sort of society we are constructing, and the sort of person we are becoming, then we have to start thinking about our duties and responsibilities to others. What do we really owe to our professions? What do we really owe to our employers? What do we really owe to our society? What do we really owe to ourselves? And how do we reach a balance among all of those duties and responsibilities?

These are questions that people have worried about for centuries. In 399 B.C. Socrates was put on trial in Athens for having "corrupted the youth of the city." He argued in his defense that all he had done was to ask the young people who attended his classes to consider the goals and standards of their lives. There was nothing wrong with this, he claimed, and ended with the closing statement that "The unexamined life is not worth living."[1] You can certainly interpret that expression following your own understanding, but perhaps he is saying that everyone should examine their duties and obligations to their professions, their organizations, their communities, and themselves. If so, it is necessary to get down to basics.

The most basic question in ethics is, "Do you have an obligation to leave the world a little better than you found it, or can you simply take what you want now, and let other people worry about making up for any shortfall later on?" Many people do recognize a personal obligation to other people to some extent, but have never thought strongly about its nature and terms and have never applied that general duty to their specific responsibilities to their professions, their organizations, their communities, and themselves. And, it has to be recognized that there are some other people who choose to ignore this injunction to "leave the world a little better than they found it." The question once again is do we cede to those people the first place in financial rewards and managerial positions, and only hope that eventually they will become concerned with the quality of their lives and the nature and terms of their obligations to others. Perhaps we need something more than reciprocity of treatment and quality of life as the reason to be moral.

TRUST, COMMITMENT, AND COOPERATIVE EFFORT

Beyond reciprocity of treatment and quality of life, the third argument in favor of moral action in management is that of cooperative effort. Organizations are composed of individuals and groups who have to cooperate to be successful. In business firms we call those individuals and groups stakeholders.

The term *stakeholder* was clearly composed to contrast with the more familiar *stockholder*. A stockholder is a person who owns a company. A stakeholder is a person who is associated with a company and, in a famous phrase, "can affect or is affected by the achievement of the organization's objectives."[2] The stakeholders in a business firm include the factory and office workers, functional and technical managers, senior executives, scientists and engineers, suppliers, distributors, customers, creditors, owners, and local residents. All, clearly, have an interest, a "stake," in the future of the firm. All, equally clearly, must contribute their efforts through cooperation and innovation if that future is to be successful and secure.

But, why should these various individuals and groups contribute their best efforts, and be cooperative and innovative, for an organization that appears not to care about them? You are a worker on an assembly line in a factory. I am the manager of that factory. I recently downsized some of your friends who also worked on that assembly line. I have gradually made changes that increased the speed of that same assembly line. I continually argue that your hourly wages are too high and your health-care benefits too large. But now let us say that you have an idea for a simple change in the design of the product that you are manufacturing that would greatly facilitate the assembly and reduce the cost. After all, you work on that assembly line day after day and hour after hour. You know far more about possible improvements in the manufacturing processes for that particular product than I ever will. Do you tell me about your idea?

The argument of this chapter is that under current conditions you probably will not tell me about your idea to greatly increase efficiency and reduce cost in my factory. Why? I would assume that you would not tell me because you would not trust me. You would think that I would take credit for the idea, ask for and receive a large bonus from the owners for having invented it, and fire a few more of your friends because your idea saved so much time and effort that they were no longer needed. I might even fire you so that I would not have to worry about your telling others that the idea for which I have received so much credit and reward was in reality your own.

What should I do in order to get you to tell me about your new idea? Perhaps I can do nothing now, but perhaps earlier I should have established an attitude that everyone within the company could expect to be treated in ways that could rationally be explained to be "right" and "just" and "fair." Perhaps I should have been moral.

Maybe the basic answer to the "Why be moral?" question is the need for a manager to build trust, commitment, and effort among all of the individuals and groups associated with his or her organization. Maybe trust is the essential first step, and perhaps we can't get commitment and effort without that trust. And, maybe trust is built upon our making and explaining our decisions and actions in a way that most people—we can probably never convince all—can agree to be "right" and "just" and "fair." This is the first basic argument of this chapter, that, as shown in Figure 5–1, trust of this nature requires a recognition of moral responsibility, an application of moral reasoning, and a possession of moral character or courage:

- Moral responsibility is the recognition of moral problems. Perhaps this is the most essential managerial function of all: Before we can start to think seriously about a moral problem we first have to comprehend that people are actually being hurt or harmed or are having their rights denied by our company's decisions or actions. Many managers don't want to know if this is happening. If they don't know, the reasoning goes, they can't be held responsible. Perhaps, however, the only true social responsibility managers can be said to have is to know what is happening to the members, the stakeholders, of their organizations.

- Moral reasoning is the process of examining and then resolving these recognized moral problems in a way that will be convincing to others. We can't just say, "Well, this will certainly benefit us so I know you'll understand," or "I feel badly that this is happening to you, but we want to move forward." We as managers have to logically explain our decisions and actions and rationally consider the economic outcomes, the legal requirements, and the ethical duties of the situation. Otherwise we cannot build the trust, commitment, and effort among all the individuals and groups associated with the firm that will enable us to move forward.

- Moral character is the possession of courage to first recognize a moral problem and then propose a "just" solution. Many managers are not willing to face up to moral problems. They are not willing to say, "This is what is happening to some of the individuals and groups associated with our firm. These are the alternatives. And, this is what I recommend and why I recommend it." They fear that their action will not be popular in some parts of their firm. That is why courage is a part of character and why integrity—the willingness to act on principle—is essential to build trust among all of the stakeholders in extended organizations.

FIGURE 5–1

Building Trust, Commitment and Effort within Organizations

Corporate management in extended organizations

{

Recognition of moral problem
    What is "duty"?

Application of moral reasoning
    What is "right"?

Possession of moral character
    What is "integrity"?

}

Trust
Commitment
Effort

EXTENDED ORGANIZATIONS

What is an "extended organization"? The term is used in Figure 5–1 on the development of trust, commitment, and effort, and is included in the subsequent discussion of those characteristics. Extended organization is an extension of the stakeholder concept. Companies have become not only much larger, but also more dependent upon a wider ranger of other firms and institutions, beyond the formal boundaries and hierarchical controls of the firm. Material and component suppliers, for example, are clearly outside the formal boundaries and direct controls of a producing firm, yet they can easily influence the quality and cost of that company's goods and services. Many suppliers now participate in the original design of those goods and services, almost on a partnership basis, and most are now relied upon for just-in-time inventory systems where failure to deliver could shut down the product lines of their customers. Figure 5–2 provides an extended view of business organizations.

Wholesale and retail distributors, as another example, are also outside the formal boundaries and hierarchical controls of a company, yet they can influence the price of the product, the level of service, and the degree of satisfaction of the final customers. Many distributors are now relied upon not only for the prompt transmission of information about current sales trends, but also for the accurate anticipation of future customer needs. Both are obviously essential for the long-term success of the producing firm.

Commercial banks, investment companies, research laboratories, and educational institutions are further examples of organizations that are outside the command and control hierarchy of a producing firm, yet can influence the long-term success of that company. They provide personnel, technology, equity, and debt. Their cooperation is essential, given the changed conditions of management. Companies with uneducated employees, obsolete methods, or inadequate funds cannot compete in a global environment.

Lastly, industry trade associations, public interest groups, and domestic and foreign political agencies are further examples of organizations that are outside the formal command and control hierarchy of the firm yet can affect the performance of each company. These associations, groups, and agencies help in determining four areas: (1) the national financial policies that set tax rules and interest rates; (2) the national regulatory policies that influence product/process designs and environmental requirements; (3) the national social policies that establish educational achievement levels and health-care costs, and (4) the national infrastructure systems that include the communication networks and the transportation methods.

If you doubt that companies are now dependent upon the governmental policies and national systems listed above, think for a minute about the domestic automobile manufacturers who must meet mileage, safety, and emission standards in their cars and provide educational training and health-care benefits for their workers. It was recently claimed that health-care benefits added

FIGURE 5–2

An Extended View of Business Organizations

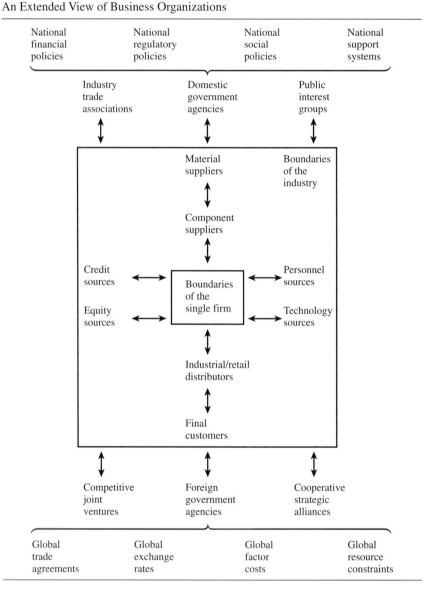

$1,100 to the cost of each American car, a charge not included in the cost of au-
tomobiles produced in Europe or Japan where the health-care system is financed by public, not private, revenues. Companies are starting to compete
based upon their country's educational and health-care systems, in addition to
their own product designs, manufacturing costs, and advertising messages.

COOPERATION, INNOVATION AND UNIFICATION

Let us say that you accept for now that companies have become much larger, more extended, and less susceptible to the hierarchical "command and control" of the formal management structure. What does that mean for management, and particularly what does that mean for the need to be moral, to recognize and resolve the mixtures of benefits and harms and the balances of rights and wrongs that occur in the decisions and actions of the firm? The argument of this chapter is that moral management is necessary to build cooperative effort among the separate stakeholders in large, extended organizations in order to achieve the cooperation, innovation and unification that are needed for success. There are three basic steps in this progression between moral management and organizational success. Each may be called a "thesis" of the chapter:

- *Trust builds committed effort.* The first major thesis is that (1) treating people in ways that can be considered to be "right" and "just" and "fair" creates trust; (2) trust builds commitment, (3) commitment ensures effort, and (4) effort is essential for success. Certainly there will be disagreements among the stakeholder groups on exactly what distribution of benefits and allocation of harms, on precisely what recognition and denial of rights, can be considered to be "right" and "just" and "fair" in any given situation. Certainly some stakeholder groups will prefer one decision or action, while other stakeholder groups will prefer others. But, the first thesis of this chapter is that as long as all of the groups together can agree that the decision process itself has been "right" and "just" and "fair"—that is, that the decision process has considered the interests and rights of each of the groups according to known and consistent principles—then there should be an increase in trust and commitment among all of the stakeholder groups, and that increase in trust and commitment should, in turn, lead to an increase in effort.

- *Committed effort is essential for success.* The second major thesis of this chapter is that the effort that results from stakeholder trust and commitment goes far beyond that which is based only upon financial incentives or commercial contracts. Stakeholder trust and commitment result in a willingness to contribute "something extra," a readiness to act with both energy and enthusiasm for the benefit of the firm. A story by Edward Carlson, then president of United Airlines, illustrates very succinctly this willingness to contribute something extra. Mr. Carlson is quoted as saying, "The president of a company has a constituency much like that of a politician. The employees may not actually go to the polls, but each one of them does elect to do his or her job in a better or worse fashion every day."[3] Employees at all levels electing to do their jobs in better rather than worse fashions is exactly what is meant in this text by contributing something extra. That committed attitude among all of the stakeholders—not just the employees, but suppliers, distributors, agencies, associations, and partners—is essential for the success of organizations today.

- *Success is becoming increasingly difficult to achieve.* The third major thesis of this chapter is that this committed attitude, this willingness to contribute something extra, this readiness to act with energy and enthusiasm for the benefit of the full organization on the part of all of the stakeholders, is more important now than in the past due to the changed conditions of global competition. Companies have become more aggressive. Technologies have become more advanced. Products have become more complex. Markets have become more diverse. Processes have become more oriented towards quality and cost. Customers in both the industrial and consumer segments have become more insistent upon value and choice. Changes in competitors, technologies, products, markets, processes, and customers have become more frequent. And the thoughtfulness, speed, and cost of the firm's reactions to those changes—or even better in their anticipations of them—have become more critical.

UNIFY AND GUIDE

In summary, it is the argument of this chapter that it is no longer possible to manage organizations that must respond intelligently, quickly, and efficiently to technological, product, market, process, or customer changes on a "command and control" basis. Innovation is required, but corporate managers cannot command innovation. Cooperation is essential, but corporate managers cannot control cooperation. Something more is needed, and that "something more" is the trust, commitment, and effort that comes from moral management.

Let us assume that you accept for now the proposal that the old "command and control" form of management is no longer viable. Let us further assume that you also agree that the stakeholder groups—the people who are affected by and in turn can affect the performance of the organization—are now too diverse in their various activities for easy assimilation, and that they now extend too far beyond the hierarchical boundaries for easy direction. The question is, then, what takes the place of the outmoded "command and control" model? What generates a sense of trust, commitment, and *directed* effort?

Directed effort is obviously important. Undirected effort results only in chaos and confusion. But directed effort has to be the result of trust and commitment as well as of direction and planning. This leads us to the fourth major thesis of this chapter. Moral reasoning—the process that leads to a determination of what is "right" and "just" and "fair" in the treatment of others—is not peripheral to corporate management. It is central to corporate management.

Moral reasoning is not something to be considered, if at all, only after the important strategic, structural, technical, functional, and operational decisions have been made. Moral reasoning is not something to be published as a code of conduct that will be handed to each employee on his or her first day at work, and then promptly forgotten. Moral reasoning has to become an integral part of the managerial process. It has to be combined with the other managerial decisions and actions at all levels of the firm to ensure trust, commitment, and directed effort.

The need for trust, commitment, and directed effort leads us to a form of management that might be called "unify and guide" rather than "command and control." Unification is the key. Unification means bringing all of the stakeholders of the firm—those within the company, those within the industry, and those within the society—together into an innovative and cooperative whole. Unification requires recognizing the impacts of company actions—both benefits and harms—upon the stakeholders of the firm and then distributing those impacts through a process that is thought to be "right" and "just" and "fair." Unification, based upon trust, commitment, and effort, is the moral responsibility of management. But it has to be combined with the practical responsibility of guidance.

A NEW METHOD OF MANAGEMENT

Perhaps what is needed is a changed method of management, one that will extend the concepts of trust, commitment, and effort and the results of cooperation, innovation, and unification throughout the firm. The changed philosophy would balance the economic benefits, legal requirements, and ethical duties of the management and be expressed in the values, goals, and missions of the company. This approach is portrayed in Figure 5–3.

What is involved in this new method of management? It is based upon a changed philosophy that attempts to balance economic outcomes, legal requirements, and ethical duties. These, of course, have been the topics of the last three chapters, but let me attempt to summarize these three approaches very briefly:

- *Economic outcomes*, based upon impersonal market forces. The belief here is that a manager should always act to maximize the product revenues and minimize the factor costs of his or her firm, for those actions will in turn generate the greatest material benefits with the least time, money, and material costs to his or her society. This approach is considered to be legitimate only so long as all of the markets are fully competitive (that is, they cannot be manipulated) and all of the costs are fully included (that is, none are ignored because they are external to the firm). The problem is that this approach does not accurately recognize the nature (desire for justice and liberty) nor completely value the worth (need for dignity and respect) of individual human beings. It is a start, but only that. Something more is needed.

- *Legal requirements*, based upon impartial social and political processes. The belief here is that a manager should always act to obey the law for the law can be considered to represent the collective moral standards of the members of his or her society. A manager may not like a law that his or her fellow citizens have passed, but the rationale is that he or she should obey that law for otherwise there will be chaos, with no material benefits for anyone. This approach is considered to be legitimate only as long as each of the stages in the social and political processes by which individual moral standards are coalesced into national legal requirements can be considered to be impartial. They should constitute a "social contract" in which people act for the well-being of society rather than the self-interests of themselves. The problem is that this approach recognizes the desire for justice and liberty and the need for dignity and respect, but the method for achieving those goals is difficult to apply. This approach is a continuation on the earlier economic outcome start, but only that. Again, something more is needed.

FIGURE 5–3

Proposed Relationships between Managerial Decisions and Actions and
Organizational Cooperation, Innovation, and Unification

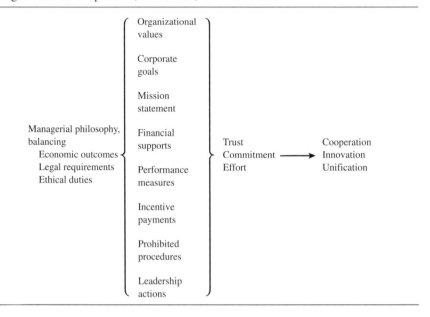

- *Ethical duties,* based upon rational thought processes. The belief here is that a
  manager should always act in accordance with a set of objective norms of behavior or universal statements of belief that can be logically shown to invariably lead
  to a "good" society in which everyone cooperates for the benefit of a common
  goal. This is a society that is not "good" due to material benefit/cost relationships
  (economic outcomes) or social order/freedom balances (legal requirements), but
  "good" due to all of the members following rational principles of conduct that
  eliminate subjective self-interest and substitute objective social interest. The result should be the achievement of justice and liberty and the provision of dignity
  and respect. The problem is that these rational principles of conduct can conflict,
  and there is no agreed-upon order of priority to resolve those conflicts. Again, a
  continuation, not an ending.

The argument of this text is that none of these approaches is complete and
final in and by themselves, but that taken together, in balance, they can lead to
managerial decisions and actions that are "more right," "more just," and
"more fair" than any approach used by itself. We as managers cannot claim
that any one of our decisions or actions is absolutely "right" and totally "just"
and completely "fair," but it is possible to logically explain the moral basis of
those decisions and actions to others.

The further argument of this text is that a sequence of these decisions and
actions that can be shown to be "more right," "more just," and "more "fair"
than all reasonable alternatives should, over time, lead to trust, commitment,

and effort among all of the participants—the stakeholders—in the organization. That trust, commitment, and effort among all of those participants or stakeholders should, again over time, lead to cooperation, innovation, and unification. That cooperation, innovation, and unification should, once more over time, lead to success for both business firms and service organizations operating under competitive global conditions. Why should a manager be moral? It is necessary for success. Let me repeat the earlier graphic representation of these organizational relationships in Figure 5–4.

This approach will be further discussed in Chapter 6, "How Can a Business Organization be Made Moral?" The argument in that chapter will be that it is necessary to infuse the managerial balance among economic outcomes, legal requirements, and ethical duties throughout the firm, rather than leaving that changed philosophy isolated, at the top. For now let me describe very briefly the first three steps in that process of infusion: the need to establish organizational values, corporate goals, and a firm mission statement combining the values and goals. The mission statement is the reason for the company to exist. If you accept that trust, commitment, and effort are essential to the success of the firm for they lead to cooperation, innovation, and unification, then that reason for existence has to reflect values and goals that are meaningful for each and relevant to all of the stakeholder groups:

FIGURE 5–4 _____

Proposed Relationships between Managerial Decisions and Actions and Organizational Cooperation, Innovation and Unification

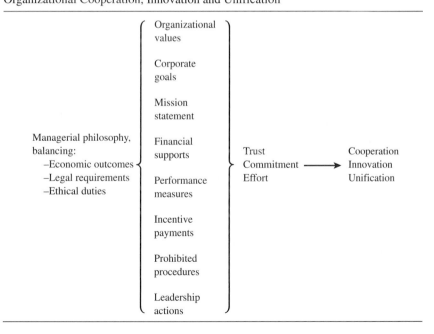

- *Corporate Values.* To avoid easy generalizations think of corporate values as the duties the senior executives of the firm should—in your view—owe to the various individuals and groups associated with the firm who can, in one way or another, affect the future performance and position of the firm. These individuals and groups would include owners of all types (institutional and individual), employees at all levels, customers in all segments, suppliers, distributors, creditors, local residents, national citizens and global inhabitants. What—again in your view—is important to each of these groups? What—once more in your view—should the senior executives of the company recognize as being important to each and to all of those groups? In short, how can the company begin to think about unification based upon similarities rather than separation based upon differences? For each of the cases that follow this chapter, list four or five of these groups in the order of the importance you believe they should hold to the firm, and give some indications of the nature of the duties you believe are owed to each.

- *Organizational Goals.* To avoid easy generalizations think of company goals as the endpoints the senior executives of the firm should—in your view—set for the various dimensions of performance that are possible. What—again in your view—should the senior executives want to accomplish along such dimensions as financial performance, technological achievement, industry position, market share, customer satisfaction, manufacturing efficiency, employee loyalty, environmental protection, public reputation, and social contribution? What—once more in your view—should the various groups associated while the firm want to accomplish on each of these dimensions? Remember that scientists and engineers doubtless would like technological achievement, while the owners and creditors might prefer financial performance. The two may not be as dissimilar as they at first appear; if the organization is well guided there will be an obvious connection between the two. For each of the cases that follow in this chapter, list four or five of these dimensions in the order of importance you believe they should hold to the firm, and give some indications of the nature of the end-points set for each dimension.

- *Mission Statement.* Think of the mission statement as the means of combining the duties that the firm has to others with the goals that it has set for itself. What role, as a result of this combination, should the firm attempt to play within the market, the industry, the economy, and the society? It is frequently difficult to express managerial values and organizational goals in explicit numerical terms. Consequently, many firms compromise with a mission statement that speaks only generally about the duties they want to observe and the end points they want to achieve, but much more specifically about the means they want to use and the standards they want to follow. The intent is to define the future of the firm, the scope of its activities, and the character of its people so that everyone will clearly understand, "This is where we're going to go, this is what we're going to do, and this is how we're going to do it." Think in terms of a document that will create a challenge for everyone associated with the firm. Think also in terms of a document you would be *proud* to hand to employees, to show to customers, to send to suppliers and distributors, and to include in the annual report for owners.

Following this chapter are a series of cases on companies that most people will agree have done nothing "wrong." Instead, they appear to have balanced the economic outcomes, legal requirements and ethical duties of their decisions and actions in a way that many people find to be "right." Were these companies more or less successful as a result of those actions? Put together a list of the corporate values and the organizational goals that you think would accurately reflect the thinking of the senior executives, and prepare a mission statement that you think would create both a point of challenge and a source of pride to everyone associated with the firm.

Footnotes

[1]Plato, "Apology" in *The Dialogues* [of Socrates], trans. B. Jowett. New York: Random House, 1987.

[2]R. E. Freeman, *Strategic Management: A Stakeholder Approach.* Boston: Pitman, 1984, p. 46.

[3] Thomas Peters, and Robert Waterman, *In Search of Excellence: Lessons from America's Best Run Companies.* New York, Harper & Row, 1982, p. 289.

CASE 5–1

Johnson & Johnson and the Worldwide Recall of Tylenol

Johnson & Johnson is a long-established manufacturer of health-care products and pharmaceutical drugs. The company is best known by consumers for products such as Band-Aids and Tylenol tablets, but it is better known by physicians for minimally invasive surgical instruments and highly sophisticated diagnostic systems. It is a firm that has grown consistently over time, with a stock price that went from $12 per share in 1989 to $107 per share in 1999.

The company has a very unusual mission statement, or affirmation of the purpose of the firm, which focuses on corporate duties rather than financial profits. This statement has been widely distributed among active employees, and it is not considered to be "window dressing," or a hypocritical desire to appear socially concerned while everyone really focuses on the bottom line. This was proven a number of years ago when a person in Chicago, for reasons that have never been discovered, put tablets containing arsenic in unsold bottles of Tylenol on store shelves throughout that city and the suburbs. Six people died. It could not quickly be proven that this had occurred purposely at the retail stores in Chicago, and not accidentally at the manufacturing plant in New Jersey. Consequently Johnson & Johnson removed every package of Tylenol from every store in America and abroad in a matter of days, at a cost of over $100 million, to protect its customers. Those packages were later replaced, free of charge, to all retailers and to any customers who returned unused portions of purchased packages, with new drugs in tamperproof containers. The senior executives at the time explained that this prompt and complete response was required by the Credo or Mission of the firm:

> We believe that our first responsibility is for the doctors, nurses, and patients, to mothers and all others who use our products and services.
>
> - In meeting their needs everything we do must be of high quality
> - We must constantly strive to reduce our costs in order to maintain reasonable prices
> - Customer orders must be serviced promptly and accurately
> - Our suppliers and distributors must have an opportunity to make a fair profit
>
> We are responsible to our employees, the men and women who work with us throughout the world.
>
> - Everyone must be considered as an individual. We must respect their dignity and recognize their worth
> - They must have a sense of security in their jobs. Compensation must be fair and adequate and working conditions clean, orderly and safe
> - Employees must feel free to make suggestions and complaints
> - There must be equal treatment for employment, development and advancement for those qualified
> - We must provide competent management and their actions must be just and ethical
>
> We are responsible to the communities in which we live and work, and to the world community as well.
>
> - We must be good citizens—support good works and charities and bear our fair share of taxes
> - We must encourage civic improvements and better health and education
> - We must maintain in good order the property we are privileged to use, protecting the environment and natural resources
>
> Our final responsibility is to our stockholders. Business must make a sound profit.
>
> - We must experiment with new ideas. Research must be carried on, innovative programs developed, and mistakes paid for
> - New equipment must be purchased, new facilities provided, and new products launched
> - Reserves must be created to provide for adverse times
> - When we operate according to these principles, the stockholders should realize a fair return

Class Assignment. The prompt and complete action by Johnson & Johnson was exceedingly well received by consumer advocates within the United States, but there was some grumbling among financial analysts and fund managers. The general feeling among many of the professionals on Wall Street was that $100 million was too large an amount to spend for all stores in all parts of the world. "They should have just taken the product off the shelves in Chicago where the deaths actually occurred, at maybe a cost of $2 million" was a common comment. What is your opinion? Should they have recalled just the Tylenol in the Chicago area and waited to see what would happen, or were they correct in removing the product from all stores everywhere?

1. If you believe that Johnson & Johnson took the correct action by spending $100 million, put together a presentation that the president of the company should make to the Association of Institutional Investors at its next annual meeting justifying that large expenditure.

2. If you believe that Johnson & Johnson was wrong in spending $100 million to recall all of the Tylenol, put together a presentation that the president of the company should make to a Congressional committee explaining that the company took the action only to avoid lawsuits and that the result was a waste of perhaps $98 million that might better have been spent on other health-care needs within the United States. Wind up by requesting a new law that would encourage much smaller recalls until the extent of a problem in product safety became much clearer.

CASE 5–2

Herman Miller and the Protection of the Environment

Herman Miller is a furniture manufacturing company located in Zeeland, just west of Grand Rapids, Michigan. It has traditionally taken a very employee-oriented organizational stance with a strong participatory management process. It has also traditionally taken a very innovation-oriented strategic posture. The company has been very successful in the design, production, and marketing of new furniture and panels for open office and computer usage settings. Employees at all levels, from the factory floor to the executive suite, are expected to participate in the continual improvement of company operations and to experiment with new products, new processes, and—just recently—new recovery methods.

In 1993 the company, with the agreement of employees, made a commitment to totally eliminate all trips to the dump by the year 2003. One of the first steps to implement this goal was the recovery and utilization of waste fabric. Herman Miller made and continues to make an extensive line of cloth-covered office partitions and matching chairs that, even with computerized cutting patterns designed to optimize utilization of the material supplied in 48-inch wide bolts, resulted in 800,000 pounds of small pieces of scrap fabric on an annual basis. For years that material had been taken to a landfill. Starting in 1994 it was shredded and shipped to North Carolina where it was made into insulation for car roof and door panel linings. This saves the company $50,000 in dumping fees, but unfortunately it costs the company about $100,000 above the minimal sales revenues (the material has to be almost given away to the buyer; it can be sold for only pennies per pound) for the shredding and trucking. Senior executives believe that modern manufacturing companies must do more to preserve the physical environment, even at a cost to profits, and they are willing to absorb that net $50,000 loss ($50,000 saving in dump fees less $100,000 cost in shredding and trucking).

As a further example, the company found it was impossible to recycle the 750,000 styrofoam coffee cups Miller employees discarded each year. Consequently they were banished from the firm and the company distributed 5,000 ceramic mugs. The only problem, the executive in charge of recycling now admits, was that they made the new cups too attractive, with the company logo in bright clear color. Now, he explains, it costs more to replace the ceramic mugs that are taken home by visitors as well as employees each year than to buy the styrofoam cups that were thrown away. He feels that the company has taken the correct action, however, saying that the firm is ahead environmentally if not financially.

The company is now recycling leather, vinyl, foam, office paper, phone books, and lubricating oil, and it has reduced the trash it hauls to landfills by 90 percent since the start of the program. As an offshoot of this internal recycling program, in 1995 Miller began an external reuse program. The company offered to buy back, recondition, and then resell any office furniture that it had originally manufactured that was no longer needed by the customer. This program was so successful that Miller recently adopted "cradle to grave" design requirements. Company engineers are now expected to specify materials, such as aluminum and wood, that come apart easily during the reconditioning process and that take little energy and produce few pollutants in recycling. These materials tend to be more costly than the usual steel and plastic, but company managers believe that the investment will pay off in the future.

In 1996 the firm built a $4 million waste-to-energy plant that saves $750,000 a year in fuel and landfill costs. That is not enough to generate a return on capital above operating costs, the company now admits. However, the general feeling of both executives and workers seems to be that they live in a very attractive section of the state, and they have a duty to preserve the environment despite the cost. Western Michigan, close to the shore of Lake Michigan, is a rural area with extensive farms and forests, and executives and workers alike appear to take pride in leading in the preservation effort.

In 1997 the company designed molded plastic shells for its office and home furniture products that are shipped by truck to replace the styrofoam and cardboard packaging that is commonly used by other firms in the industry to protect furniture from damage during transit. These plastic shells reduce both the labor and material costs of packaging, but they have to be returned, which adds to the freight expense. The additional freight is said to be a bit more than the savings in labor and material, but again the company feels that this is a commitment for the future.

In 1998 the company invested $800,000 in two incinerators to burn 98 percent of the toxic solvents that escape from the finishing booths in which wooden furniture parts are stained and varnished. These furnaces go far beyond what is required by the Clean Air Act, but once more company executives defend the investment, saying that the best way is the ethically correct way. They believe that eventually governmental regulations will be increased to meet rising public expectations, and then the company will have the knowledge and the equipment to be cost leaders.

In 1999 Miller plans to totally eliminate the current use of tropical hardwoods such as teak and mahogany and substitute domestic species such as birch and maple even though the latter are much more expensive both to purchase and to use. It takes more time and effort to cut out the natural defects in the wood because boards from local sawmills have many more knots and splits; the trees are much younger and smaller than those from tropical forests. However, replanting the forest is an accepted practice in the Midwest, but not in the tropics. The reason advanced by the company for the proposed change is that it doesn't want to continue destroying the tropical forests. They want, executives explained, to help in forcing those countries to adopt good forestry practices.

Class Assignment.   Financial analysts at large brokerage firms have reported that Herman Miller "wastes" about $1 million per year in special efforts dedicated to preserving the environment. They have recommended strongly that those funds be used to "grow the business" or to be distributed as dividends to the owners. The recommendations of brokerage analysts are taken seriously by most business firms; their recommendations do influence potential investors and affect stock prices.

1. Where do you stand on this "protect the environment despite the cost" issue? Do you believe the money—$1 million is a relatively large amount for this company; profits in 1998 were only $35 million—is "wasted" as the financial analysts claim and instead should be used to grow the business and reward the owners? Or do you believe that the money is well spent?

2. If you believe that the company should continue its environmental preservation efforts, put together a presentation that you would make to the Association of Financial Analysts at their annual meeting if you were the president of Herman Miller. Can you convince them that continuing these expenditures is the "right" thing to do?

3. If you believe that the company should stop its environmental efforts, put together a presentation that you—again if you were the president of Herman Miller—would make to the Sierra Club, a group of very active environmentalists, at their annual meeting. Can you convince them that ending these expenditures is the "right" thing to do?

CASE 5–3

Merck Corporation and the
Cure for River Blindness

Merck is a large (62,300 employees) pharmaceutical company located in Whitehouse Station, New Jersey. The company is primarily known for the productivity of its research and development effort. Literally thousands of prescription drugs have been conceived by their scientists, formulated in their labs, improved through first animal and then human testing, guided through governmental approval, and eventually manufactured and marketed worldwide. The result has been excellent financial performance. Profits for the company in 1994, the date of the case, were slightly over $2 billion for the year. The company, however, proposed to spend $100 million of that to produce and distribute what was called an "orphan drug" for the prevention and cure of a tropical disease known as "river blindness."

Orphan drugs are pharmaceutical prescriptions with little or no commercial potential. Unfortunately they occur very frequently in medical research. Usually they treat a very rare disease, for which the market size is too small or the insurance coverage too limited to enable the firm to recover its costs of development, testing, approval, manufacturing, and marketing. Most pharmaceutical companies simply discard orphan drugs at the outset, while they are still in the concept stage. Merck was unusual. It would, upon occasion, complete the full process, from concept to distribution. But, because most of the orphan diseases Merck addressed were very rare, its expenses were at least partially limited. This would not be the case for river blindness, which afflicted large numbers of people in desperately poor regions of the world. Neither patients nor governments in those regions could afford to pay for the drug. It would have to be given away, at no charge.

River blindness, formally known as onchocercias, is a disease that afflicts some 18 million people in the mountainous areas of Central Africa and Central Asia. It is caused by the bite of a tiny black fly that breeds only in fast-moving rivers and streams; that is the reason for the restriction of the illness to hilly or mountainous terrain with substantial rainfall. That is also the reason for the lack of effectiveness of the most common form of disease control in the tropics: aerial spraying. It is almost impossible to maintain adequate pesticide strength in the rapidly flowing waters of mountain brooks and streams to kill the black fly larvae. Mosquitoes, which transmit malaria to humans in a similar

---

Source: This is a shortened version of an earlier case prepared by the Business Enterprise Trust, and it is used with permission. Cost estimates were derived from local sources.

fashion by drawing blood, are much easier to control through aerial spraying because they breed in stagnant ponds and swamps where pesticide strength can be kept much higher for much longer periods of time.

When the black fly bites a human being to draw blood it frequently enables the larvae of a small parasitic worm carried by the fly to enter the human blood stream. The parasitic worm by itself is not overtly harmful, but when those worms reach maturity they release millions of microscopic offspring, known as microfilariae, which swarm throughout the body tissue. They tend to cluster in the skin, where they cause terrible itching and eventually lead to lesions, infections, and disfigurement. The itching is so severe that many victims resort to suicide. Then, after several years of torment the microfilariae invade the eyes, and the patient becomes blind.

River blindness is a loathsome disease. Until the early 1990s, there was no cure and not even much hope of finding a cure. The nations in Central Africa and Central Asia afflicted by the disease are all Third World countries, without the financial resources to support pharmaceutical research. The peoples infected with onchocercias within those countries are all desperately poor—partially as a result of the debilitating disease—and lack the money to pay for medical treatment. Further, it is scientifically difficult to devise a drug that will kill the parasitic worms in the bloodstream and the microfilariae offspring in the body tissues without killing or severely harming the patient.

In the mid-1980s researchers in the veterinarian drug unit of Merck were working with a range of microbiotic cultures in an attempt to develop a treatment for the parasitic worms that affect cattle, hogs, horses, and other farm animals in the United States. One of these new cultures, code-named Mectizan, had been written off as a failure. It seemed to have no potential as a cure for any major animal diseases, though it was remarkably effective when used against the microfilariae of an exotic and relatively harmless gastro-intestinal parasite found in horses.

One of the researchers, Dr. William Campbell, noted a marked genetic similarity between the microfilariae found in horses that seemed to cause little damage and the microfilariae found in humans that led to river blindness. Dr. Campbell decided to take advantage of a scientific freedom policy at Merck that enabled him to spend up to $500,000 of company funds and invest up to a year of his own time to pursue a prescription drug concept before any formal evaluation of the commercial potential of the drug would be required. He quickly, within a few months, was able to show that the new culture, Mectizan, worked, and worked well, on the river blindness microfilariae growing in a tissue culture derived from human beings. There was, however, no guarantee that it would work equally well on the parasites growing in an actual human being without adversely affecting the health of that human being.

It was necessary to find an animal species, preferably a mouse or rat instead of a dog or cat, for health impact rather than target impact testing. Many people object, on humanitarian grounds, to the use of intelligent and affectionate domestic animals such as dogs and cats for medical research. Dr. Campbell was able to create, by genetic modification, a mouse that could be infected with the microfilariae responsible for river blindness. Mectizan, the new drug, worked remarkably well upon these microfilariae without—apparently—harming the mice. Perhaps a cure for river blindness which, once again, afflicted 18 million people worldwide was possible. But, the review for commercial potential, required at the end of the experimental stage for each new drug, quickly confirmed what everyone, including Dr. Campbell, already knew. These people and the nations they inhabited were too poor to pay for the cure. Despite this lack of commercial potential the Board of Directors of Merck voted to go ahead with human testing.

There were both moral and financial problems with the human testing of Mectizan. Only volunteers were to be used, of course, but in this instance it was not clear that nonliterate tribes people from central Africa and Central Asia would fully understand the risks of their agreeing to participate in the tests. They would hope to be cured, and that was indeed a possibility. They would expect not to be harmed, through that was unfortunately also a possibility. And to ensure the scientific validity of the testing process, approximately half of the volunteers would have to be given a noneffective substitute for the drug—a placebo—to ensure that it was truly the drug, and not some other factor in the environment, that generated the cures.

It would further be necessary to supervise the tests very closely, on the site. It was clearly not possible, given that there was no knowledge of possible adverse reactions, for researchers to simply go to one of the afflicted areas, pass out an equal number of Mectizan pills and ineffective placebos, and say, "So long, we'll see you again three months from now if you're still living." Physicians and nurses had to be there, to judge the reactions, to measure the results, to treat the reactions, and to reassure the patients. Those physicians and nurses would be at considerable risk of contacting the disease themselves. Air-tight and air-conditioned dormitories and treatment centers could be built, at very considerable cost in those remote and poor regions, to protect the medical personnel against the black flies that carry the disease, but there was no assurance that this protection would be complete. And transportation to the remote areas where the disease occurred would add further risks and expenses. The financial costs of these preliminary human tests were estimated at $50 million.

Merck went ahead with the investment for the preliminary human tests. The company recruited medical and scientific personnel from within and from various religious and relief organizations. The tests were outstandingly successful. Next, the drug had to be approved by a governmental licensing agency, which required a totally new series of tests under the supervision of that agency. Merck selected the French Directorate of Pharmacy and Drugs to supervise these new tests, rather than the U.S. Food and Drug Administration, because findings of the French government were more highly valued by African and Asian officials and physicians than equivalent findings of the U.S.

government. France had been the colonial power in the mountainous regions of Central Africa and Central Asia primarily affected by the river blindness disease, and the French had left a legacy of at least partial respect for their medical personnel. The French Directorate, however, provided no funding. The financial costs of the new regulatory tests added another $50 million to the Merck investment.

Again the tests were outstandingly successful, and government approval was quickly granted by the French and grudgingly recognized by the Americans. Now the international marketing department of Merck was drawn into the planning phase, and it further confirmed what everyone had long known: There was no conventional market for the drug. The victims were too poor. The countries in which they lived were too undeveloped. The international communities were too unfeeling.

The president of Merck approached the U.S. government. The State Department said that it approved wholeheartedly of the effort, but claimed that distribution of the drug was the responsibility of the U.S. Agency for International Development, a division of the Treasury Department that made grants and loans for Third World development projects. This agency also expressed admiration for the proposal, but explained that its budget was committed for the next 10 years to capital improvement projects for roads, railways, and dams.

The president of Merck then approached the World Health Organization, a division of the United Nations headquartered in Geneva, Switzerland. That agency, in essence, replied that it would accept donations of the drug but would pay nothing to offset its development and manufacturing expenses, and it would arrange for distribution only to the extent of shipping the materials, once received free of charge, to the governments of the nations involved. This was totally unacceptable to Merck. Company executives feared that government officials in the developing nations of Central Africa and Central Asia would, despite the clear poverty of the victims, sell the drugs for whatever property or labor could be obtained in return. And, company executives believed that the distribution had to be supervised by trained medical personnel. It was thought that victims of the disease, tormented by the itching and frightened of the blindness, would take an overdose on the basis that, "If 1 is good, 2 or even 10 will be that much better."

Members of the Board of Directors at Merck were faced with the possibility that the orphan drug Mectizan that their company had developed and tested at a cost that the company had absorbed of somewhat over $100 million would not be made available to the estimated 18 million people who needed it very badly. They voted an additional $100 million per year to ensure its distribution and use.

Now there were murmurs of dissent from many of the financial analysts associated with the brokerage firms, investment banks, and mutual funds of Wall Street. None of them said publicly that Merck should halt the distribution of the drug. The disease was too awful, the victims too poor, and the need too great for open opposition to be voiced. But, $100 million a year for the foreseeable future—Mectizan did not provide an immunity to the disease, only a cure that had to be made available to each new victim—seemed to many of the analysts to be too large an expense for the company to bear. The analysts claimed that Merck's first duty was to its stockholders, and that the company should delay distribution until governmental and international funding became available. There were numerous letters to financial journals saying, in essence, that business firms were not charitable organizations and should not act as if they were.

Class Assignment.   Dr. Roy Vagelos, a physician who was president of Merck, reported to the Board of Directors that he had made determined efforts to secure funding from the U.S. government, from the French government, from the United Nations, and from numerous charitable foundations. All had said that their funds were committed to other projects, primarily those associated with large-scale economic development. The cure of this disease, even if that could be expected to substantially assist the economic development of the two regions, appeared to be very low on everyone's global list of priorities.

1. Where do you stand on the distribution of Mectizan? Assume that the cost estimates are correct and that distribution will cost $100 million per year. Assume that the drug is very effective and will help 18 million people per year. Should Merck act now and contribute that money on its own, or should it wait and hope for eventual governmental funding?

2. If you believe that Merck should go forward with its plan to spend $100 million per year for the foreseeable future in an effort to cure river blindness in Central Asia and Africa, put together a presentation that you believe Dr. Vagelos should make to the Association of Financial Analysts at its next annual meeting. Convince this group that the expenditure is "right."

3. If you believe that Merck should delay and wait for governmental or international funding, put together a presentation that you believe Dr. Vagelos should make to "Doctors without Frontiers," a group of physicians who volunteer their time to respond to medical emergencies in developing nations. Convince them that the delay is the "right" thing to do.

CHAPTER 6

How Can a Business Organization Be Made Moral?

This book has made five basic arguments. The first is that moral problems in business are complex and difficult to resolve because some individuals and/or groups associated with the firm are going to be hurt or harmed in ways outside their own control, while others will be benefited or helped. Further, some of those individuals and/or groups associated with the firm will have their rights ignored or denied, while others will have their rights recognized and expanded. There is a mixture of benefits and harms, of rights exercised and rights denied, and this mixture makes it very difficult for business managers to decide upon a course of action that they can confidently say is "right" and "just" and "fair" when faced with moral problems.

The second basic argument is that business managers cannot rely upon their moral standards of behavior, or the intuitive ways they just automatically feel about what actions are "right" and "just" and "fair," to make their decisions when faced with moral problems. Moral standards of behavior differ between people, depending upon their personal goals, norms, beliefs, and values, which in turn are dependent upon their religious and cultural traditions and

FIGURE 6–1 _____

The Complex Nature of Moral Problems in Business Management

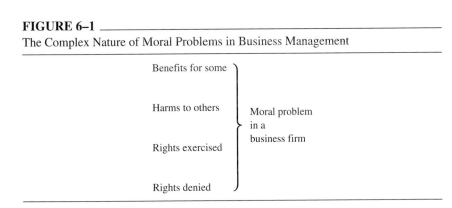

their economic and social situations. The individuals and groups in a global economy come from very different traditions and live in very different situations, and consequently their moral standards of behavior, which are subjective, cannot be used to convince others that the course of action they recommend is "right" and "just" and "fair."

The third basic argument is that business managers have to recognize that the individuals and groups associated with their firms will have different moral standards as to what they believe to be "right" and "just" and "fair." Consequently it is not enough for a manager to simply reach a decision on what he or she believes to be a proper balance of benefits and harms, of rights recognized and denied, in any given situation. Managers have to go further and *be able to explain convincingly why that balance should be viewed as "right" and "just" and "fair."* A convincing explanation requires objective methods of analysis rather than subjective standards of behavior. These

FIGURE 6–2

The Derivation of Subjective Standards of Moral Behavior in Management

Religious/Cultural traditions

↓

Personal goals
Personal norms
Personal beliefs
Personal values

} Subjective standards of moral behavior

↑

Economic/Social situations

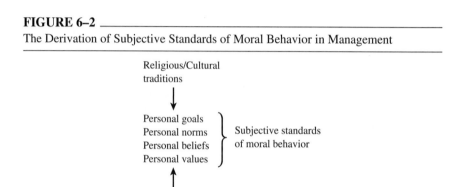

FIGURE 6–3

The Application of Objective Methods of Moral Analysis in Management

Understand all moral standards

Recognize all moral impacts
- Benefits to some
- Harms to others
- Rights exercised
- Rights denied

} Define complete moral problem

{ Determine the economic outcomes

Consider the legal requirements

Evaluate the ethical duties }

Propose convincing moral solution

objective methods of analysis include (1) economic outcomes based upon impersonal market forces; (2) legal requirements based upon impartial social and political processes, and (3) ethical duties based upon rational human goals.

The fourth basic argument is that if this analytical procedure is followed, with a moral solution that is logically convincing to the individuals and groups associated with the firm, the result will be an increase in trust, commitment, and effort among those individuals and groups. Business firms have not only grown in size recently; they recently become "extended" in form. That is, they are now dependent for their success upon a much wider range of individuals and groups within the company, the industry, and the society. The committed efforts of all those individuals and groups, many of them outside the formal structure and consequently the hierarchical control of the company, are essential for the success of the firm. They have to be willing to provide "something extra," a degree of commitment that goes beyond mere gratitude for a paycheck, to generate that success. That willingness comes from trust in the integrity of the management.

The fifth, and last, basic argument is that it is not enough for the senior executives in a firm to recognize moral problems, develop moral solutions, and possess moral integrity in order to build trust, commitment, and effort among all of the individuals and groups associated with the firm. Instead, this sense of integrity has to spread throughout the firm, and that requires a mission statement based upon organizational values and corporate goals and sustained by financial supports, performance measures, incentive payments, prohibited procedures, and leadership actions. Given the increasing intensity of global competition, companies cannot continue to operate successfully without the resulting cooperation, innovation, and unification among all the individuals and groups associated with the firm.

The extension of this changed method of management that combines or balances economic outcomes, legal requirements, and ethical duties throughout the firm is to be the topic of this last chapter. As in the first chapter, we

FIGURE 6–4

Building Trust, Commitment and Effort within an Organization

	Recognition of moral problems What is "duty"?	
Corporate management in extended organizations	Application of moral reasoning What is "right"?	Trust Commitment Effort
	Possession of moral character What is "integrity"?	

FIGURE 6–5 _____

Proposed Relationships between Managerial Decisions and Actions and
Organizational Cooperation, Innovation and Unification

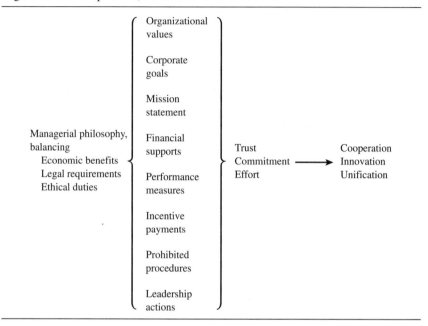

will start with an example. In the first chapter this example was of a major
moral problem in which it was not clear what decision or action the company
—Hydro Quebec—should take. In this last chapter the example will be of a
major moral disaster in which it is very clear what decisions and actions the
company—Exxon Corporation—should have taken, but didn't. We will start
with the wreck of the Exxon Valdez, then use that as an example of how to extend moral responsibility throughout the firm.

EXAMPLE OF A MAJOR MORAL DISASTER

At 9:30 P.M. on Thursday, the 22 of March, the oil tanker *Exxon Valdez* left the
oil terminal at Valdez, Alaska, loaded with 1.26 million barrels of oil. The
Valdez is the largest tanker owned by Exxon. It is nearly 1,000 feet long and
weighs, fully loaded, 280,000 tons.

When the ship left port, it was under the command of Captain William
Murphy, the harbor pilot. Harbor pilots are responsible for steering both in-
coming and outgoing tankers through the Valdez Narrows, a half-mile-wide
approach to the port of Valdez. After exiting the Narrows and achieving the
sea lanes in Prince Williams Sound, Captain Murphy turned over command to
Captain Joseph Hazelwood and left the ship. Captain Murphy testified later

that he had smelled alcohol on the breath of Captain Hazelwood, but that he made no comment and took no action. He knew that it was common practice for both the officers and crew of oil tankers to drink while in port.

Captain Hazelwood, immediately after assuming command, radioed the Coast Guard and requested permission to alter course to avoid large chunks of ice that had broken loose from the Columbia Glacier and were floating in the outbound shipping lane. The permission was granted. Captain Hazelwood then turned over command of the vessel to Third Mate Gregory Cousins and went below to his cabin. Mr. Cousins was not licensed to pilot a ship in the sea channels approaching Valdez. Mr. Cousins and others later testified that it was common practice to turn over command of oil tankers to nonlicensed officers.

Captain Hazelwood had set the automatic pilot to steer the ship southward into the inbound shipping lane, and he had instructed Mr. Cousins to maintain the course until after the ice chunks from the glacier were passed and then to return northward to the outbound lane. No inbound traffic was expected, and permission for this course change had been granted by the Coast Guard, so no danger was anticipated. At 11:55 Mr. Cousins ordered a course change of 10 degrees right rudder to bring the tanker back to the proper lane within the channel. There was no response. At 12:04 the lookout, who was on the bridge rather than at the normal station on the bow of the tanker, sighted the lighted buoy marketing Bligh Reef, a rock outcropping only 30 to 40 feet beneath the surface. Mr. Cousins ordered emergency hard right rudder. Again there was no response. In the hearing that followed the accident, it was determined that either Captain Hazelwood had not informed Mr. Cousins that he had placed the ship on automatic pilot, or that Mr. Cousins and the helmsman had not remembered to disconnect the automatic pilot, which prevented manual steering of the vessel.

At 12:05 A.M. the Exxon Valdez ran aground on Bligh Reef. The hull was punctured in numerous places, and 260,000 barrels, approximately 11 million gallons of crude oil, spilled from the badly ruptured tanks. It was the largest oil spill in the history of the North American petroleum industry.

At 12:28 A.M. one of the officers on the ship radioed to the Coast Guard that it was aground on Bligh Reef. "Are you leaking oil?" a Coast Guard operator asked. "I think so," was the reply.

At 3:28 A.M. members of the Coast Guard boarded the Exxon Valdez and reported that oil was gushing from the tanker. "We've got a serious problem," radioed the Coast Guard officer onboard the tanker. "There's nobody here. . . Where's Alyeska?"

"Alyeska" was the Alyeska Pipeline Service Company, which both managed the oil pipeline that brought crude oil 800 miles from the oil fields at Prudhoe Bay to Valdez and ran the oil terminal at Valdez. It was responsible, through a formal agreement with the state of Alaska, for the containment and recovery of all oil spills within the harbor and sea lanes. That agreement was expressed in a detailed written plan, 250 pages long, that listed the equipment and personnel that Alyeska was to keep available and the actions it was to take to react promptly to oil spills.

The stated goal of the written plan was to encircle any serious oil spill with floating containment booms within five hours of the first report of the occurrence and to recover 50 percent of the spill within 48 hours. The stated goal was well known within the area and accounted for the perplexity of the Coast Guard officer. When he reported, "There's nobody here," he was referring not to the captain and crew of the tanker, but to the oil spill recovery team and equipment from Alyeska.

The Coast Guard officer also noted the smell of alcohol on the breath of Captain Hazelwood and reported to his base in very blunt terms that he suspected the captain was drunk. He was unable to establish the degree of intoxication, due to the lack of a testing kit, but he did request the assistance of the Alaska State Police to conduct the tests as soon as possible. Those tests were conducted the following morning, and they did establish that the level of alcohol in Captain Hazelwood's bloodstream at the time was twice the legal limit.

At 6:00 A.M. on Friday, March 23 (six hours after the accident), officials from Exxon flew over the grounded tanker for the first time, and they reported a massive oil slick streaming away from the tanker. They contacted the Alyeska oil terminal and ordered a quicker response and greater effort. The problem, the manager at that terminal reported, was that the single barge capable of handling the long containment booms had been out of service for two weeks and had been unloaded for repairs. Workers were preparing to reload the barge, he said, but the only employee who was capable of operating the crane needed for reloading had not yet reported for work. Later that morning the loading was completed and the barge was taken in tow by a harbor tug. At 2:30 P.M. the barge arrived at the wreck site, carrying all of the containment booms that were available at the terminal and a number of centrifugal pumps to help in removing the remaining oil from the Valdez.

At 7:36 A.M. on Saturday, March 24th (31 and a half hours after the accident), Exxon began pumping oil from the *Valdez* to a second tanker moored alongside, the *Baton Rouge*. At about the same time, seven Alyeska "skimmers," or barges with vacuum equipment designed to siphon oil off the surface of the water, arrived at the site. The skimmers, however, were designed to recover oil that had been bunched in a compact mass by containment booms. Those booms were still not in place due to a shortage of tugs and to some degree of confusion in the means of unloading the booms and placing them in the sea. By nightfall, only 1,200 barrels of oil had been recovered.

By 11:00 A.M. on Sunday, March 25 (59 hours after the accident), the *Exxon Valdex* was finally encircled by containment booms. It had taken two and a half days to get the booms in place, despite the original plan that called for full containment of any spill within five hours. Most of the oil was now outside the booms in a slick that covered 12 square miles, and the wave action had begun to convert the crude oil to an emulsified "mousse" mixture of oil and water that quadrupled the volume. This emulsified mixture now lay five to nine inches thick upon the surface of the sea. The specific gravity of the emulsified mixture was very different from the specific gravity of either water or oil, and the skimmers were no longer effective except when working on fresh seepages close to the grounded tanker, within the booms.

At 6:00 A.M. on Monday, March 26 (78 hours after the accident), the Coast Guard admitted that the situation was out of control. The first two days had been calm, but Sunday night winds as high as 73 miles per hour had arisen and driven the emulsified oil and water mixture 37 miles from the wreck site. It was swathing the islands and beaches throughout Prince William Sound with solid bands of black petroleum "gunk," the accepted term for the residue that is left after the more volatile elements in crude oil have evaporated. The skimmer barges and boom-tending boats had been forced to retreat to sheltered water. Flights into the Valdez airport, bringing additional supplies and people, had been halted. Most of the oil that had remained in the unruptured tanks of the *Exxon Valdez* had been pumped out, but it was now thought to be impossible to recover any further substantial amount of the spill. Eventually marks of this spill stretched 700 miles along the coast, spoiling fishery resources, wildlife refuges, and national parks in one of the most scenic regions of the country, and killing sea birds, fish, and mammals in one of the prime marine habitats of the world.

> Nearly two months after the biggest oil spill in American history, Alaskan officials say not a single mile of beach has been completely cleaned and that the death tolls of birds, fish and mammals continues to mount.
>
> Large patches of oil, untended in rough and remote seas, are still washing up on pristine Alaska beaches more than 500 miles from the reef in Prince William Sound where the *Exxon Valdez* went aground March 24.
>
> The oil from the spill of 11 million gallons hit 730 miles of coastline, Alaskan state officials said today. Of that, only four miles have been declared cleaned. Less than one mile is totally free of oil, the officials said.
>
> * * * * *
>
> The ecological toll of the spill thus far includes more than 11,000 birds of 300 different species, 700 Pacific seal otters, and 200 bald eagles, according to a tally by the State Department of Environmental Conservation.
>
> Biologists say that the actual number of dead wildlife could be three to five times higher than those found because many of the animals have been washed out to sea or taken by predators.
>
> * * * * *
>
> On some beaches in Prince William Sound the oil is more than three feet thick, lodged in the rocks and providing a reservoir of fresh contamination at every high tide. (*The New York Times*, May 19, 1989, p. 1)

The causes of the accident, while obviously related to the intoxication of the captain and the subsequent command of the ship by an unlicensed third mate, were thought to be more complex than that simple explanation. Two additional factors were mentioned in the early hearings of the Federal Transportation Safety Board that investigated the oil spill.

- *Tired crew members.* The crew members on the tanker were said to have been exhausted from working long hours and not fully alert. The *Exxon Valdez* normally carried a crew of 20 persons. This crew size was considered to be typical for crude oil tankers, but it was substantially smaller than that required by Coast Guard regulations and union requirements on merchant cargo ships. The oil companies had argued that the new technologies automated the operations of the tankers and eliminated the need for a larger crew. The modern equipment, however, had to be manned and maintained, and consequently the automation did not keep the officers and crew from working extensive amounts of overtime and frequently going long stretches with little or no sleep. Crew members on the *Exxon Valdez* testified that they had worked an average of 140 hours of overtime per month per person for the six months prior to the accident. One hundred and forty hours of overtime per month and 20 days at sea per month plus the regular 8-hour watches works out to be 15 hours per day.

> Many of the crew members were exhausted, a routine feeling on Exxon ships, they testified. (*New York Times*, May 22, 1989, p. 10)

- *Ignored sailing rules.* There were definite violations of sailing rules. Captain Hazelwood advised the Coast Guard that he was taking the ship on a southwesterly course, into the inbound shipping channel, to avoid floating ice chunks. That was considered to be perfectly proper and normal under the circumstances, though permission was never granted for this maneuver except when the inbound lanes were completely free of other shipping. Captain Hazelwood, however, did not advise the Coast Guard that he then altered course ever further to the south, out of the inbound shipping lanes and into waters close to Bligh Reef, nor that he had engaged the autopilot. Permission for the further course change would almost certainly have been refused, had the Coast Guard been informed, and Coast Guard rules are very definite that autopilots should never be used except in the open sea. Both improper actions certainly contributed to the final grounding of the ship.

> Your children could have driven a tanker up through that channel. (Statement of Paul Yost, commandant of the U.S. Coast Guard, quoted in *The Wall Street Journal*, March 31, 1989, p. 1)

Within Alaska, public reactions to the accident and to the lackadaisical practices that apparently led to the accident centered on the potential damage to the fishing resources and consequently on the harm to the livelihood of a substantial portion of the state's population. The Alaska coast from Prince William Sound northward is known as the richest salmon and crab fishing ground in the world. Exxon assured the fishing boat operators that they would be compensated for any losses they suffered as a result of the oil spill, and explained that the company had insurance that would protect it against claims for negligence up to $4,500 million.

Outside of Alaska, public reactions to the accident and to the lackadaisical practices revealed in the hearings focused on the fouling of the environment and the destruction of the wildlife:

Already thousands of birds have died, and biologists fear that a significant portion of the Sound's 12,000 sea otters—which lose buoyancy when just 10 percent of their body is covered in oil—may be in jeopardy.

Those who know these bejeweled waters—rich in fish, fowl and fauna like few other places on earth—believe the damage will be monumental and long lasting. (*The Wall Street Journal*, March 31, 1989, p. 1)

Right now I'm still finding dead sea otters on the beach (61 days after the accident). Bald eagles feed on them, so I'm finding dead eagles. . . . Here I am, a scientist with a Ph.D., and as I watch these oiled birds trying to take off I start to cry. (Statement of biologist at the Kenai Fjords National Park, quoted in the *New York Times*, May 19, 1989, p. 1f)

Public reactions to the accident also were not mollified when the chairman of Exxon, Mr. Lawrence Rawl, decided not to go to Alaska and supervise the cleanup operations directly. Instead, he remained in New York City, and made no direct comment upon the oil spill or cleanup operations for seven days. Other officials with Exxon also refused to comment. The first statement by the president of Exxon U.S.A., the holding company for Exxon Shipping that owned the grounded tanker, was made on May 9:

We do not know what caused this accident. . . . Exxon's response was prompt and consistent with the previously approved contingency plan. (Mr. Bill Stevens, quoted in the *Detroit Free Press,* May 9, 1989, p. 7A)

In fairness to Exxon, it should be explained that company officials felt that public reactions to the oil spill were extreme and did not take into account several mitigating factors. First, they thought that the public did not really understand that the company could not be held responsible for the intoxication of Captain Hazelwood. Second, they thought that the public did not fully realize that the company had been prevented from using chemical dispersants on the oil.

Chemical dispersants, it should be understood, do not destroy the oil. Instead, the effect of the dispersant is to lower the surface tension of the oil to the point where it will break up and disperse in the water in the form of tiny droplets. The problem is that these tiny droplets are in a size range that is easily ingested by marine organisms on the lower end of the marine food chain, and therefore gradually impact marine creatures on the higher end of that chain. The extent of that impact has never been studied under all climatic conditions. It is known that dispersants make an oil spill much less visible; there is no certainty that they make it any less toxic.

Despite the lack of certainty about the effect of the dispersants, company officials thought that chemicals should have been used as soon as it was apparent that the containment and recovery efforts had failed and before the beaches were fouled and the wildlife killed. Mr. Rawl, the chairman of Exxon, in an interview with *Fortune* magazine, said environmentalists acting with the state of Alaska had prevented the company from applying the dispersants promptly:

One of the things I feel strongly about—this catching hell for two days' delay—is that I don't think that we got a fair shake. The basic problem we ran into was that we had environmentalists advising the Alaskan Department of Environmental Conservation that the dispersants could be toxic. (Lawrence Rawl, quoted in the *New York Times*, May 22, 1989, p. 10)

Mr. Lee Kelso, director of the Alaskan Department of Environmental Conservation, disagreed strongly that his department was responsible for any delay in the use of the chemical dispersants:

Exxon was free to use dispersants on the vast majority of the oil slick, and did not do so. (Statement by Lee Kelso, quoted in *The Wall Street Journal,* April 3, 1989, p. 1)

Mr. Lee Raymond, president of the Exxon Corporation, said that he blamed "ultimately the Coast Guard" (*The Wall Street Journal,* April 3, 1989, p. 12) for the delay in the use of dispersants, explaining that it had required a test before granting permission.

Coast Guard officials denied that they had required testing, saying that it was only common sense to gauge the effectiveness of the treatment under the wind, wave, and water temperature conditions that existed at the time.

Government reactions to the oil spill centered not on the causes of the accident, and not on the consequences of the oil spill or the dispute about testing, but on the slowness and ineffectual nature of the cleanup. The federal attitude seemed to be that accidents do occur, that seamen have been known to consume excessive amounts of alcohol in the past, and that under conditions of stress people may forget about test conditions and requirements. But, in the view of the government in Washington, there was no excuse for the inability of Alyeska and then of Exxon to deal promptly and effectively with the spill itself.

The contingency plan that had been developed by Alyeska and approved by the state of Alaska envisaged containment within five hours and recovery of a minimum of 50 percent of the oil by skimmers within 48 hours. Containment, as stated previously, took 59 hours and estimates of the amount of oil actually recovered ranged from 0.4 to 2.5 percent. A number of reasons for the ineffectiveness of the response by Alyeska and Exxon were given in hearings held by the National Transportation Safety Board.

It should be explained, before discussing the results of these hearings before the National Transportation Safety Board, that the Alyeska Pipelines Service Company is not a subsidiary of the Exxon Corporation. It is a consortium owned by the seven oil companies that have drilling rights on the North Slope of Alaska and ship crude oil from Prudhoe Bay to Valdez. Representatives of all seven companies serve on the board of directors. Exxon is the second largest owner, and it is said to participate actively in the management of the company.

The first reason given for the slowness of response was a shortage of equipment. The oil spill contingency plan required Alyeska to maintain two barges loaded with containment booms and ready for use. At the time of the spill, only one barge was available. The other had been scrapped as old and obsolete, but its replacement was still in Seattle. There was a requirement in the contingency plan that Alyeska notify the state Department of Environmental Conservation if any equipment was out of service for any period of time. Alyeska now concedes that it failed to provide this notification.

The barge that was available had been damaged by a storm in January. It was still considered to be seaworthy, but the containment booms had been unloaded to facilitate repair. Repairs had been delayed, according to testimony by Alyeska officials, because the company had been unable to locate a licensed marine welder. Environmentalists at the hearing displayed the Valdez telephone book that listed four companies that claimed to provide licensed marine welding services.

Seven thousand one hundred feet of containment booms were stored at the oil terminal. The contingency plan did not specify an exact lineal footage that was to be kept in stock, but it can be understood that 7,100 feet would be enough to contain a spill around a 1,000-foot tanker only if the booms could be placed quickly, before the oil spread out upon the surface of the water. Three thousand feet would be required just to encircle the hull.

Ten skimmers, which are large suction units that can be mounted on barges and used in essence to vacuum oil from the surface of the sea, were available as promised in the contingency plan. However, replacement parts were not kept in stock, and equipment breakdowns were common as the machines were not designed to work on the emulsified mixture of oil and water that was formed rapidly through wave actions on the noncontained spill.

Other equipment that was needed either was missing or could not be found quickly. Heavy ship fenders, essential for the second tanker to come alongside the *Exxon Valdez* and pump out its remaining oil, couldn't be located for hours because they were buried under 14 feet of snow. Half of the required six-inch hose needed for the pumping never was found and replacement had to be flown in from Seattle. The emergency lighting system to illuminate the boom-laying and oil-pumping work at night was finally discovered off base, being readied for use in the Valdez winter carnival.

As a final example of the shortage of equipment, it was determined after the accident that there never had been enough chemical dispersant stored in Valdez to treat the oil spill, even had there been no disagreement or misunderstanding about permission to use this material:

> Records made available this week show there was prior approval to use dispersants in the area of the spill and that only 69 barrels of dispersants were on hand in Valdez for a job that called for nearly 10,000 barrels.
> Six days after the spill, Exxon still had only a fraction of the amount needed to fight the disaster, according to records and the company's testimony this week. (*New York Times*, May 22, 1989, p. 10)

In addition to the shortage of equipment, there was also a shortage of personnel. The oil spill contingency plan required Alyeska to have a crew of 15 persons on duty at all times. These were not oil spill experts. These were hourly paid workers responsible for the normal operations of the terminal, but according to the plan they should have included all of the skills and trades necessary to respond to emergencies, whether oil spills at sea, oil leaks on land, or oil fires at the terminal.

At the time of the spill, only 11 workers were on duty. Unfortunately, none of those people knew how to operate the crane, which was needed to load the barge with the long and heavy containment booms. A crane operator was finally located, but he was also the only one who knew how to drive the fork lift, and he spent the morning after the accident, when speed in response was essential, running back and forth between the fork lift and the loading crane.

Lastly, there was a lack of training. Alyeska had dismissed its oil spill response team in 1981. This was a group of 12 persons originally set up to contain and then clean up spills throughout Valdez Harbor and Prince William Sound. The duties of the spill response team were assigned to regular employees at the plant. At the time of dismissal, Alyeska had claimed that this arrangement would be superior as they would have "120 people trained in oil spill response rather than 12."

> Some of the cited 120 scoff at this. One senior employee says he has had "zero oil spill training, none." He recalls being summoned to two spills over the years. "I didn't know what the hell I was supposed to do, and when I found the guy I was supposed to report to, he did not know what the hell we were supposed to do either. We just stood there watching." (*The Wall Street Journal*, July 6, 1989, p. 1)

Some of the operating managers within the oil industry have been greatly concerned by this tendency to replace specialized teams with personnel from the general work force:

> You either have a team of people who are dedicated to a specific task, and trained to perform that task under any and all conditions, or you have nothing. The Valdez terminal didn't have that trained team, and it showed.
>
> We run into this same problem continually with fire drills. Previously, every refinery had a fire department, with fire engines, a fire chief and a fire crew. Now, they just have the engines and, if they are lucky, they still have a chief who knows what he is doing and can teach the others. We are not lucky, and we don't still have a chief. It is company policy to run a drill once every six months. The bell rings, and all of the 9:00 to 5:00 desk jockeys jump on the truck, and away they go. When they get there, they don't know how to turn on the hydrant, they don't know how to work the pump, they don't know how to lay the hose and fight the fire, and they don't know what is safe and what isn't. We have not had a fire since the department was disbanded, but when we do it is going to get very bad very fast.
>
> I can understand exactly what happened at Valdez. They had not had a major spill in 18 years, but when they did it got very bad very fast. (Statement of oil industry executive made in confidence to the case writer)

The shortage of equipment, the shortage of personnel, and the lack of training were caused, it now appears, by deliberate policy decisions reached by the senior management of Exxon Corporation, who pushed strongly for cost reductions at Alyeska during the mid-1980s. These policy decisions were not taken arbitrarily. They were in response to a change in the basic economic conditions of the oil industry.

Oil prices fell from $32 per barrel in 1981, at the height of the power of the Organization of Petroleum Exporting Countries (OPEC) to $12 per barrel in 1987, and then rose slightly to stabilize in the range of $15 to $20 per barrel. The large oil companies are vertically integrated, with divisions for the exploration, production, and refining of crude oil, and for the distribution and marketing of oil products. The lower price for crude oil brought exploration nearly to a halt and severely reduced the profits that come from production.

The large vertically integrated oil companies reacted slowly to the changed economic conditions, but the reaction—when it came—was dramatic and harsh. Costs were reduced. Employees were discharged. The changes at Exxon were particularly dramatic because the company for years had prided itself on a generous, almost paternal attitude towards its employees. In January 1986 Mr. Clifton Garvin, chairman of Exxon Corporation since 1975, commented to *Fortune* magazine about personnel polices at the time that his company's selection as one of the 10 "most admired" firms in the United States:

> Exxon hasn't existed 104 years without having developed a lot of strengths. No. 1 is the people who are in this company. We have more than our fair share of good people. And particularly over the past five years, those people have done well. We also have the financial strength to weather difficult times. In the unsettled recent past of the oil industry, we have been able to adjust to the ups and downs of OPEC and crude-oil pricing. (Statement by Mr. Clifton Garvin, quoted in *Fortune*, January 6, 1986, p. 20)

Six months later, Exxon Corporation was in the midst of an extensive restructuring effort that would eventually change the company from one of the "most admired" to one of the most disliked:

> Exxon is giving workers until May 30 to decide whether to resign. If it doesn't get enough volunteers, it will resort to involuntary terminations. Based on Exxon's earlier announcement of a 26 percent budget cut, guesses on the final body count range from 15 percent to more than a third of all its employees. Analysts figure that the restructuring will provide Exxon with gains in efficiency and profitability, and that by conserving cash the company will be better able to buy oil properties if prices stay low. (*Business Week*, May 5, 1987, p. 32)

The generous, almost paternal attitude of the company towards Exxon employees had disappeared. Nearly one-third of all the company's workers, almost all of those over 50 years of age, were told they had to retire early or be fired:

> With oil companies cutting production in the face of falling crude oil prices and a hard-noised head chopper named Lawrence Rawl in the president's chair, at least part of Exxon's worldwide workforce of 145,000 seemed destined for the block. In late April, the world's largest oil company offered 40,500 employees the option to retire early or quit with no compensation. (*Fortune*, May 16, 1986, p. 11)

The new chairman of Exxon, Mr. Lawrence Rawl, who replaced Mr. Clifton Garvin in the spring of 1986, apparently believed that he had been selected by the board of directors to reduce costs and increase earnings, despite the probable impact upon employee morale:

> Rawl isn't saying, but the prospect of shaking people up does not rattle him. His operating style, he brags, is treading on toes. "That's my M.O." Like most top Exxon executives, he has been essentially invisible to the outside world during his 34-year climb up the corporate ladder. Inside the company, however, Rawl has earned a reputation as a waste cutter and head chopper.
>
> "The current structure of the Exxon Corporation has been in place for about 20 years," he complains. With the restructuring of international operations under way, he will turn next to Exxon's corporate headquarters in New York City, where, he says, "We still have things to do." . . . Says Rawl: "I'm bottom line oriented. I look at the revenues and then I look at everything that comes in between. When I find something that looks a little bit soft, I take a hard look. When the good times are rolling you can ignore some of that stuff. But when times get difficult, you've got to do something." In fact, he concedes, "You should do it anyway. That's what shareholders pay us for." (*Fortune*, April 14, 1986)

The cutbacks in staff extended throughout Exxon to the Exxon Shipping Company—the 20-person crews on that company's oil tankers reportedly were to have been reduced to 15 persons had the accident not intervened—and to the Alyeska Pipeline Company:

> When oil prices began falling in 1981, the owners of Alyeska ordered it to save even more on costs. In late 1982, Alyeska managers prepared what they thought was a lean budget and presented it to a meeting of the owner's committee in San Francisco. According to former Alyeska officials who were briefed on the meeting at the time, committee members cited a figure, roughly $220 million, and asked if the budget was under that; told that it wasn't, they rejected it out of hand.
>
> "There was an overall attitude of petty cheapness that severely affects our ability to operate safely," recalls Mr. Woodle who came over from the Coast Guard to run the terminal's marine operations just in time to see their budget slashed by about a third. "I was shocked at the shabbiness of the operations." (*The Wall Street Journal*, July 6, 1989, p. 1)

MANAGEMENT OF A MORAL COMPANY

The oil spill from the Exxon Valdez coated 750 miles of Alaska coastline. It severely impacted the livelihood of commercial fishers, almost destroyed the food sources of native Indians, and it resulted in the death of 40 percent of bald eagles in Alaska, killed 80 percent of sea otters in Prince William Sound, and eliminated 200,000 birds along the coast. It nearly ruined the reputation of the Exxon Corporation, and it resulted in a $2.4 billion fine by the federal government and a $2.8 billion penalty in a civil trial. Senior executives truly wish that the careless accident and delayed cleanup had never happened. (see Figure 6–6).

FIGURE 6–6

The Wreck of the Exxon Valdez and the Cleanup of the Resulting Oil Spill

How could it have been avoided? The argument of this chapter is that it would have required a series of changes, starting with a different philosophy or method of management, as shown in Figure 6–6. The balance of this chapter will discuss the stages in that figure, with a short explanation of the recommendations of each stage, and then a brief comment about the performance of Exxon relative to those recommendations.

Philosophy of Management

If the total focus of corporate management is placed upon financial benefits for the stockholders, with little or no attention paid to potential harms for the other stakeholders, the result—according to this text—will be a lack of trust, commitment, and effort. A company is dependent upon a range of individuals

FIGURE 6–7

Proposed Relationships between Managerial Decisions and Actions and
Organizational Cooperation, Innovation and Unification

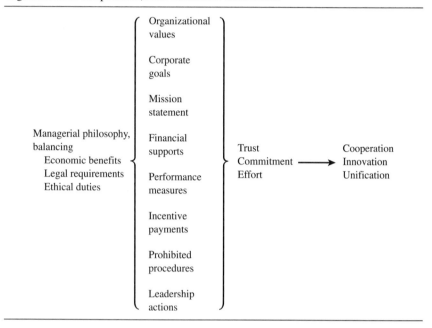

and groups within the company, the industry, and the society whose cooperation, innovation, and unification are essential for success. What is needed is a
balance between three analytical methods that recognize the interdependen-
cies of these individuals and groups:

- *Economic outcomes,* based upon impersonal market forces. Always act to optimize economic outcomes for the firm because that will generate maximum material benefits for the society, *provided* all product and factor markets are truly
  competitive and all internal and external costs are fully included.

- *Legal requirements,* based upon impartial social and political processes. Always
  act to obey the law because that will come as close as possible to following the
  collective moral judgments of members of society, *provided* those requirements
  can be justified by Social Contract (ignorance of self-interest) concepts.

- *Ethical duties,* based upon rational human goals. Always act in accordance with
  objective norms of behavior or universal systems of belief *provided* those norms
  and beliefs can logically be shown to lead to a society that combines justice and
  liberty and that treats individuals with dignity and respect.

Clearly at the time of the wreck Exxon was being managed with sole attention to the financial benefits of the stockholders. Mr. Rawl openly admitted
that he was "bottom line" oriented, that he planned to fire employees and cut

expenses to increase profits, with no concern for those to be fired in the company or to those to be harmed in the community. Under economic outcomes, the company did not recognize the external costs that were imposed upon the commercial fishers, the native Indians, and the active environmentalists. Under government requirements, the company did not obey the law, in the form of the spill response contract with the state of Alaska. Under ethical duties, the company was not open, honest, truthful, and proud of its actions and did not select the greatest net benefit for society or act in a way it would be willing to have all others act. The result was a clear lack of trust, commitment, and effort by employees on the tanker—no one was willing to try to remedy the violations of sailing rules that led to the careless accident—and at the terminal—no one was willing to try to change the shortages of equipment and training that led to the slow response. That lack of trust, commitment, and effort brought about, eventually, a huge cost to the company and a heavy charge to the society.

Corporate Values

To avoid easy generalizations think of corporate values as the duties the senior executives of the firm should—in your view—owe to the various individuals and groups associated with the firm who can, in one way or another, affect the future performance and position of the firm. These individuals and groups would include owners of all types (institutional and individual), employees at all levels, customers in all segments, suppliers, distributors, creditors, local residents, national citizens, and global inhabitants. Think about what issues are probably important to each of those individuals and groups. Then, think about the extent to which the senior executives of the firm should recognize those factors that are important to each of those individuals and groups. In short, think about how the company should begin to plan for unification based upon similarities rather than separation based upon differences.

Clearly Exxon owed profitable operations to the owners, but it also owed them the duty of avoiding large fines and penalties. Perhaps Exxon could not have owed continued employment to all of its workers, given the changed conditions of the oil industry, but it could have provided those workers with better conditions such as less forced overtime on the oil tankers and improved training such as better instruction for the response teams. It would be hard to argue that it did not owe an unharmed environment to the local residents and forthright information on the level of preparation to the state officials. None of these duties, beyond profits owed to the shareholders, apparently were recognized by the senior executives at Exxon.

Organizational Goals

To avoid easy generalizations think of company goals as the endpoints the senior executives of the firm should—in your view—set for the various dimensions of performance that are possible. What—again in your view—should the senior executives want to accomplish along such dimensions as financial performance, technological achievement, industry position, market share, customer satisfaction, manufacturing efficiency, employee loyalty, environmental protection, public reputation, and social contribution? What—once more in your view—should the various groups associated with the firm want to accomplish on each of these dimensions? As with the corporate values there will be differences among these groups. Scientists and engineers doubtless would like to emphasize technological achievement, while the owners and creditors probably would prefer to focus on financial performance. The two may not be as dissimilar as they at first appear; if the organization is positioned correctly within the industry there will be an obvious connection between the two. Again, think about how the company should begin to plan for unification based upon similarities rather than separation based upon differences.

Exxon placed total emphasis upon financial performance and set very explicit goals along that dimension. The accident, and the total of $5.2 billion in fines and penalties, could have been avoided with greater emphasis upon technological achievement (better methods of tanker control and spill cleanup), employee morale (less drinking by tanker officers and more training for terminal employees), environmental protection, and public reputation. The basic question in proposing goals for a corporation is whether it is possible to plan for profits or whether it is necessary to plan for the activities that lead to profits. Exxon, it is very clear, planned for profits.

Mission Statement

The mission statement is the means of combining the duties that the firm holds to others with the goals that it has set for itself. What role, as a result of this combination, should the firm attempt to play within the market, the industry, the economy, and the society? It is frequently difficult to express managerial values and organizational goals in explicit numerical terms. Consequently, many firms compromise with a mission statement that speaks only generally about the duties they want to observe and the endpoints they want to achieve, but much more specifically about the means they want to use and the standards they want to follow. The intent is to define the future of the firm, the scope of its activities, and the character of its people so that everyone will clearly understand, "This is where we're going to go, this is what we're going to do, and this is how we're going to do it." Think in terms of a document that will create a challenge for everyone associated with the firm. Think also in terms of a document you would be *proud* to hand to employees, to show to customers, to send to suppliers and distributors, and to include in the annual report for owners.

Exxon, at the time of the wreck of the Exxon Valdez, did not have a mission statement. Instead, it had a Code of Conduct which is reproduced below:

Our company policy is one of strict observance of all laws applicable to its business:

A reputation for scrupulous dealing is itself a priceless company asset

We do care how we get results

We expect candor at all levels and compliance with accounting rules and controls

It is the established policy of the company to conduct its business in compliance with all state and federal antitrust laws

Individual employees are responsible for seeing that they comply with the law

Employees must avoid even the appearance of violation

Competing or conducting business with the company is not permitted, except with the knowledge and consent of management

Accepting and providing gifts, entertainment, and services must comply with specific requirements

An employee may not use company personnel, information, or other assets for personal benefit

Participating in certain outside activities requires the prior approval of management

What would have happened had Exxon Corporation had a mission statement similar to the one adopted by Johnson & Johnson, which was printed in Chapter 5? Here the order of priorities was very clear: customers, suppliers, distributors, employees, and local residents come first, with company owners at the very end. Just having a different mission statement that emphasized duties and goals in set rankings rather than policies and prohibitions without priorities probably would not have avoided the wreck or improved the cleanup. But, it is the argument of this text that having such a mission statement bolstered by proper financial supports, performance measures, incentive payments, prohibited procedures, and leadership actions would have made a substantial difference.

Financial Supports

Within every firm, in very simple terms, someone has to sell the products (marketing), manufacture the goods (production), and supervise the cash flows (finance). In slightly more complex terms, someone also has to gather the data (information systems), develop the people (human resources), and apply the technologies (research and development). In somewhat further complex terms, someone has to select the strategy (strategic planning), define the tasks (activity planning), and design the structure (organizational planning). People at all of these levels, from the least to the most complex, need money, or more properly the authority to spend money, in order to follow the policies and achieve the goals set in the mission statement.

Financial supports provide that authority to spend money to accomplish results. This money comes in two forms: capital and cost. Capital represents the long-term investments needed for buildings, equipment, and inventory; those amounts are "capitalized" or recorded as an asset on the balance sheet. Cost represents the short-term expenditures required for employee salaries and outside services; these amounts are "expensed" or deducted from revenues on the income statement. The issue in Financial Supports is whether the capital is allocated and the costs are budgeted to maximize the profits for the company or to fulfill the duties and meet the goals listed in the mission statement.

It is very clear that Exxon had not made the long-term capital investments that were needed for equipment and inventory to be able to contain and then recover the oil spill. Only one of the two barges specified in the contract with the state of Alaska to transport the containment booms to the site of a spill was available, and that had been damaged and not repaired. An adequate number of containment booms were not available. Spare parts for the skimmers were not in stock. Only 69 barrels of chemical dispersants were on hand, not the 10,000 barrels that were required. Obviously the emphasis here had been on profits, not duties and goals.

It is also very clear that Exxon had not budgeted the short-term cost amounts that were needed for personnel and training to be able to contain and then recover the oil spill. The specialized oil spill recovery teams had been disbanded. Only 11 general purpose workers were on duty at the time of the wreck, not the 16 specified in the contract with the state of Alaska, and those employees had not been specifically trained to respond to oil spill emergencies. There was a lack of cohesion in the containment and recovery efforts caused, in the view of the marine managers of the Valdez terminal, by "an overall attitude of petty cheapness that severely affected our ability to operate safely" (*The Wall Street Journal*, cited previously). Obviously here also the emphasis had been on profits, not duties and goals.

Performance Measures

Performance measures are the means of evaluating the performance of the persons assigned to the various critical tasks designed to implement the strategy and achieve the mission of the firm within capital investment and expense budget constraints. Many of these performance measures are financial in nature, simple restatements of the capital allocations and revenue/expense budgets. Others are numerical and related to such aspects of job performance as unit output, customer satisfaction, product performance, workplace safety, employee morale, and environmental preservation. Setting these performance targets for people assigned to critical tasks is felt to be an important aspect of corporate management; it is frequently said that, "If you can't measure 'em, you can't manage 'em." The issue in performance measures, as in financial supports, is whether the measures are set to maximize the profits for the company or to fulfill the duties and meet the goals of the mission statement.

None of the published accounts of the hearings and trials that followed the wreck of the Exxon Valdez spoke specifically of the performance measures that were in use by the Exxon Corporation. It can be assumed, however, given the restrictions on capital allocations and limitations on budgeted expenses, that all of them focused on profits. It would appear that none of the managers at Valdez were measured on the availability of response equipment and inventory or on the training of recovery employees.

Incentive Payments

Incentive payments are the means of rewarding the performance of the persons assigned to the various critical tasks designed to implement the strategy and achieve the mission of the firm. They are the method by which the people supervising the programs and managing the divisions are rewarded for meeting the performance targets to which they have been assigned. These rewards can be financial (bonuses or commissions), positional (promotions and raises) or reputational (recognition and praise). They are usually tied very closely to the performance measures; if those measure achievement of revenue, cost, or profit goals the incentive payments reward that achievement. These rewards for meeting performance targets often have an impact upon the occurrence of moral problems, particularly if the size or the importance of the incentives for the manager can overcome that person's judgment as to what is best for the firm. Bonuses and commissions that form a very high percentage of a manager's total compensation package often lead towards cutting corners and taking risks.

> Again, none of the published accounts of the hearings and trials that followed the wreck of the Exxon Valdez spoke specifically of the incentive payments. It can be assumed here also, however, that all of them focused on rewarding the managers who met their profit and cost objectives. Had those managers received a bonus, or a promotion, or even just recognition and praise, for having response equipment and inventory on hand, or for having trained employees ready to react, the spill probably would not have been left uncontained for 59 hours rather than the 5 hours specified in the contract with the state of Alaska.

Prohibited Procedures

Prohibited procedures are a published listing of behavioral standards, of procedures or actions that simply will not be tolerated by the company. This listing of behavioral standards, often termed a code of conduct, generally differs in two important ways from the mission statement. The mission statement usually is very idealistic; the conduct code frequently is very realistic. The mission statement is very general; the code is very specific. Examples of prohibited acts that are often included in a code of conduct are "Employees of this company may accept no gifts, lunches, dinners, or other forms of entertainment with a value over $25," or "Employees of this firm must never falsify accounting records or expense accounts." There often is an emphasis upon financial standards, not mission priorities, in these prohibited procedures.

The code of conduct of the Exxon Corporation was reproduced earlier in this chapter. Essentially it says that laws should never be broken, bribes should never be paid, and benefits should never be accepted. It does not, however, say that ship's officers should never be intoxicated, safety equipment should never be unavailable, or safety training should never be neglected.

Leadership Actions

Often it is possible for the leader of an organization to take a dramatic action or issue a memorable statement that will indicate to members of the organization the relative weight to be given to profitable outcomes versus social impacts. It is easy, in many business organizations, to forget the values, goals, and priorities of the mission statement if those differ from a total focus on financial performance. It is hard, in most business organizations, to get people, even diligent employees, to carefully read memos or attentively listen at meetings about social performance. This is particularly true in large organizations in which there are hundreds of memos and numerous meetings. Senior executives, however, simply by the way they publicly choose to spend their time or voice their concerns, can clearly indicate their priorities.

Apparently no senior executive at Exxon had been at the Valdez terminal to publicly inspect spill response capability or had attended environmental meetings to energetically endorse spill prevention technology since Lawrence Rawl became chairman. Mr. Rawl did not go to Prince William Sound after the grounding of the tanker, which seems to indicate his position on the financial performance versus social performance question. Prior to the wreck there were many things senior executives could have done, had the company included environmental protection in the mission statement, to convey the importance of that protection. Inspection of sites, interviews with employees, and presentations of awards would all have been possible. These were not done, and the result was not only severe damage to the environment but huge charges against Exxon.

The next three cases involve companies that focused totally on profits. Persons within those companies took actions that were profitable over the short term, but brought harms to customers, employees, and local residents. Eventually those actions became publicized, which brought large losses in public reputation, customer loyalty, and employee support, and eventually resulted in substantial governmental fines and legal claims. Set up a new mission statement, and then the financial supports, performance measures, incentive payments, prohibited procedures, and leadership actions that would have prevented those harmful actions by lower-level employees in each of these firms.

CASE 6–1

Two Companies in Need of Redirection

Two short cases that depicted moral problems encountered by recent graduates of a program in business administration were included earlier in this text. These cases—"Sarah Goodwin" and "Susan Shapiro"—depicted very fundamental moral problems for in each instance they placed the career of the individual in jeopardy if she refused to accept the situation. The recent graduates had to decide what they would or would not accept; that is, they had to decide where they would "draw the line."

Now you have been promoted. Put yourself in the place of the president of one of those companies. Just to help your memory, the moral problems involved (1) a retail store that was shipping defective food products to the ghetto for sale to the poor; and (2) a chemical company that continued to operate a production process even though it was harmful to the health and well-being of the employees.

Assume that you are the president or a very senior vice president, clearly at a managerial level where you can make whatever decision you believe would best serve the interests of your company. You also have a reputation as a "doer," a man or woman who has managed company operations very successfully in the past, with continually rising sales and increasing profits, and consequently a person who tends to get his or her own way in dealing with both superiors and subordinates. In short, no one will openly oppose your suggestions. That does not mean, however, that people further down in the organization, at the functional or operating levels, will automatically accept your directions just because they are your directions. You probably will have to recommend some fairly major changes in the organizational mission, structure, and systems of the firm.

Assume lastly that you have just found that the situation described in the case not only exists in your firm, but is widespread within your firm. That is, if you decide to be the president of the chemical company, you now understand that almost all of your chemical plants have production processes that are technically legal but medically and environmentally harmful. You are shocked. You say to your spouse that night, "I had no idea this was going on, but it obviously is and I've got to do something to stop it."

Class Assignment.   What are you going to do? Chapter 6 of this text suggested that you think along the following terms to ensure a more moral approach to management and to build greater cooperation, innovation, and unification among all levels of an organization.

Proposed Relationships between Managerial Decisions and Actions and
Organizational Cooperation, Innovation and Unification

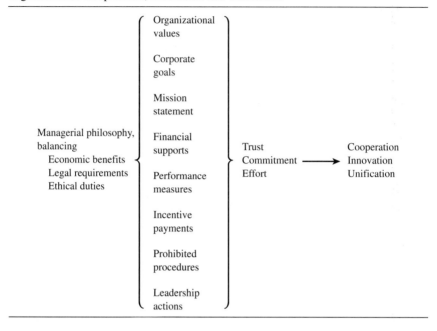

CASE 6–2

McKinstry Advertising and Settling Disputes

You are the president of the McKinstry Advertising Agency, a medium-sized
firm that specializes in preparing the marketing strategies, performing the
market research studies, arranging the distribution channels, and designing the
advertising and promotional materials for industrial companies that have
developed offshoot consumer products. You obviously serve a very specific
niche. Your clients are industrial companies—that is, they sell primarily to
other manufacturing firms and government agencies—that have developed
products for the retail trade as unintended outcomes of their R&D programs.
Dow Chemical Company, while not a client of your agency, is an almost ideal
example of this type of firm. It is an industrial firm that has developed and
currently produces and markets such consumer products as Dow Bathroom
Cleaner and Ziploc Bags, which in total amount to only 5.8 percent of Dow's
total sales.

Your clients tend not to be as large as Dow Chemical Company nor as
well established in consumer marketing. Most have had very little experience

in retail sales, and they generally are not very sophisticated in advertising methods. They tend, therefore, to rely heavily upon the advice of the account executives and advertising experts at your agency and to develop relationships with those people that are far more permanent and personal than is common in the "what have you done for me lately" culture of the consumer products advertising industry.

The "permanent and personal" relationships that are typical of your company but not of consumer advertising in general seem to be the cause of a major problem that you have recently encountered. One of your larger clients developed a new type of radar detector. Radar detectors, also known as "fuzzbusters," are simple but extremely sensitive radio receivers that are tuned to the wavelength of the police radar. When a car equipped with a detector first enters the radar field a warning light flashes or a buzzer sounds enabling the driver to slow down, if necessary, before the speed of the car can be calculated by the police equipment. The use of radar detectors thus enables drivers to avoid being stopped and fined for speeding.

Speeding is alleged to be responsible for many traffic accidents. There is no question but that traffic accidents are a major problem within the United States. There were 27.7 million traffic accidents involving passenger cars in 1990 and 6.1 million traffic accidents involving trucks in the country. These 33.8 million traffic accidents resulted in 46,400 deaths, 1.8 million severe injuries that required hospitalization, 7.8 million moderate injuries that required attention by medical personnel, extensive slight injuries, uncounted personal traumas, and huge financial losses.

Speeding was said to be a factor in 65 percent of all of those accidents in 1990 and in 87 percent of the accidents during that year that caused deaths and severe injuries due to the greater impacts that came from the higher speeds. But, it has to be admitted that neither statistic is totally reliable. Police estimate speed based upon the length of skid marks and the extent of physical damage, but those estimates obviously are inexact. Further, "speeding" is defined as any vehicle velocity above the posted limit, and it is claimed that the posted limit is considerably below the safe capability of modern cars and highways in many instances.

Vehicle speed, moreover, is only one of the factors that cause traffic accidents. Alcohol intoxication is believed to be associated with 28 percent of all accidents and 48 percent of all accidents that result in death and severe injury. Often speed and intoxication together are held to be the cause. Again, though, there is a problem in measuring intoxication. The percentage of alcohol in the bloodstream that impairs physical response time and personal judgment varies with the body weight, physical conditioning, and drinking history of the individual. Police and medical attendants use a test that takes into account only body weight and, further, it is said by representatives of the licensed beverage (that is, beer, wine, and liquor) industry that the legal threshold for intoxication has been set much too low. Most drivers would be considered to be "driving under the influence" if they consumed two to three glasses of beer or wine within 30 minutes of an accident.

In summary, it cannot be said that the exact causes of most severe traffic accidents are known with certainty but it is believed that speeding and drinking, jointly or separately, play some role in the events that lead up to those accidents. Also to blame, in many instances, are the design of the highway, the condition of the weather, the maintenance of the vehicle, the time of the day (many severe accidents occur at dusk with poor lighting and tired drivers), and the presence of radar detectors. A study by the Ohio State Police Department found that radar detectors were present in at least one of the vehicles involved in 69 percent of all severe traffic accidents on the highways of that state in 1990. Studies in other states have confirmed that finding, with some estimates of the relationship running as high as 75 percent.

The use of radar detectors is illegal in many if not most states, but neither the manufacturing nor the marketing of the units has ever been banned by the federal government, which, of course, is the sole authority that could regulate their interstate trade. The U.S. Constitution forbids any state from restricting "imports" from any other state. Therefore, an unusual situation often occurs in which the use of the radar detector sets may be illegal within a given state, but the sale of those sets is not illegal and cannot be prohibited by that state.

The manufacture and marketing of radar detectors was an expanding industry, with total sales revenues reaching $67 million in 1991, until the police in a number of states began to use lasers rather than radar to apprehend speeders. Lasers project focused beams of light waves rather than focused beams of radio waves, and consequently they cannot be "picked up" by most radar detectors.

Your client, as an offshoot of contract research for the defense industry, has developed a new technology that does "pick up" the light waves far enough away from the source so that drivers can slow down. A full explanation of the technology is not needed; it is probably sufficient to say that the device works on the principle that the light waves from a police laser interfere with a certain spectrum of exceedingly short-range radio signals broadcast from the detector set in the owner's car. That interference can be detected even though the police car is out-of-sight, perhaps a quarter-mile ahead on the highway, and the police laser is not targeted on this particular car. The proposed design also picks up the interference from a police car's older radar device equally well.

The electronics firm that developed the new radar/laser detection came to the account executive they knew at your agency and requested a marketing plan supported by market research. The marketing plan was finished; it had a heavy emphasis upon direct distribution supported by extensive advertising. The market research was completed; it showed that the first entrant into this field with a new technology could rapidly build market share. The client requested that a young associate who had prepared a very successful advertising program for one of their earlier products be assigned to design the promotional materials for this new one.

The associate, Marilynn Schaefer, refused, saying privately that she felt that it was not "right" to market radar and/or laser detectors that led to more numerous and more severe highway accidents and to greater incidents of death, suffering, and injury. The design director proposed other employees at the associate level within the creative segment of the firm, but the client's representative wanted Marilynn Schaefer to do the work. She continued to refuse, though expressing her reasons only to the account executive, George Sarbo. Eventually the conflict between these two people reached the stage at which George said to Marilynn, "Either work on this account for me or don't work at this agency for anyone" and fired her.

Marilynn Schaefer immediately came to you, as president of the agency, saying that it was not right to fire a person because of her moral beliefs. George Sarbo quickly followed, saying that for 20 years he had followed the stated agency policy of providing clients with personalized service, and that if Marilynn did not want to do so she could not work for him and she should not work for the agency. He also said that if Marilynn were retained at the agency he would leave. You realize that George Sarbo is one of only three account executives at your firm, that he has a very loyal following of clients, and that he might well be able to take those clients with him if he indeed did decide to leave. You also realize that Marilyn Schaefer is one of the more creative employees in the design department. You do not want to lose her either.

Proposed Relationships between Managerial Decisions and Actions and Organizational Cooperation, Innovation and Unification

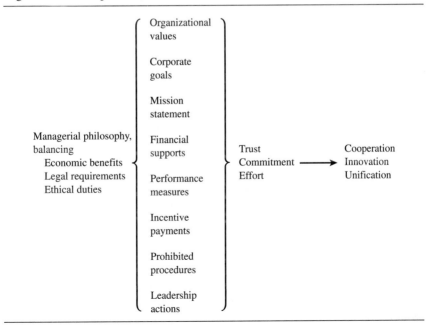

Further conversations with both of the participants in the dispute and with the industrial client on the following day showed no change in their positions. The client's representative clearly felt that the delay in assigning Ms. Schaefer to work on the needed adverting was due only to the press of other accounts upon her time; he stated that he felt that he was "owed" her assistance on this project.

Class Assignment.   As president of the agency, what should do you do? The text in Chapter 6 suggested that you think in terms of considering moral issues before they arise, and then building greater cooperation, innovation, and unification throughout the firm

CASE 6–3

Boston Company and Firing the Chairman

The Boston Safe Deposit and Trust Company, generally called the Boston Company for short, was founded shortly after the Civil War to provide trust management and investment custody services for wealthy New England families. The latter half of the 19 century and the early part of the 20 century were periods of rapid industrial growth within the region. Textile mills, machine tool factories, railroad equipment companies, and specialty chemical plants all expanded. Many of these were family owned, and the Boston Company established a reputation as the premier financial institution to manage the wealth of their well-born clients.

By 1960, however, the industrial prosperity of New England had come to an end. The textile mills had moved to the South, in search of less expensive labor. The machine tool factories had moved to the Midwest to be close to their major customers: the automobile, farm machinery, and home appliance industries. The specialty chemical plants, which primarily produced paint, varnish, and the early plastics, had moved to Texas and Louisiana to make use of the petrochemical feed stocks discovered in those states. The railroad equipment companies had simply closed when cars, trucks, and airplanes replaced the railroads as the major modes of transportation.

The Boston Company opened offices in Chicago, Houston, and Los Angeles in an attempt to move closer to the new centers of wealth, but it found that its reputation had less meaning in those new areas and, it was said, many of its potential customers found their manner to be stodgy and old-fashioned. Its investment performance had been excellent. Investment officers at the Boston Company had recognized very early the growth potential of microelectronics, data processing, pharmaceutical drugs, and packaged foods, and had moved their clients' money into the common stock of companies in those industries.

Somehow, however, this record of growth in the pension funds and trust funds under their control exceeding that of the common stock indexes was not enough. The Boston Company remained profitable, polite, and stagnant.

In an interesting sidelight, the Houston office formed a consulting group to advise on investments in oil and natural gas exploration and production; this became known as the Boston Consulting Group, but this division was sold by the Boston Company shortly after it was moved back to Boston. After the sale the Boston Consulting Group went on to become one of the largest and most profitable corporate-level consulting firms in the country.

In 1981 the Boston Company itself was purchased by Shearson Loeb Rhoades (later to be known as Shearson Lehman Brothers), a division of American Express. Shearson Loeb Rhoades was a large investment bank and brokerage firm with offices throughout the country. The intent of the merger was to market the mutual funds and investment services offered by the Boston Company through the branch offices of Shearson Loeb Rhoades. It was a strategy that was almost immediately successful, given that Shearson Loeb Rhodes appointed an aggressive new chairman to oversee, as the *Institutional Investor* (July 1987, p. 129) put it, "Boston Company's transformation from a banking and trust culture" to a more activist investment banking outlook with much higher performance goals.

Mr. von Germeten, the 41-year-old chairman and CEO appointed by Shearson Loeb Rhoades, brought in a new director of marketing, a new director of finance, and a new treasurer. Together they set out to remake the company. Young people were recruited, often with backgrounds in quantitative finance. Older people were let go, unable to keep pace with the changes. The Boston Company continued its focus on the wealthy, limiting its clients to those with over $1 million in net worth, but the sources of this wealth changed from basic manufacturing to the real estate, retail sales, and entertainment industries. In short, the bank began to appeal to celebrities:

> When Donald Trump bought his yacht *The Princess* in 1988, he didn't have to throw a lavish celebration party. His lender threw it for him. Boston Company, the American Express subsidiary that loaned Trump the $29 million purchase price, spared no expense. Champagne and caviar flowed as top executives from the area toured the 282-foot yacht in Boston Harbor. For Boston Company Chairman James N. von Germeten, the Trump loan represented the transformation of his firm from a stodgy trust-fund manager for New England's old-line elite to a big-time backer of the nouveaux riches, especially celebrities and real estate developers. (*Business Week*, July 22, 1991, p. 58)

The Boston Company financed expensive homes as well as yachts; it built up a $4.2 billion portfolio of "jumbo" mortgages in amounts ranging from $350,000 to $3.5 million. These large mortgages were generally unavailable from other financial institutions and consequently carried higher-than-normal interest rates. Large personal loans were also issued to the bank's wealthy clientele, often with special collateral or repayment provisions that again permitted higher-than-normal rates. The record of successful management of client funds also continued, which allowed higher-than-normal fees to be charged for that management area.

The emphasis throughout the period 1982 to 1988 was on growth. Deposits increased 18-fold; mortgages and loans 10-fold; private trust funds 8-fold; public pension funds 6-fold; after-tax earnings 12-fold. Clear targets for growth in assets, loans, revenues, and profits were set for each of the divisions within the company, and large cash incentives were arranged to reward the managers who met or exceeded those goals:

> A large part of the firm's success, particularly in active investment management, stems from company-wide incentive compensation schemes von Germeten introduced. It began with portfolio managers and analysts but has since expanded. Now, he points out, all managers have pools to "incentivize" their staffs, and bonuses have been as high as 100 percent of salary. (*Institutional Investor*, July 1987, p.131)

Growth in assets, revenues, profits, salaries, and bonuses were accompanied by a growth in "perks," which were felt to be necessary to attract the wealthy clients and reward the successful managers:

> Mr. von Germeten brought a go-go style to the Boston Company's State Street headquarters. The company soon was throwing lavish parties complete with caviar and ice sculptures. Mr. von Germeten, unlike his predecessor, rode around Boston in stretch limousines; when in London, he opted for a Rolls Royce.
>
> In November, he flew out to Los Angeles, where Boston Company opened a new office with a party so lavish it featured a 66-piece orchestra. A guest at the party says he was flabbergasted to find that Boston Company had hired dozens of parking valets to whisk away celebrities' Mercedes and Jaguars.
>
> As the Boston Ballet finished a Saturday matinee of *The Nutcracker* last month, a mock balloon descended from the stage rafters, carrying, of all people, James N. von Germeten, Boston Company's flamboyant president. The thousand-odd Boston Company employees who had bought out the hall looked on, dumb-founded and slightly embarrassed. Mr. von Germeten, in full business suit regalia, didn't miss a beat however. He happily mingled with the dancers and took a bow with the ballerinas.
>
> Such a dramatic entrance deserved an equally dramatic exit, and that exit occurred just two months later: Mr. von Germeten was asked to resign on January 20, 1989, when the Boston Company was forced to recognize $45 million of "accounting irregularities" that had falsely inflated profits for the prior year. (*The Wall Street Journal*, January 30, 1989, p. 1f)

In explanation of this request, it was revealed that the comptroller of the Boston Company had refused to "sign off" on the internally prepared financial statements for the third quarter of 1988. She maintained that revenues were being recognized before they occurred and that expenses were being recorded after they became due, which, of course, had the effect of substantially increasing profits for the period. The comptroller claimed that this had been happening on a much smaller scale for years, but that it had now reached the stage where she could no longer agree, as an accounting professional, that the statements represented fairly the financial position of the firm.

Mr. von Germeten claimed, in response, that he had immediately informed executives at Shearson Loeb Rhoades about the allegations, but surprisingly there was no accounting follow-up, no audit of the books by a public accounting firm. Ms. Aronin, the comptroller, was persuaded to stay and not make her statement public as she had originally threatened to do. In November, however, Mr. Patrick Thewlis, the manager of the Boston Company's internal investment portfolio, which had been exceedingly profitable for the prior five years, committed suicide at his home. A public audit of the $1.1 billion fund was required by law, given the circumstances of the manager's death, and that audit quickly revealed an unrecorded loss of $10 million on a $100 million investment in esoteric securities known as collateralized mortgage obligation residuals. These are securities whose value fluctuates sharply with changes in interest rates; they were, in essence, a bet that interest rates would go down. Instead, they went up.

This stark evidence of an unrecorded loss in an unsuitable investment for a trust company obviously supported the earlier allegations of the comptroller, and a public audit of the entire company was quickly arranged:

> By mid-December, the company's outside auditors, Coopers & Lybrand, and accountants from Shearson were crawling all over Boston Company, and they didn't like what they found. On December 23, Shearson announced that Mr. von Germeten, Boston Company Chief Financial Officer Joseph Murphy, and Boston Company Treasurer Michael Walsh had been put on paid leave. Shearson also said it had uncovered $10 million to $15 million of accounting irregularities—a figure that later tripled when the investigation was completed in January. (*The Wall Street Journal*, January 30, 1989, p. 1f)

Outside directors of the firm—those not associated with either Shearson Loeb Rhoades or the Boston Company—were dismayed by the size of the loss caused by accounting deceptions and by the size of the investment in unsuitable securities. Both were felt to have been caused by the pressures from senior executives to meet quarterly goals for revenue and profit increases:

> A Boston Company director says the deceptive accounting began soon after the stock market crash of October 1987, when Boston Company was in danger of falling short of its performance goals. Missing the goals would mean sharply lower management bonuses, which sometimes approached $1 million [each] for top executives, company sources say. (*The Wall Street Journal*, January 30, 1989, p. 1f)

The outside directors of the firm met on January 20 and accepted the resignations of Mr. Murphy and Mr. Walsh (chief financial officer and treasurer, respectively). Mr. von Germeten, however, refused to resign, and in a series of interviews sought to minimize the severity of the accounting problems and his involvement in them:

> "At no time during this year did I believe there was improper accounting going on," he is reported to have said. "I'm not an accountant. I'm required to follow the judgments and advice of other people. This was a series of judgmental errors by professional accountants." (*The Wall Street Journal*, January 20, 1989, p. C14)
>
> In a series of interviews this month, Mr. von Germeten insisted he hasn't done anything wrong. He has accused Shearson of conducting a "witch hunt" in its investigations, and he has said that any earnings problems merely reflect "judgmental errors by accountants." Asked whether subordinates might have thought he wanted rapid growth no matter what it took, Mr. von Germeten said: "That's what the pressures of business are all about." (*The Wall Street Journal*, January 30, 1989, p. A1)

Mr. von Germeten was not without support in the financial community. Many fellow executives and some people in the media thought that he had been instructed by the owners to achieve growth in sales and profits, and he had done so "in spades," and that now he was being condemned for lower-level activities over which he had no control:

> Another troubling issue is executive responsibility—and motivation. Some clients and Shearson insiders believe Boston Company felt compelled by Shearson to produce extraordinary results at a time when most other units of Shearson, an American Express Company subsidiary, were struggling. During the probe, says one Shearson source, Murphy and Walsh "claimed that they were under tremendous pressure from von Germeten. Von Germeten claimed he was under tremendous pressure from Phillips." (*Business Week*, February 6, 1989, p. 87)

> I'm one of those who think that James von Germeten is getting a raw deal from Shearson. He did exactly what they told him to do. He raised profits from $10 million in 1982 to $150 million in 1988. Certainly there were losses from the accounting errors. Certainly there were losses from the investment mistakes. Certainly they've now had to repossess Trump's yacht, and write off about $90 million in their jumbo mortgage portfolio [as of January 1991]. But you've got to compare that to the overall return to Shearson, which was immense.

> You cannot hold the chief executive officer of a business firm responsible for everything that happens within that firm. You have to hold him [or her] responsible for profitable operations, and as long as he [or she] produces the targeted rate of return, maintains the expected competitive position, and follows the letter and spirit of the law, then you have to support that executive. Boston Company broke no laws. No institution or private investors were hurt. No government funds were lost. Instead, von Germeten transformed an old-line trust company into a modern money machine. He is being condemned for mistakes made by subordinates far down in the corporate structure, in the process of that transformation. He should be retained as president. (Statement of industry observer, made in confidence to the case writer)

Proposed Relationships between Managerial Decisions and Actions and
Organizational Cooperation, Innovation and Unification

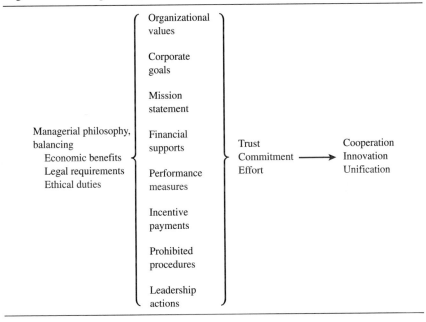

Class Assignment.   The assignment for the class discussion can be broken
into two sections: What should be done about von Germeten, and what should
be done about Boston Company?

1. You are a senior executive at Shearson and a member of the committee that
    oversees the Boston Company. What action would you take regarding James
    von Germeten's refusal to resign? Assume that you are the oldest member of
    that committee and doubtless will be the one assigned to meet with him and an-
    nounce the committee's decision. What will you say at that meeting?

2. Assume now that you are Mr. von Germeten (if the committee decides to retain
    him as president), or the replacement for Mr. von Germeten (if the committee
    decides to fire him). What actions would you take? Specifically, it is a common
    rule of management consulting that a senior executive can only accomplish
    three things in any one year. What three things would you want to accomplish in
    your first year as president?

3. The text in Chapter 6 suggested that you think in terms of settling moral issues
    before they arise, and then building cooperation, innovation and unification
    throughout the organization. Would you use this framework of analysis?

Index